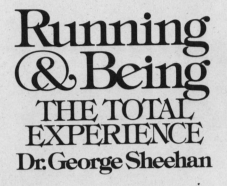

Running & Being
THE TOTAL EXPERIENCE
Dr. George Sheehan

Running & Being

THE TOTAL EXPERIENCE

Dr. George Sheehan

Drawings by Nora Sheehan

WARNER BOOKS

A Warner Communications Company

WARNER BOOKS EDITION

Copyright © 1978 by George A. Sheehan, M.D.
All rights reserved including the right of reproduction
in whole or in part in any form.

Library of Congress Catalog Card Number 77-18271

ISBN 0-446-38185-3 (U.S.A.)
      0-446-38186-1 (Canada)
This Warner Books Edition is published by
arrangement with Simon and Schuster, Inc.

Warner Books, Inc., 666 Fifth Avenue, New York, N.Y. 10103

W A Warner Communications Company

Printed in the United States of America

Not associated with Warner Press, Inc. of Anderson, Indiana

First Printing: October, 1978

10 9 8 7 6 5 4 3 2

To Joe Henderson and Rich Koster, who encouraged when encouragement was needed, praised when praise was due, and were silent when that was the kindest thing to do.

Contents

Introduction

My design is thin and linear. I am a nervous, shy noncombatant who has no feeling for people. I do not hunger and thirst after justice. I find no happiness in carnival, no joy in community. I am one with the writers on The New Yorker *whom Brendan Gill described. They touched each other only by accident, were secretive about everything, and never introduced anyone properly.*
—GEORGE SHEEHAN

GEORGE SHEEHAN is an uncommon man. Doctor. Writer. Runner. He is more than the sum of his visible activities.

Uncelebrated, underpublicized, he is equally unconcerned. He is unquestionably a philosopher, and much of his journalism is both poetic and mystic.

But most of all, Sheehan is himself. Through pain and sweat and honesty, he has discovered who he is and he has become that person. Totally. He is an eloquent, joyful man. Not one, perhaps, for these times—but one who has made himself comfortable in them.

To write of Sheehan is as compelling as it is frustrating. His definition of himself and his vision of the world around him deserve a wider and much more versatile audience than that which currently enjoys him.

But to attempt to interpret, to explain Sheehan is an exercise in inadequacy—if only because he does it so much better himself.

Biographically, George Sheehan is a fifty-nine-year-old cardiologist in Red Bank, New Jersey, a peaceful community fifty miles from Manhattan. He was reared in Brooklyn, the oldest of fourteen children. He has twelve children of his own.

In spite of these numbers, he is and always has been one of life's private people. His wife, Mary Jane, says of him, "He has never needed anyone else. He doesn't find most people interesting, and he's uninterested in the conventional."

Sheehan is a paradox. He is private but he is equally humble. He communicates with the world through his writing: a column called "The Innocent Bystander."

And he communicates with himself on the roads. Running is his essence. Through it, he has discovered the marvel of his own human spirit. He has become himself. He has fulfilled himself.

And from this experience, his running, has come rare articulation, a special, individual prism that is his window to the world. Individual, but far-reaching.

From an ever-mounting stack of Sheehan columns—a major problem was simply staying ahead of a man as relentless in his writing as he is in his running—the following sampler is offered:

On sport and character: "Sport will not build character; it will do something better. It will make a man free. It has this tremendous potential for self-revelation. What we want to know is who we are, and sport can tell us quickly, painlessly and as surely as any other human activity. Besides, I would rather be one than have it."

On the decline of heroes: "Where have all the heroes gone? They've gone with the simplicities and the pieties and the easy answers of another era. Our lack of heroes is an indication of the maturity of our age. A realization that every man has come into his own and has the capacity of making a success out of his life. Of being able to say, 'I have found my hero and he is me.' "

George Sheehan may or may not be his own hero, but he certainly is his own man. He lives life at his own pace, ignoring what he refers to as "the full-court press" which destroys the human game plan of so many of his fellows.

In his sixth decade, Sheehan runs for approximately an hour every other day during his lunch hour. He travels seven and a half miles along a winding, hilly river road, and then "towels off," because "honest sweat has no odor."

He lunches on "Tab and yogurt," does his work in a sports shirt, Levi's and canvas shoes, and is "a great napper. Naps are one of the most neglected parts of modern civilization," he states flatly.

Sheehan ran competitively in school, but then abandoned it for tennis until about fifteen years ago. Now, besides his daily adventures along the river ("I look for answers on the roads. I take my tools of sight, hearing, touch, smell, taste and intellect and run with them. I discover a total universe, a world that begins on the other side of sweat and exhaustion."), he runs in the Boston Marathon, and almost every Sunday he races in New York's Central Park.

"Racing is the lovemaking of the runner," he says. "It's hard to pass up. A runner has few friends, and they are always other runners. The place to meet them is at the races."

Modestly he maintains, "As a writer, I'm like Eddie Stanky, a .230 hitter. My theme is mostly the idea of play. Of bringing back your body, of becoming yourself, a total man. When I write, I tell who I am, what I'm like, what I've discovered running. I'm not embarrassed to expose myself. I don't care what I write as long as it's true."

He was and is a sports fan. But he sees danger in the pervasive spectating of today's America.

Sheehan believes that Americans must "spill out of the TV room after an event, and act on what they have seen." As for himself, he has been known to spill back onto the road for a second run of the day after being stimulated by a televised sporting event.

What George Sheehan is, really, is not any different from the rest of us. But what he does in the common situation, how he sees it and himself, sets him apart.

Sheehan writes, "Fitness is my life; it is indispensable. I have no alternative, no choice, but to act out this inner drive that seems entirely right for me."

Running is euphoria for Sheehan. "But then comes the Hill," he writes,

> and I know I am made for more. And by becoming more, I am challenged to choose suffering, to endure pain, to bear hardship. . . .
>
> At first the gentle swell carries me. . . . But gradually the Hill demands more and more. I have reached the end of my physiology. The end of what is possible. And now it is beyond what I can stand. The temptation is to say, "Enough." This much is enough. But I will not give in.
>
> I am fighting God. Fighting the limitations He gave me. Fighting the pain. Fighting the unfairness. Fighting all the evil in me and the world. And I will not give in. I will conquer this hill, and I will conquer it alone.

And George Sheehan will be himself. And, in writing about it, a gift to us all.

St. Louis Globe Democrat   RICH KOSTER

Prologue

THERE ARE TIMES when I am not sure whether I am a runner who writes or a writer who runs. Mostly it appears that the two are inseparable. I cannot write without running, and I am not sure I would run if I could not write. They are two different expressions of my person. As difficult to divide as my body and mind.

Writing is the final form of the truth that comes from my running. For when I run, I am a hunter and the prey is my self, my own truth. Not only my own truth felt and my own truth known, but my own truth written. Good writing is true writing. A thing written as true as it can be done. And that truth must be sought deep inside of me. "Look into your heart," said the poet, "and write." The hunt, then, is in my heart, my inner universe, my inner landscape, my deepest inner forest.

To reach these recesses, these hiding places below the conscious, I must first create a solitude. I must achieve the aloneness that is necessary for the creative act whether one is a master or a common man like myself. Because nothing creative, great or small, has been done by committee. And having reached this solitude, this privacy, this detachment, I must await the coming of truth and know how I am to write it.

But all of this, of course, begins much earlier. First an idea interests me. Then I put it in my head and allow it to germinate for a while. Each day I take it out and inspect it for substance. If it stands up I go to the typewriter for a day or two and accumulate pages of copy. Thurber referred to this effort as "mud" and saw it as the necessary first step to the finished product.

Next, I try to organize this raw material. Attempt to discover its essence, its true meaning, what it is all about. This is almost always a failure. What I have written until then is only information. It can make me neither laugh nor cry. It has yet to be transformed into something true, something alive. That must wait until I am on the roads. Only when I am on the run does this happen.

What running does is allow it to happen. Creativity must be spontaneous. It cannot be forced. Cannot be produced on demand. Running frees me from that urgency, that ambition, those goals. There I can escape from time and passively await the revelation of the way things are.

There, in a lightning flash, I can see truth apprehended whole without thought or reason. There I experience the sudden understanding that comes unmasked, unbidden. I simply rest, rest within myself, rest within the pure rhythm of my running, rest like a hunter in a blind. And wait.

Sometimes it is all fruitless. I lack the patience, the submission, the letting go. There are, after all, things to be done. People waiting. Projects uncompleted. Letters to be answered. Paperwork to do. Planes to be caught. A man can waste just so much time and no more waiting for inspiration.

But I must wait. Wait and listen. That inner stillness is the only way to reach these inner marvels, these inner miracles all of us possess. And when truth strikes, that brief, blinding illumination tells me what every writer comes to know. If you would write the truth, you must first become the truth.

The mystery of all this is that I must let it come to me. If I seek it, it will not be found. If I grasp it, it will escape. Only in not caring and in complete nonattachment, only by existing purely in the present, will I find truth. And where truth is will also be the sublime and the beautiful, laughter and tears, joy and happiness. All there waiting also.

All this, of course, defies logic. But so does life. We live, then explain things after the fact, and imperfectly. Somehow, perhaps not the way I have said, running gives me the word, the phrase, the sentence that is just right. And there are times when I take a column on the road and it is like pulling the handle of a slot machine. Bang comes down the first sentence. Bang comes down the second, and the paragraphs unfold. And then Bang, jackpot, the piece is finished, whole and true and good.

But writing is never easy. And no matter how well done, never to one's satisfaction. Writing, someone said, is turning blood into ink. Whatever, the idea of suffering is so natural to both writers and runners it seems to be a common bond.

And therefore no surprise when one turns out to be both.

1. Living

No athlete every lived, or saint or poet for that matter, who was content with what he did yesterday, or would even bother thinking about it. Their pure concern is the present. Why should we common folk be different?

YOU WIN, the experts agree, if the game is played in your rhythm. You lose if it isn't. Every basketball fan knows that. "We put on the press," a coach once told me, "not so much to create turnovers, but to upset our opponent's rhythm. To get them moving and not thinking." Most basketball fans know that, too.

But how many of us know that the same thing is happening in our lives every day? How many of us see that we are letting someone else set the rhythm of our lives, or that we face the equivalent of the Boston Celtic full-court press when we get out of bed each morning?

The clock is where it all starts. This mechanical divider of time controls our action, imposes our work day, and tells us when to eat and sleep. The clock makes every hour just an hour. It makes no distinctions between morning and afternoon. Aided by electric daylight, it doles out apparently equal minutes and seconds until *The Late Show*. And then, Good night.

The artist, especially the poet, has always known this to be wrong. He knows that time shortens and lengthens, without regard to the minute hand. Knows that we have a beat foreign to

17

this Greenwich metronome. Knows also there is an ebb and flow to the day that escapes the clock, but not us. And realizes that this rhythm, this tempo, is something peculiar to each individual, as personal and unchanging as his fingerprints.

The artists know this. The scientists have proved it. In *Biological Rhythms of Psychiatry and Medicine,* Bertram S. Brown writes, "Rhythm is as much a part of our structure as our flesh and bones. Most of us are dimly aware that we fluctuate in energy, mood, well being and performance each day, and that there are longer, more subtle variations each week, each month, each season, each year."

There was a time when we could sit and listen to these rhythms, but now they can hardly be heard over the din of the mechanical clocks set up by school and business and society. Now we have commuting and TV, three-day weekends and twelve-hour workdays, March migraines and April ulcers, twenty-one-year-old addicts and forty-five-year-old heart attacks.

Is anyone listening to his innards? But then, who listened to Socrates: "Know thyself"; or to Norbert Weiner: "To live effectively is to live with adequate information"; or to the Japanese philosopher Suzuki: "I am an artist at living, and my work of art is my life."

But that's what we must do to face that Celtic press every morning. Listen to what our body is trying to tell us. Know ourselves. Get adequate information. Become artists. Otherwise, someone else will control the pace, the game, and the score.

The Celtics are there and the press is on. They make us fit the job. Make us fit the hours. Make us fit the demands. Make us change to their tempo. March to their drummer. All the while, destroying our game plan. Our way of becoming all we are. Choking off what we do best.

They have made us prisoners of their artificial time, their mechanical clock. And all the while, they are planning the final irony. When we retire, they will give us a watch.

"Living the good life," wrote Nikolai Berdyaev, "is frequently dull and flat and commonplace." Our greatest problem, he claimed, is to make it fiery and creative and capable of spiritual struggle.

I agree. Life, except for a favored few, like poets and children and athletes and saints, is pretty much of a bore. Given the choice, most of us would give up the reality of today for the memory of yesterday or the fantasy of tomorrow. We desire to live anywhere but in the present.

I see that in myself. I start the day with an agenda of things to be done that makes me completely oblivious of what I'm doing. I arrive at work with no memory of breakfast and no idea of what kind of day it is. I am in perpetual concern or rumination about the future.

Numbers of people do the same thing in reverse. They avoid reality by living in the past. Nostalgia is their way of life. For them the good old days will never be equaled. Or emulated, for that matter, since these people rarely bestir themselves to any activity.

But for those active in mind and heart and body, the child and the poet, the saint and the athlete, the time is always now. They are eternally present. And present with intensity and participation and commitment. They have to be. When the athlete, for instance, turns his attention from the decision to be made this second and every second, he invites disaster. Should his concentration falter, should his mind wander to the next hole, the next set, the next inning, he will be undone. Only the now exists for him.

And the saint, for all his talk of heaven and the hereafter, knows that everywhere is right here, that all of time is right now, and that every man exists in the person in front of him. He knows that every instant he must choose and continue to choose among the infinite possibilities of acting—and being. He has no time to think on the future.

Nor has the poet. He must live on the alert. Always aware.

Always observant. When he does this well, he teaches us how to live more fully. "The feeling of life is in every line of the poem," writes James Dickey of the *Odyssey* by Kazantzakis, "so that the reader realizes time after time how little he himself has been willing to settle for in living; how much there is on earth, how inexplicable, marvelous and endless creation is."

For such a man, Perfection Past is no temptation. Nor is it for the saint or the athlete. Their characteristic fall from grace is in the contemplation of future triumphs. Heaven, perhaps, or a masterpiece, or a world's record. No athlete ever lived, or saint or poet for that matter, who was content with what he did yesterday, or would even bother thinking about it. Their pure concern is the present.

Why should we common folk be different? Are we not all poets and saints and athletes to some degree? Yet we refuse to make the commitment. Refuse to accept our own reality and work with it. So we live in the might-have-been world of the past and the never-will-be world of the future.

What we need is an element of present danger, an intimation of tragedy, some feeling of powerful implacable forces at our doorstep. We need a threat to the commonplace which will suddenly and for all time intensify its value.

Some years ago, that happened to me. I had run a personal best marathon in Oregon, and came home full of what I would accomplish at the Boston Marathon. Five days later, I came down with the flu, and everything of importance fell into place. I no longer cared what I ran at Boston, or indeed if I ran at Boston at all. What I cared about first was health, and then being able to run again. Just to run and feel the sweat and the breathing and the power in my legs. To feel again what it was like to toil up hills and to push through pain. Just that and perhaps that good tired feeling after a race. No past runs or future triumphs would comfort me. I was ready to repent and hear the Good News.

I knew then what every poet and child, every athlete and saint knows. The reason they say this is for all the marbles is because it is always for all the marbles. And the reason they say there is no tomorrow is because there is never, at this very moment, a tomorrow. We are always at risk, always at hazard.

"The trouble with this country," the late John Berryman once told fellow poet James Dickey, "is that a man can live his entire life without knowing whether or not he is a coward." For the burly Berryman and ex-fighter-pilot Dickey, ordinary day-to-day living did not provide the arena for the ultimate test, the moment of truth. For at least Dickey, war is the Big Game.

"Nothing," he writes, "gives you such a feeling of consequence and performing a dangerous and essential action in a great cause."

Where, indeed, can we find those qualities in our nine-to-five existence? "There were a lot of people in the service," says Dickey, "who cried when they were discharged because they knew they would have to go back to driving taxicabs and working in insurance offices." This perception of the heightened life of the soldier is expressed even by the late James Agee. Greatness, said Agee, emerges only under difficult circumstances, and it is war that produces these circumstances.

"The fact is," writes Agee, "that in war, many men go well beyond anything that any sort of peace makes possible for them."

But peace is where courage is. It lies somewhere between the wartime obliviousness to danger and the prudence of intellect that helps us preserve the race. Courage, if we go back to its Latin root, means that the seat of the intelligence is in the heart. That the heart determines a man's action, rather than his reason or his instincts. And if the heart has its reasons the mind does not know, it also has reasons the body does not know.

Our day-to-day living may seem mindless to the mind and of no consequence to the body, but the heart tells us different. The heart is where faith lies. Where we find the supreme act of courage, the courage to be. To take arms against oneself and become one's own perfection.

"Courage," according to Paul Tillich, "is the universal and essential self-affirmation of one's being." It therefore includes the unavoidable sacrifice of elements which are part of us, but prevent us from reaching our actual fulfillment.

In everyday language, this means that if the most essential part of our being is to prevail against the less essential, we may have to give up pleasure, happiness and even life itself. Courage, then, has nothing to do with a single act of bravery. Courage is how one lives, not one specific incident. Just as mortal sin is a life style, not one startling transgression.

Some, like Berryman and Dickey's men in *Deliverance*, still ask for that one supreme test. They go from peak experience to peak experience. Shooting rapids, making parachute jumps, climbing mountains. Looking for fear that can be met and overcome fairly. Looking for something of consequence done for a great and essential cause.

Can day-to-day living provide that? Can day-to-day living become the Big Game? It can if you increase the stakes. Take Pascal's wager that God exists. Even if men had no reason for believing in God, said William James, they would postulate one as a pretext for living hard and getting out of the game of existence the keenest possibilities of zest.

"Every sort of energy and endurance, of courage and capacity for handling life's evils," claimed James, "is set free in those who have religious faith." Religion, he concluded, will always drive irreligion to the wall.

It will because suddenly we are doing something for a great and essential cause. And everything we do is of consequence and demands our perfection, physically and intellectually and psychologically. But always keeping sight of the truth that each of us is unique, each affirming his own self. Therefore we are not submissive. We are not concerned with right and wrong but with verities like good and evil.

So you see it is not as Berryman said. We are, in fact, always being called upon to be whoever we are, hero or coward. The challenge is always there. But it is not the reckless pursuit of catastrophe, it is the acceptance and perfection of the persons we are meant to be. In that perennial process so frequently fatiguing, often depressing and occasionally painful, courage is the bridge between our minds and our bodies.

"There are days when you can't get the ball in the basket, no matter how hard you try," a basketball coach once told me. "But there is no excuse for not playing good defense."

I've known those days. Days when every shot is forced. Every idea manufactured. Days when invention and wit and originality disappear. When nothing is new or bright or wonderful. The air is the same. The people are the same. The problems are the same. And on those days I start to press and everything gets that much more difficult. The feel is gone. And with it the touch, the ease, the brilliance that play brings.

The offense, you see, is play. The defense is work. When I am on offense, I create my own world. I act out the drama I have written. I dance the dance I have choreographed. I sing the song I have composed. Offense is unrehearsed, exuberant, free-wheeling. Offense is an excitement which provides its own incitement. Its own compulsion. Its own driving force. It generates its own energy.

Offense, then, is an art. It cannot be forced. It is a spontaneous, joyful unification of the body and the mind. Therefore there are days it won't happen. The circuits of the brain will not open. The playful right hemisphere remains inaccessible.

Defense needs none of this. Defense is dull, boring, commonplace. It is the unimaginative plodding attention to duty. It is grit and determination and perseverance. It requires—can I use that word?—simply an act of the will. There is never a day you can't play defense. All you need is the decision to put out. To give one hundred percent.

On defense I am another person, the real person. Offense is a showplace for talent and even genius. What defense discloses is character. There effort and energy are a matter of the will. There I am asked, "Will I or won't I have it so?"

So defense is a matter of pride. The determination to be the person I am. The decision to give my word of honor, to take an oath that what has to be done will be done.

I try not to be proud of my offense. My play, my creativity, is a gift freely given and perhaps just as readily taken away. How many poets have turned to drink in an effort to restore that childlike way of looking at things? One has to be superstitious of such feats. The mystic never presses his luck. He accepts the vision, tells few if any, and does not expect to see it again.

I enjoy my play. Enjoy having the ball. But I know that my talent is something I carry. The real test comes when that is absent. When I am filled with fatigue and boredom and the desire to be off on a vacation or a short drunk. We all know this and react differently. In an army survey, sixty-four males averaging twenty-two years of age rode exercise bicycles at fifty-five percent of their maximum oxygen capacity. They were told to ride until it became so discomforting that they felt it necessary to stop. They stopped at times varying from one and a half to ninety-eight minutes.

Defense therefore narrows down to character, the ability to persist in the direction of the greatest resistance. There are teams, and successful ones, that no longer look solely to talent. They recruit on character. It is a long season. There are days on end of giving of yourself, and talent is not enough. Only character can fix my will to the idea that anything less than my best is unworthy of me and the game and the people I play it with. Only character can take defense and make it worth every iota of my mental and physical energy. Only character can make me function when my existence seems to be, as Emerson said, a defensive war.

I know all that, as I suspect you do. But I still play defense like almost everyone else. Knowing that eventually there will be a turnover and I will get the ball. And I dream of suddenly seeing that new idea plain like a man coming open. And I hit him and then see his shot, that long perfect parabola. Knowing that when the ball leaves his hand, like the idea not yet written, it will hit nothing but cords.

But dreams are not the stuff defense is made of. Nor are men, for that matter.

2. Discovering

*Who I am is no mystery. There is no need to tap
my phone or open my mail. No necessity to
submit me to psychoanalysis. No call to
investigate my credit rating. Nothing to be
gained by invading my privacy. There is, in fact,
no privacy to invade. Because like all human
beings I have no privacy. Who I am is visible for
all to see.*

WHEN I WAS YOUNG, I knew who I was and tried to become
someone else. I was born a loner. I came into this world with an
instinct for privacy, a desire for solitude and an aversion to loud
voices, to slamming doors and to my fellow man. I was born
with the dread that someone would punch me in the nose or,
even worse, put his arm around me.

But I refused to be that person. I wanted to belong. Wanted to
become part of the herd, any herd. When you are shy and tense
and self-conscious, when you are thin and scrawny and have an
overbite and a nose that takes up about one third of your body
surface, you want friends, you want to join with others. My
problem was not individuality, but identity. I was more of an
individual than I could handle. I had to identify with a group.

I was not unusual in this. Youth rebels, but rebels into other
conformities. Moves from Christianity to Communism. From
Brooks Brothers suits to T-shirts and jeans. From meat and po-

tatoes to macrobiotic diets. From crewcuts to long hair. But no one is going it alone. No one is facing just who he is.

We all know this to a degree. We refuse to accept the true self so painfully evident to the young, a self so tragically concealed from the old. "There is only one complete, unblushing male in America," wrote Erving Goffman in *Stigma,* "a young, married, white, urban, northern, heterosexual, Protestant father of college education, fully employed, of good complexion, weight and height, and a recent record in sports."

Anyone who fails to qualify in any one of these ways, comments Goffman, is going to view himself from time to time as unworthy, incomplete and inferior.

I spent the next four decades with these feelings of being unworthy and incomplete and inferior. Combating my own nature. Trying to become someone I was not. Concealing the real me under layer after layer of coping and adjusting and compensating. All the while refusing to believe that the person I had initially rejected was the real me. All the while trying to pass as a normal member of a normal society.

Then I discovered running and began the long road back. Running made me free. It rid me of concern for the opinion of others. Dispensed me from rules and regulations imposed from outside. Running let me start from scratch.

It stripped off those layers of programmed activity and thinking. Developed new priorities about eating and sleeping and what to do with leisure time. Running changed my attitude about work and play. About whom I really liked and who really liked me. Running let me see my twenty-four-hour day in a new light and my life style from a different point of view, from the inside instead of out.

Running was discovery, a return to the past, a proof that life did come full cycle and the child was father to the man. Because the person I found, the self I discovered, was the person I was in my youth. The person who was hypersensitive to pain, both physical and psychic, a nominal coward. The person who did not wish his neighbor ill, but did not wish him well either. That person was me and always had been.

And that person, wrote Dr. William Sheldon in his *Varieties of Human Physique,* was as normal as anyone else. In fact, wrote Sheldon, most people built like me act that way. Function follows structure, wrote Sheldon, and there is a relationship between body build and personality. To act any other way would be foreign to my nature. Sheldon's constitutional psychology was the scientific confirmation of what I had already learned about myself on the roads.

But could he tell me more? I dug into his *Atlas of Men* and there I was. Somatotype 235 (Mesomorphic ectomorphy), the fox among men. (Sheldon used an animal symbol for each body type.) The number 235 is somatotype shorthand for little or no fat (2); a moderate amount of muscle (3); and a predominance of skin, hair, nervous tissue and thin bones (5). (The limits being one to seven.)

Just like the fox, whom Sheldon described as delicate, lean and fast, a brittle, meat-hungry hunter of great speed and resourcefulness and endurance. If cornered, defiant and courageous beyond his real strength, but normally a furtive, secretive way of life. With a little less muscle and aggressiveness, I would be a squirrel. A little more and I would be a wolf.

So who is the 235? Like the fox, he is a defiant loner who makes his own rules. "The 235," writes Sheldon, "is too brittle for direct fighting, too exposed to thrive in the over-stimulation of ordinary social life, but he has a sense of confidence and a subconscious knowledge that he has a long life ahead."

This eventually leads him to a defiant way of life and often to the mental hospital, with now and then a savior emerging from the ranks. Like Prometheus, he sometimes has enough strength and endurance to triumph over the establishment.

I am not all that sure about being a 235. But there are days when I run when I know I am a fox. Days when I feel the Hound in pursuit. When I appeal to all swift things for swiftness and flee Him in the mist of tears and under running laughter. When I am hunted, but I know there will be no kill. Know that in the end, the Hound does run with the fox. He will not take me until I know what I need to know, and do what I am supposed to do.

No practiced eye is needed to distinguish a marathoner from a middle linebacker, and both of these from the nonathlete who would prefer to float around in the water conversing with his companions. Each is built for his task. The fragile, thin and small-boned distance runner can carry his light frame for miles and miles. The athletic and muscular football player is, as Don Meredith once said, hostile and agile and all those wonderful things. And the soft, round and fat swimmer rides high in the water and takes to it like a dolphin. In sports, your body determines your role. Function follows structure.

Life is no different. Our work, our life style, should be like our play. "To maintain one's self on this earth is not a hardship," wrote Thoreau, "but a pastime; as the pursuits of the simpler nations are still the sports of the more artificial." So the dominant component in physique that makes a person a distance runner also determines his approach to people and society, to eating and travel, to education and discipline, to the goals and values and behavior that marks his "good life." It should come as no surprise, therefore, that his "good life" is quite different from that of an aggressive football player and the relaxed socializer.

Yet educators, psychologists, theologians, social scientists and philosophers continue to lump us under that great umbrella, Man. Man, they tell us, using "we" and "our" and "us" and other collective words indiscriminately, should, would, will, ought or must do this or that.

They try to set up an all-embracing system of ethics and psychology. Tell us how to act and react. Lump the marathoner and the middle linebacker and the plump nonathlete into one composite human being.

It doesn't work in sports. It won't work in life. The centuries-old injunction "Know thyself" still applies. And the best way to know yourself is through an analysis of your body structure and the way it moves.

The Greeks were the first to notice this. Aristotle would have diagnosed me by the shape of my nose. Hippocrates looked at the body build and predicted subsequent disease. Later, men were classified by body humors, sanguine, phlegmatic, choleric and melancholic. Through the years men have been the connection between the way a man is constructed and the way he acts. As in all of nature structure determines function.

It wasn't until three decades ago, however, that Sheldon finally made this constitutional psychology a legitimate science. Sheldon saw that we were made up of different ratios of the three primary layers of tissue in the embryo: the ectoderm (skin and nervous tissue), the endoderm (intestines), the mesoderm (bone and muscle). Depending on the ratio and the predominating tissue, he was able to predict physical abilities, reaction to stress, aesthetic preferences, personality, temperament, and appropriate life style.

To read Sheldon is to have a whole new world opened to you. And to accept Sheldon is to accept yourself and your own peculiarities and to learn to live with the peculiarities and to learn to live with the peculiarities of others. To see yourself as normal and lovable no matter how odd you appear. And to see others as normal and lovable also, however difficult that is to comprehend.

Mostly we have gone wrong because we have failed to investigate this relationship between the shape of a man and how he behaves. We have not seen that physique and temperament are two aspects of the same thing. That structure must somehow determine function and with it the laws of each human being and his inner harmony. It identifies, to use Emerson's expression, the music of one's own particular dance of life.

Should his structure be analyzed correctly, a person would discover what kind of a body he has and therefore what kind of person he is. Learn his strengths and weaknesses, his likes and dislikes, how he relates to people and things, and even his appropriate life style. With such an analysis, he would come to know his own individual physiology, psychology and philosophy. ("A man's religion or philosophy," wrote Ellen Glasgow, "is as natural as the color of his eyes, or the tone of his voice.")

He would then perceive whether he is built for flight or fight or negotiation. Whether he was born to dominate his fellow men or socialize with them or avoid them completely. Such a study would tell him his work, his play, and whether he should marry, and if so to whom.

These are the restrictions on our inalienable rights of life, liberty and the pursuit of happiness. Our bodies define and determine that life, that liberty, and the form of that pursuit. Each is different for each person, and the body, writes Sheldon, is the objective record of the person. The task before us, says Sheldon, is to convert that record into speech.

For Sheldon there is no body–mind problem, no conscious versus unconscious, no break between the physical and the mental. He sees only structure and behavior as a functional continuum.

"My aim," he wrote, "is to develop every individual according to his best potential, protecting him from false ambition, the desire to be someone he never can be, and, even more important, never should be."

Without Sheldon you will try to reform yourself or others. Either despising yourself or viewing others as hopeless ruffians or sloppy bores. At least two thirds of the people in the world will set your teeth on edge if you don't understand each body build and the natural way these people act.

Mankind, said Sheldon, is divided into three races. But these races have nothing to do with color or geography or blood types. There is the athletic race, the muscular mesomorphs (the doers); the relaxed and amiable race of endormorphs (the talkers); and the thin small-boned race of ectomorphs (the thinkers).

These races have their special qualities, and harmony between these races is a lot more difficult then you might suspect. Each reacts differently and in ways the others may well find annoying or distressing or even dangerous. The mesomorph reacts to stress by going into action. He is best described by words like *dominant, cheerful, energetic, confident, competitive, assertive, optimistic, reckless,* and *adventurous.* The leisurely endomorph, on the other hand, reacts to stress by socializing. He is more likely to be described as *calm, placid, generous, affectionate, tolerant, forgiving, sympathetic, and kind.*

The ectomorph is none of these things. He is *detached, ambivalent, reticent, suspicious, cautious, awkward, and reflective.* He finds ideas much more interesting than people. And he reacts to stress by withdrawal.

In a world where concern for one's fellow man is basic, he preserves himself by being uninvolved. Like Einstein, he was made to pull in a single harness. Like Thoreau, he has found no companion so companionable as solitude. And with him, as Kazantzakis said, "People sense I have no need of them, that I am capable of living without their conversation. There are very few people with whom I could have lived for any length of time without them feeling annoyed."

His solution, of course, is not to impersonate the achiever or those who love community. This would be a pseudolife. Even if he succeeds, he fails. He must realize that the life that men praise and regard as successful is, as Thoreau said, but one of a kind.

And let his body lead him to the kind for him.

Who I am is no mystery. There is no need to tap my phone or open my mail. No necessity to submit me to psychoanalysis. No call to investigate my credit rating. Nothing to be gained by invading my privacy. There is, in fact, no privacy to invade. Because like all human beings I have no privacy. Who I am is visible for all to see.

My body tells all. Tells my character, my temperament, my personality. My body tells my strengths and weaknesses, tells what I can and can't do. If I were in a big black box and all you knew about me were my measurements, my lengths and breadths and circumferences, you would still know what kind of man I am.

William Sheldon used just such techniques in his *The Varieties of Human Physique*, describing the dominant temperaments that went with the primary physical components.

Sheldon was saying something all painters, but especially caricaturists, know. Man reveals himself through his body. "When I draw a man," wrote Max Beerbohm, "I am concerned simply with the physical aspect of him. I see all his salient points exaggerated and all his insignificant points proportionately diminished. In those salient points, a man's soul reveals itself. Thus, if you underline these points and let the others vanish, one is bound to bare the soul."

What each of their subject's bodies reveal to Sheldon's tape measure and Beerbohm's pen is the range of human reactions to stress, be it psychic or physical. And the even wider range of pleasures and desires. Yet each must be considered normal for that particular individual. Otherwise, he would be leading someone else's life. In effect, playing someone else's sport. My life is authentic only when I feel, think and do what I and I only must feel, think and do.

This is nowhere more evident than in the thin, detached, introspective, solitary long-distance runner. In an egalitarian, competitive society where there is no excuse for failure, he scores well below the median in need to achieve. He lacks the necessary psychological energy and enterprise and willingness to take risk.

This is a lot to learn, you might say, from one long look. But Sheldon is not alone in this idea. There are many who think that the body, the product of heredity and our genes, is still the dominant force in who we are and what will happen to us. So we hear of type-A personalities having heart disease; and of predicting coronary attacks from body build.

There are many who will not accept this. The Freudians, who think we were born with a clear slate and then childhood and our parents did us in, see this as an aberration. So do the dreamers of the American Dream, who say we can be anything we want to be. They see Sheldon's theories as deterministic, a threat to freedom.

I see it differently. My body shows me what I am free to be. It does not set a boundary but shows me a fulfillment. And liberates me from a depressing past and an impossible future.

Who are you? Take a look.

I am a runner. Years ago that statement would have meant little more to me than an accidental choice of sport. A leisure time activity selected for reasons as superficial as the activity itself.

Now I know better. The runner does not run because he is too slight for football, or hasn't the ability to put a ball through a hoop, or can't hit a curve ball. He runs because he has to. Because in being a runner, in moving through pain and fatigue and suffering, in imposing stress upon stress, in eliminating all but the necessities of life, he is fulfilling himself and becoming the person he is.

I have given up many things in this becoming process. None was a sacrifice. When something clearly became nonessential, there was no problem in doing without. And when something clearly become essential, there was no problem accepting it and whatever went with it.

From the outside, this runner's world looks unnatural. The body punished, the appetites denied, the satisfactions delayed, the motivations that drive most men ignored. The truth is that the runner is not made for the things and people and institutions that surround him. To use Aldous Huxley's expression, his small guts and feeble muscles do not permit him to eat or fight his way through the ordinary rough-and-tumble.

That he is not made for the workaday world, that his essential nature and the law of his being are different from the ordinary and usual is difficult for everyone, including the runner, to comprehend. But once it is understood, the runner can surrender to his self, this law. And become, in the puritan sense, the "free man," the man who is attached only to the good.

In this surrender, the runner does not deny his body. He accepts it. He does not subdue it, or subjugate it, or mortify it. He perfects it, maximizes it, magnifies it. He does not suppress his instincts, he heeds them. And goes beyond this animal in him toward what Ortega called his veracity, his own truth.

The finished product is therefore a lifetime work. This giving up, this letting go, the detachment from attachments, is an uneven process. You should give up only what no longer has any attraction to you, or interferes with something greatly desired. That was Gandhi's rule. He advised people to keep doing whatever gave them inner help and comfort.

I have learned that also. Whatever I give up, whatever innocent indulgences, ordinary pleasures or extraordinary vices, I do so from inner compulsion, not in a mood of self-sacrifice or from a sense of duty, I am simply doing what comes naturally.

For the runner, less is better. The life that is his work of art is understated. His needs and wants are few, he can be captured in a few strokes. One friend, a few clothes, a meal now and then, some change in his pockets; and, for enjoyment, his thoughts and the elements.

And though he's on the run, he's in no hurry. Concerned at times with tenths of a second, he actually responds to the season, moving through cycle and cycle, toward less and less until body and mind and soul fuse, and all is one.

I see this simplicity as my perfection. In the eyes of observers, however, it appears completely different. My success in removing myself from things and people, from ordinary ambition and desires, is seen as lack of caring, proof of uninvolvement, and failure to contribute.

So be it. A larger view of the world might include the possibility that such people are necessary. That the runner who is burning with a tiny flame on some lonely road does somehow contribute. And while a world composed solely of runners would be unworkable, a world without them would be unlivable.

3. Understanding

*I am who I am and can be nothing but that.
"Do not mistake me for someone else," said
Nietzsche. Do not mistake me for a listener or
citizen or friend. And when I get that look in my
eye that says I'm going "away," do me a favor.
Let me go.*

WHEN I RUN THE ROADS, I am a saint. For that hour, I am
Assisi wearing the least and meanest of clothes. I am Gandhi,
the young London law student, trotting ten or twelve miles a
day and then going to a cheap restaurant to eat his fill of bread. I
am Thoreau, the solitary, seeking union with the world around
him.

On the roads, Poverty, Chastity and Obedience come naturally. I am one of the poor in spirit who will see God. My chastity is my completion in the true Eros which is play. And the Ten
Commandments are the way the world works.

But off the roads, that all changes. Anyone who has lived with
a distance runner knows that. They see in him what was said of
Moses by the advisers of an Eastern king. Looking at his picture, they said, "This is a cruel, greedy, self-seeking dishonest
man." The king was puzzled and asked Moses, who said the
experts were right. "That's what I was made of," he said, "I
fought against it and that's how I became what I am."

Unfortunately, I am a long way from that final victory. And, like most distance runners, I have all the bad features of a saint without any of the redeeming ones. Pity the family and friends who have to care for us.

"Caring" is the word, because the average distance runner is a helpless creature who can with difficulty change a light bulb. He is unable to fend for himself in a competitive world and has long since given up trying. From long experience, he expects that things will be done for him. Meals provided. Laundry done. Errands run. All of the amenities taken care of so he can do his thing. And do it to his heart's content.

So my poverty is not poverty. My needs may be little, like Saint Francis. But unlike him, the little I need, I need very much. The little I want, I want very much.

My breakfast is simple. But it must be perfect. Do not cut my English muffin with a knife or I may not talk to you for the rest of the day. My clothes may be rejects and hand-me-downs, but lose them or even have them in a laundry at the wrong time and my day may be ruined. And so it goes from shoes to yogurt, everything has to be just right or the day becomes dark and dreary. And not only for me, but for the people around me.

If I do resemble Assisi, it is in the matter of money. I never have any. I expect others to take care of me. Pay my entry fee. Take care of my lunch. Only in absent-minded moments will I reach for a check. Rarely through the years have I been caught with enough change to buy a chance for charity.

And if poverty is still a battle, what about chastity? Even more of a struggle. Like thousands of scrawny, pinch-faced Irishmen, I have fought my body since my First Communion. Known that the body belongs to the Devil. Read Joyce or O'Casey or even Yeats, who wrote in his diary that he set these things down so other young men might not think themselves peculiar.

So, off the roads, chastity comes from the highest form of fear—the fear of eternal damnation. "Others, I am not the first," wrote Housman, "have wished more mischief than they durst." Only beyond such restraint is the reconciliation of body and soul and then the true Eros and the love of friends and, finally, the agape where in the giving we receive.

And finally, what of obedience? Discipline in running, discipline in training, comes easily. Discipline in real life is another story. The mind and the will and the imagination are not as easily controlled as the legs and the thighs and the panting chest. Running, of course, helps. The art of running, as Eugene Herrigal wrote of the art of archery, is a profound and far-reaching contest of the runner with himself. And that contest should lead to his perfection.

When I was young, I was afflicted with what my aunt called "convenient deafness." I still am. I have the ability to tune out what is going on around me. It is normal for me to retreat inside myself and become less and less aware of my surroundings. If I am in a group and not talking, do not suppose I am listening. I am "away." I am off in another world. Off in my natural habitat, my mind.

Being "away" is the true freedom. I escape to where I want to be, thinking what I want to think, creating what I want to create. Wherever I am, whomever I am with, it doesn't matter. The greatest bore in the world may be holding the stage, but I am untouched. I am, as Yeats once said, like a child in the corner playing with his blocks.

And being "away" from making a fool of myself. When I am with people I am always saying too much or too little. Something better left unsaid, or stupid, or soon regretted. If it takes me ten hours to write a six-hundred-word essay, how could I possibly say something out of hand that I would ever care to have repeated?

I am a descendant of similar people of the mind. Men like Kierkegaard and Emerson and Bertrand Russell. Those who saw themselves early as different and, at first, disastrously so. "I was a shy, solitary prig," say Russell. Ungenerous and selfish, cautious and cold, was how Emerson described himself. Kierkegaard made much the same analysis. "Ideas," he wrote, "are my only joy, human beings an object of indifference."

Such people, according to Ortega, have very little knowledge of women, business, pleasure and passion. They lead an abstract life, he said, and rarely throw a morsel of authentic live meat to the sharp-pointed teeth of their intellect.

The way out of that abstract existence is to go out. If not to other people, at least to the body. And so they became great walkers, outdoor people. Emerson's journal has a reference to a forty-mile walk from Roxbury to Worcester, and Russell wrote of his pleasant relaxation after his twenty-five-mile walks.

And that, I suppose, is why I run and find there the authentic life. "First be a good animal," said Emerson. And in running I am that animal, the best animal I can be. Doing what I am built to do. Moving with the grace and rhythm and certainty that I seem to have possessed from all time.

And there I find joy. Kierkegaard was mistaken in that. There is no joy in ideas. Joy comes at the peak of an experience and then always as a surprise. I cannot have joy on demand. At best, I go where I have felt it before. And that is mostly on the river road, moving at a pace I could hold forever and my mind running free. So that I am in this alternation of effort and relaxation, of systole and diastole. And then I have that fusion where it all is play and I am capable of anything. I become a child.

It will not surprise you that the thinkers believe that our true journey is back to our childhood. One mystic wrote that man's perfection and bliss lay in the transformation of the bodily life to joyful play. Norman Brown declared that man is that species of animal which has as its immortal project the recovering of its childhood.

I will not apologize, therefore, for an activity that makes me a child. An activity that takes me away from women and business, pleasure and passion. An activity that is its own meaning. An activity without purpose.

So I run in joy and even afterwards there is a completeness that lingers and is even restored in the long hot shower. I am "away," not in the mind but in its warm, relaxed, tingling happy body, the feeling of running still in my legs and arms and chest. I am still enjoying who I was and what I did that hour on the road.

Some of you may wonder that a life can be felt so completely in the absence of other people. I wonder at that myself. It goes against everything I have been taught. Everything that went into the preservation of our culture.

But I am who I am and can be nothing but that. "Do not mistake me for someone else," said Nietzsche. Do not mistake me for a listener or citizen or friend. And when I get that look in my eye that says I'm going "away," do me a favor. Let me go.

The distance runner, I have observed, is usually a secretive person. I am one myself. There was a time before I came to running when I rarely looked anyone in the eye. Even now I am reluctant about it. Some, I am sure, think me shifty-eyed and not to be trusted. And to an extent they are right. I am shifty-eyed. I avoid that direct gaze. I prefer to neither see nor be seen.

Seeing, looking into another's eye's, can be a total revelation. The look, wrote Ortega, is an act that comes directly from an inwardness with the straight-line accuracy of a bullet. Erving Goffman described it as "the most direct and purest reciprocity that exists anywhere."

The look, then, is in the present tense. It has nothing to do with past or future, with were or will be. The look is now. It is direct. Like a poem it must not mean, but be. We look through, not with, our eyes. Our eyes, therefore, are what we are. My eyes are me.

The eyes, then, reveal and in revealing appeal for revelation. Richard Avedon, the photographer, says of himself and his subjects, "We are there eye-to-eye, completely open, naked to each other." He is there, he says, asking them to give and they are trying to give, to demonstrate themselves. And when that ultimate revelation is achieved, he says, "Thank you." Then the strangers again become strangers. Eyes then glaze over. Looks become unfocused. The connection is broken.

The look, then, tells no less than who I am. It says, "This is the real me." It tells truth in the sense the Greeks used the word: to bare. The look, that subtle yet tenacious look, does just that. It bares me down to the submerged inner landscape of my soul.

In times gone by I was ashamed of that truth, ashamed of the self I supposed myself to be. And, being ashamed, avoided other eyes. There was a time when I could not abide with that soul or that inner landscape. I sought only to hide it. I lived then in an either/or world. If you were not one thing, you were the other. I was always the other, the unacceptable, the sinner, the outsider. And it was all there in my eyes. One look straight into my eyes and the observer would know me for what I was. One who cared little for his fellow man. One who viewed the Other, if not as an enemy, at the very least as a threat.

In one unguarded unequivocal gaze, one sharp straight line from one heart to another, I would be illuminated like a countryside by a lightning flash. All my embarrassments, my mistakes, my playing the fool. So I learned to protect myself. To wear a mask. To talk into the air. To control others' access to me. To keep intruders away from my real self or who I thought my real self to be.

In those days the worst command I could hear was "Look me straight in the eye and tell me that." Then inevitably the truth would come out. I would be caught in the lie. "Never let them get your eyes" was the motto of a famous New York detective. If you did they knew you. In that instant all deception was over. My eyes revealed in those seconds what I have buried for years. Exposed scars and opened wounds I thought long healed.

Running has changed all that. Given a new perspective to that inner landscape. I accept my ups and downs, my ins and outs, my uncertain being and becoming. I do my best. I remain patient and enjoy. And most of all I make no judgments except about effort. There I demand the most and more.

So my look is no longer furtive. No longer unfocused and shifting over the surface. No longer directed three inches to the left of the listener's ear or just over the speaker's left shoulder. I am able to show myself to another human being, desiring to give my love and receive theirs. I no longer need to avert my gaze from anyone.

But I do. I am still the secretive runner. My looks are still for those who are like myself. Those who share my truth, my feelings, my perception of the world as happy and sad. When I lecture to runners I go from one face to the other speaking eye to eye, mind to mind, heart to heart. And I am moved as I move them.

At races it is much the same. Not so much, perhaps, before the race, when we are a little frightened and worried about the future. At that time I sometimes exhibit a spurious ease and a false assurance to mask that fear.

It is afterward that we see inside of each other. It is after we have survived a desperate thirty minutes that there is pride and happiness and union in the looks we exchange.

There even poetry fails. Poetry, said Eliot, is the best possible words in the best possible arrangement. Yet it is still less than the nonverbal that provoked it. Poetry is only the putting into words of what my eyes and yours have said.

I have always felt uneasy in the presence of authority. The sight of a police car in my rear-view mirror is enough to paralyze me from the waist down. Any legal-looking document in the mail can ruin my day. And one word from someone with a title or uniform and I snap to attention like a Marine in boot camp. My world, you see, is filled with drill instructors whom I avoid as much as possible.

Every once in a while I fail. A dozen or so years back, I made a U turn in our main street after picking up the morning paper. When I completed the turn, I was looking right into the face of the chief of police. He knew me immediately for what I was. A man who hated rules but was afraid of those who enforced them. "Don't ever do that again," he said. I never did and I never will.

But human laws are minor. Human authority can be either avoided or heeded with little change in everyday living. Nature cannot. Nature's laws can be either major or minor, but they cannot be ignored. Nature, I have found, can lean on you more than any human being. It is one thing to avoid principals and bosses and policemen, but quite another to avoid the laws that govern the universe.

Human law is soft and kindly and forgiving compared to the ones that run the cosmos. Traffic tickets and felonies, and income tax evasions and legal suits are easily negotiable compared to gravity and the laws of motion and thermodynamics. Laws, incidentally, that are omnipresent and unavoidable. I can evade a clash with my head, but not with the rules that make the world work.

That clash begins when I get into the car in the morning. It may or may not start. Either way, the car is obeying rules that govern energy and its transformation. Rules from which there is no appeal. There is no letting you off just this once, no probation, no leniency. And neither prayers nor curses will revive a dead generator.

Should I try to circumvent this need for mechanical conformity by getting a push, I only dig the hole a little deeper. Now other regulations, about force and vectors and torque, come into play. The bumpers lock.

What good pleading extenuating circumstances? Temporary insanity? A defect in toilet training? The day has barely begun and I am in the hands of tyrants, controlled by a dictator.

Should the car start, this unfeeling oppression continues. As I accelerate, my cup of coffee previously resting securely on the open door of the glove compartment falls to the floor. The coffee splashes my freshly cleaned Levi's and the books and papers on the seat beside me. I brake and the deceleration covers the floor with a fine mixture of coffee and correspondence. Before the trip is complete I have experienced the adverse effects of gravity, centrifugal force, friction and any number of other laws in nature that can wreck your day.

At those times, I think of heaven as the place where all those laws can be broken. Coffee never spills no matter how carelessly I place it down or how quickly I shift. And everything stays in place no matter how fast I take the turns. And should I forget and leave something on the roof of the car, it will remain there until I get to my destination. And I will be preserved from the violence and interference of laws both human and natural.

Actually, it is the other way around. Law preserves me from violence and interference. Because my neighbors obey policemen and legislators and bureaucrats, because my coffee and car obey the precepts of physics and science, I live in a stable world. And because of that, I am able to rise above the law and become a free man. The least I can do is obey the traffic laws and learn how to drive a car.

Generosity is not one of my faults. I have no impulse to spread my money around. No temptation to give until it hurts. I treat my neighbor as myself. Which means to use it up, wear it out, make it do. And ask for separate checks.

I wasn't brought up that way. My father made a point on entering a restaurant with a party to see the waiter immediately to make sure he got the bill. He viewed any effort by others to change this arrangement as a personal insult. In the days before the expense account and the charge card, he was the quickest draw with a wallet I ever saw.

Being a slow man with a buck is therefore not a matter of training. It seems to relate to body build and is apparently characteristic of weak, small-boned people like myself. It is an especially common finding in lonely long-distance runners. Also like myself.

Race directors know this only too well. Should they raise the entry fee a quarter, they get complaints from all sides.

And if they neglect to give out free meals or complimentary T-shirts, they will draw protests even from affluent road runners. It is not unusual, despite their dependence on their organizations, for most runners regardless of financial status to try to compete without shelling out a few dollars for an AAU card. And almost to a man they have to be dunned for their Road Runners Club dues.

You may look on this as being stingy or miserly, think of our habits as to sharing costs and helping others as un-Christian, even immoral. But that is because you are you, and we are quite different. My nickel-and-dime approach to life comes from deep inside of me. It is part of the person I am, part of the body I inhabit, part of my peculiar union of flesh and spirit.

And it is not only instinct. It is also external evidence of a personal austerity, a self-imposed mortification, an attempt at simplicity and poverty and the childlike attitude that Bernanos said was the only defense against the Devil. Against, you might say, his Devil, not yours. Except that his Devil seems to be my Devil. The distance runner's particular Devil.

Part of our problem is other people. People who, as Russell Baker wrote in his *New York Times* piece "The Summer of '39," used to hold us upside down by the heels to prove how strong they were. That was our outer world then. And we still live in a world controlled by the people who hold us upside down by the heels to prove how strong they are. It is a world primarily of money. A world of mortgages and life insurance and down payments and grocery bills. A world that is easy pickings for those who learn how to move around in it; and torture for those who don't.

I have never learned how. And never will learn how. What I have learned is to get outside the world. To need less. To reduce my wants. To be satisfied with essentials. I have learned that possessions get in my way. That money and what it can buy are distractions. I have learned that simplicity starts when income exceeds outgo.

If I were a world class runner in my age group my body fat would be less than six percent. Instead it is twice that and always will be. The reason? I am a natural-born, died-in-the-wool, nothing-can-be-done-about-it freeloader. Hungry or not, I will eat anything that is free. Last month, for instance, after a fifteen-kilometer run in which I absolutely wasted myself and went to the point of exhaustion and beyond, I nevertheless accepted and finished a postrace box lunch of orange drink and fried chicken. Yes, fried chicken.

Hand me a box lunch and, however indigestible it is, I'll gobble it up. Hand me a meal ticket and regardless of appetite I'll get on line. When all desire for food has vanished offer me anything edible and I'll manage somehow to get it down. Inside of me, as in every thin man, there is a fat man saying "Eat." And my fat man is adding "Eat, it's free."

You may not have noticed, but there are free meals not only at races, but everywhere. Everywhere, that is, if you see as free any meal that you don't pay for right there on the spot. So home meals and free access to the kitchen at night are really meals offered gratis. At those times the inner voice saying "Eat, it's free" is just as loud as when I am accepting the traditional beef stew after the Boston Marathon. I'm a freeloader in my own home.

Fortunately this tendency to eat when it's free is counterbalanced by an equal and opposite tendency not to eat when it isn't. I can go heroic lengths of time without food if I have to buy it myself. Although I look on this as being frugal, there are some places where I am thought to be a cheapskate. I will admit that I am reluctant to break a dollar, but only because there is soon very little left of the original buck. And I do fortify this reluctance to spend money on food by having no money on me to spend. There is no better way to control impulse shopping.

Buying food never did make sense to me. When I finally spend some money I prefer to have some permanent evidence of the expenditure. Doing it on something that is immediately consumed leaves me feeling cheated. For much the same reason, I suppose, I have never smoked. Buying something and then setting it on fire is incomprehensible.

So for long periods during the day I am protected by this natural miserliness or what I prefer to think of as natural austerity. When I lunch it is usually forty cents' worth of yogurt and tea, and back to work. It is only later when I arrive home that things begin to go badly.

From then on I eat as if I were a digestive athlete. I clean my plate just as I did when my mother first told about those less fortunate starving children who could live a week on what I left behind. Later I go through the kitchen like some TV-game-show winner given free access to a supermarket. During the first two commercials I can use up my five hundred calories earned so dearly with five miles on the roads. Unless somehow restrained I will go through the breadbox, get involved with the pretzels, succumb to the cheese crackers, and do away with any remaining ice cream. And still have an hour to go before the nightly news.

The answer, it seems to me, is to turn the home into a commercial establishment. Eliminate the free meal. Put everything on a pay-as-you-go basis. When I get home at night I should be faced by a menu with everything à la carte and quite expensive. And no credit cards, only cash accepted. Once I start computing cost per calories and watching the right-hand side of the bill of fare I'll quickly get back to my normal penurious self.

And for the after-dinner period there should be a checkout counter in the kitchen. Then the trip through that larder will take a lot longer as I reluctantly part with my well-worn dimes and quarters. And I'll get back to the TV room with only the best buys of the day.

On that great don't-come-and-get-it day, I'll have an answer to the fat man inside of me: "Shut up, you dummy, they're charging money for it."

The way to argue against drunkenness is not to tell lies about it. Alcohol can take you places the sober man may never see. Sobriety, wrote William James, diminishes, discriminates and says no; drunkenness expands, unites and says yes. "The sway of alcohol over mankind," he concluded, "is unquestionably due to its power to stimulate the mystical faculties of human nature."

This is what alcohol can do: Can give you a glimpse of yourself in your own particular world, of you as part of the cosmos. Drink also reveals the person you are. Whether you are the solitary schizoid, thinking great thoughts and living in fantasy. Or the gregarious manic-depressive who wants to be part of a warm and eternally friendly group. Or the muscular paranoid, ready to settle any disagreement with his fists.

What alcohol cannot do is bring these insights into purposeful action. Having glimpsed the person he is, the drinker must now find an alternate and fruitful path to his truth. To do this, he must first disentangle himself from alcohol, and then rescue himself from the lies of his daily living. So it is frequently the ex-alcoholic, who has been there and back, who experiences the new birth. It is the former lush who finally unites his divided self. It is the reformed drunk who accepts the person he is without reservation. And pursues that perfection however mediocre or even abnormal it may appear to someone else.

Becoming an ex-alcoholic, however, is not easy. Drink may be futile and ultimately degrading, but only the fortunate drinker discovers this. And it is the even more fortunate one who then comes upon a new and healthy path to the summit of his physical and mental powers. Before the liver goes, the heart enlarges, and the brain begins to deteriorate, he must get the message that there is a better way to experience himself and the universe.

My own drinking habits changed because of two such fortunate events. Back in those days when I was living it up on Saturday nights, I had always supposed that drink made me brilliant. I thought that someone should be writing down everything I said, preserving these great ideas and clever bon mots for posterity. Then, one night, someone took fifty feet of home movies of me under the influence. What I saw on the screen looked like the Missing Link rather than the intellectual I imagined myself to be. Here was photographic evidence that when drunk I was incapable of thought, much less of expressing it. Because of that film, I quit serious drinking. Not so much to become the person I was, but simply to rejoin the human race.

Distance running, my next discovery, was a positive factor and the decisive one. Negative injunctions never work. Lives are changed by do's, not don'ts. And if one is to stop drinking permanently, one must be actively involved in becoming what one is. Distance running did that for me. It reintroduced me to my body. And my body, I found out, had a mind of its own. It would no longer accept anything less that the best. Having gotten into trim, it refused to be tampered with. Having reached the peak of its powers, it dragged my mind and my will along with it.

Now the hour a day on the roads began to provide the altered states of consciousness that alcohol supplied so fleetingly. Running, I learned, gave me a natural high. What happens in those moments I am not sure. Andrew Weil, the author of *The Natural Mind,* calls it the integration of the conscious and unconscious spheres of our mental life. "This integration," he states, "is essential to the wholeness (health) of body and mind."

I'll give him no argument there, but this I know: whatever it is, it starts with the body. By first reaching a fitness which reveals the real person inside my body (just so does the sculptor find the statue inside the stone). And then through this body, this mirror of my soul, this key to my personality, this telltale of my temperament, I see myself as I really am.

I don't drink much anymore. I am never the life of any party. The hostess who invites me knows within the first five minutes she has made a mistake. I usually wander into the kitchen for a cup of coffee and then find a large book and a quiet place to read until the festivities are over. I have found out who I am. And I have no intention of impersonating anyone else.

Some people liked me better when I was drinking.

4. Beginning

If you think that life has passed you by, or, even
worse, that you are living someone else's life,
you can still prove the experts wrong.

THE PEOPLE WHO THINK they know say that given a second chance a man will make the same mess of his life he did the first time. Playwrights and novelists over the years have never given us any hope that reliving our lives would have any different result the second time around. Our scientists and psychologists seem to agree. Even such disparate thinkers as Bucky Fuller and B. F. Skinner are together on this. "We shouldn't try to change people," writes Skinner. "We should change the world in which people live." It is a thought Fuller has often expressed.

Some, of course, take an opposing view. The people who deal in Faith, Hope and Charity seem to think that one day is as good as another for changing your personal history. Philosophers since recorded time have recommended it. From Pindar to Emerson they have told us to become the thing we are; to fulfill our design; to choose our own reality, our own way of being a person. What they didn't tell us was how to do it; or how difficult it would be. When Paul said to put on the New Man, he reminded us of the unlimited potential of man; but the lives we lead constantly remind us of the obvious limits to this potential.

Clearly the Good Life is not as accessible as the books say. And yet it is not from want of trying that we have failed. We start our new lives with almost as much frequency as Mark Twain gave up smoking (thousands of times) and with about the same success.

Can tomorrow be the first day of the rest of our life? And can that life be completely different from the mess it is today? The answer, of course, has to be yes, or all those great men wouldn't have said so. But how do you go about it?

The first thing to do, it seems to me, is to retrace your steps. To go back to that period of your life when you were operating as a successful human being (although you most likely weren't aware of it). To go back to those times when your soul, your self, was not what you possessed or your social standing or other people's opinion but a totality of body, mind and spirit. And that totality interacting freely with your total environment.

Somewhere past childhood that integration of self and that response to the universe began to dissolve. We came more and more to associate who we were with what we owned; to judge ourselves by other people's opinions; to make our decisions by other people's rules; to live by other people's values. Coincidentally, or maybe not so coincidentally, our physical condition began to decline. We had reached the fork in the road. We took the well-traveled path.

One who took the path overgrown with weeds and rarely used was Henry David Thoreau. The world knows Thoreau as a man of intellect, a shrewd observer, a rebel against conventional values. What has not been emphasized was that he was an athlete, and a fine one. He was, of course, a great walker. This kept him in prime physical condition. "I inhabit my body," he wrote, "with inexpressible satisfaction: both its weariness and its refreshments." It would not be too much to say that Thoreau's other activities derived their vitality from the vitality of his body. That the self that was Thoreau depended on being as physical as he could be. And that no life can be completely lived without being lived completely on a physical level.

If Thoreau was right, the way to find who we are is through our bodies. The way to relive our life is to go back to the physical self we were before we lost our way. That tuned-in self that could listen with the third ear was aware of the fourth dimension and had a sixth sense about the forces around it. That tuned-in self that was sensitive and intuitive, and perceived what is no longer evident to our degenerating bodies.

This may come as a surprise even to physical-fitness leaders. Physical-fitness programs have long been based on the desire to lead a long life, to forestall heart attacks, to feel better generally or to improve your figure. No one ever told us that the body determined our mental and spiritual energies. That with the new body we can put on the new person and build a new life, the life we were always designed to lead but lost with the body we enjoyed in our youth.

Now, common sense will tell you that you'll never see twenty-eight again, but the facts on fitness show that almost anyone can reach levels of vigor and strength and endurance equal to most of the twenty-eight-year-olds in this country. Given the good fortune to find an athletic activity that fits him, a man can recapture his youth and a second chance to listen to what his total self held important at that time.

If you think that life has passed you by, or, even worse, that you are living someone else's life, you still can prove the experts wrong. Tomorrow can be the first day of the rest of your life. All you have to do is to follow Thoreau. Inhabit your body with delight, with inexpressible satisfaction; both its weariness and its refreshments.

And you can do it if you'll just go back to that fork in the road.

If you are seeking the solutions for the Great Whys of your creation, you will have to start with the Little Hows of your day-to-day living. If you are looking for the answers to the Big Questions about your soul, you'd best begin with the Little Answers about your body. If you would become either saint or metaphysician, you must first become an athlete.

Study the lives of those who sought their own meaning and

the meaning of the cosmos. Or read the works of the saints who lived the questions and waited for the answers in the hereafter. The common denominator of these people is asceticism, which comes from the Greek *ascesis,* meaning rigorous training, self-discipline and self-restraint.

The ascetic is no oddball recluse; he is someone seeking his optimum, his law, the life he is to lead. And asceticism is practiced by weight lifters, football players and distance runners as well as by saints and philosophers.

"First be an ascetic, which means gymnastics," wrote Kierkegaard. "Then bear witness to the truth." And he took his own asceticism into walking and there he thought out and composed his philosophy. Kant was another great walker. His neighbors could set their clocks by his passage through town.

For Thoreau, the length of his walk made the length of his writing; if shut up in the house, he did not write at all. The mind and the body, wrote Huxley, another advocate of fitness, are organically one. Motion and meditation are apparently a unity. "Sit as little as possible," wrote Nietzsche. "Give no credence to any thought that was not born outdoors, while one moved about freely—in which the muscles are not celebrating a feast, too."

But for your muscles to celebrate, and you to move about freely, you have to pay attention to details like diet and climate and training. How can one play and think and find truth when stuffed with jelly doughnuts? Nutrition is still a very controversial subject, but few will argue that we get into more difficulty eating than fasting, and that our intake of salt and refined sugar is unnatural.

Climate is something about which we don't have too many options. Some are luckier than others. When Green Bay trained in Santa Barbara for the first Super Bowl, one of the Packers asked a reporter, "What have these people done to deserve to live here?" Others have to live in their own equivalents of Leipzig, Venice and Basel, which Nietzsche found disastrous to his physiology.

Still, exercise covers a multitude of dietary and meteorological sins. The acclimatized athlete adjusts to his environment and begins to use altitude or heat or humidity to make him stronger. And his diet, through some inherent body wisdom now being allowed to operate, begins to conform with his needs, his nature.

Attend, then, to the little things, to the commonplace of diet and climate and your own form of play and sport. "I myself am my only obstacle to perfection," wrote Kierkegaard. The athlete has always known that. The athlete and the child at play have that same perception. That all things are possible and that I alone am master of my fate.

True, we must render unto Caesar. There are the forty hours we must contribute to the common good and the preservation of ourselves and our families. But beyond this door is freedom. The effort to make work more than the key to this door may not succeed in our lifetime or, indeed, in future lifetimes. But that should not bother us.

Even now work seems to distress psychologists and psychiatrists and sociologists more than the workers themselves. They have found the wisdom to accommodate to it. And they have not allowed its obvious physical, spiritual and psychological inadequacies to affect them.

Today's work does not make us the persons we can be. Work is simply the price to be paid. Having earned our daily bread, we can turn to our daily play. Having paid our dues for survival, we can pay attention to the more serious business of living. Having taken care of our bank accounts, we are now ready to take care of our bodies and the minds that go with them.

Wisdom, it says here, begins at 5 P.M.

"Is there a doctor who has the time," wrote a seventeen-year-old West German to the medical ministry, "to tell me how to live healthily?"

I'm not sure there is a doctor who would touch that question even if he had the time. Living healthily is a question few physicians seem ready to tackle. Living healthily is nothing less than arriving at old age and, in Erikson's words, "accepting one's one and only life cycle as that something that had to be and that, by necessity, permitted of no substitution."

To live healthily, therefore, is to become what one truly is and to work at it. To become in fact, as Ortega said, what you are in design. This may be a routine or rare accomplishment depending on how you view it. For myself now wandering around in my middle years seeking answers, it is like waiting for what happened to Saul on the way to Damascus.

The young, however, may get the same revelation through sport. That is one area of human activity in which they can taste of perfection. And even should they fail in that there is no better way to self-knowledge.

The athlete cannot fake it. He is a highly visible example of man maximizing himself. Or failing in the attempt. In this age of the phony and the upward failure, the athlete remains an example of excellence, grace and purity. Or at the least an honest effort to achieve those attributes.

But succeed or fail, the true athlete makes no excuses. He recognizes himself without pride or prejudice. He knows what he can or cannot do. He has found what he does best and is happy with it regardless of where he is listed in the standings. He has discovered himself, understood his strengths and weaknesses, and accepted them.

"To change the fundamental patterns of constitution and temperament is beyond our powers," wrote Aldous Huxley; "with all the best will in the world all that anyone can hope to do is to make the best of his congenital psycho-physical makeup [the particular personality associated with a given body build]."

The athlete already knows that. So he makes the best of it. Seeks fitness through positive goals rather than negative restrictions. The athlete doesn't stop smoking and start training. He starts training and finds he has stopped smoking. The athlete doesn't go on a diet and start training. He starts training and finds he is eating the right things at the right time. In just such a way other things fall into place. His sleep habits adjust. He automatically rests after eating and practices on an empty stomach. He warms up thoroughly and is satisfied with progress however slow.

He has discovered fitness and the fine line between peak performance and disaster. He becomes alert to his body signals. Palpitation, a sore throat, lightheadedness on arising, some minor joint pains, or awakening in the middle of the night—all these have meaning and alert him as a breaking twig would alert a deer in the forest. They tell him he has gone as far as he can go.

Where fitness ends, self-discovery starts. The athlete who is in complete command of the skills of his sport comes to understand the person he is through his attachment to his particular sport and his response to the stresses and strains that arise within it. He finds out what he is made of. What his true personality is.

Charles Morris in his *Varieties of Human Values* suggests there are three basic components to the human personality: Dionysian, the tendency to release and indulge existing desires; Promethean, the tendency to manipulate and remake the world; and Buddhistic, the tendency in the self to regulate itself by holding in check its desires. In psychological shorthand these components come out as dependence, dominance and detachment.

It shouldn't take all that long for a physically fit seventeen-year-old to find his or her sport and the appropriate life style to go with it. Detached, dominant, or dependent; Buddhistic, Promethean, or Dionysian.

It might even work for us aging worriers who are not at all sure that we are living, as Erikson said we must, our appropriate and only possible life cycle.

The formula for greatness, wrote Nietzsche, is *amor fati*, the love of fate, the desire that nothing be different, not forward, not backward, not for all eternity. And not merely to bear what is necessary, but to love it as well.

Offhand the statement would seem to have little application to the ordinary person, to you and me. Greatness and necessity and fate and eternity are words that thinkers tend to use, ideas that have little relation to our realities.

But when we read Keats and the poet's view, we move another step into this necessity and into our own reality. Keats saw the world as a "Vale of Soulmaking," but said we humans are not souls until we acquire identities; till each is personally himself.

The only man who truly lives, Ortega stated, is the one who follows his inner voice which says, "You are able to be whatever you want; but only if you choose this or that specific pattern will you be what you have to be."

The question, then, is not the presence of this necessity nor even its acceptance. We will certainly do that when faced with such a truth. The question is how to discover it, how to hear this voice, how to find our pattern, how to know the identity of our soul.

Our problem, then, is not the possibility of this necessity but the probability that we may never know it. That we may finish our lives without actually having lived it. That we may come to the end never having experienced it; never having heard the call. Our tragedy may be an unused soul, an unfulfilled design.

Fortunately, Nietzsche had some suggestions on what we should do to avert such a catastrophe. Attend, he said, to the little things. Take care with your nutrition. Watch your diet. Be careful about where you live and the air you breathe. Do not commit a blunder at any price in the choice of your recreation. Develop an instinct for self-defense. Make your life a matter of play.

Know that these small things are inconceivably more important than everything one has taken to be important so far. Great tasks, he concluded, depend upon small things, things which are generally considered to be matters of complete indifference.

Our salvation, then, is in the day-to-day living of what is surely the athletic life, the life committed to fitness, the life of one who knows the importance of attention to the little things, to the supposedly minor details of everyday living. The athlete is aware of all the points Nietzsche makes. Knows the response to training and diet and relaxation. The effect of tension and other people, of energy wasted on situations and relationships which make him merely a reactor. And the athlete knows more than most how one can find himself in play; and can accept himself who he was, is and will be.

Those who have found this play and with it their bodies know that life comes down to the usual matters of tasting, touching, hearing, seeing, breathing. "Our bodies are us, us," writes John Updike in discussing immortality, another grand idea. And then goes on to suggest that the only Paradise we can imagine is this Earth; the only life we desire is this one.

Fitness, then, is an imperative. How it is to be done is an individual matter, a matter, I might say, of necessity. But whether it is jogging or scuba diving, tennis or mountain climbing, its performance will involve attention to the details Nietzsche outlines. And in following this prescription we will begin to uncover the person inside, to burnish and polish and scrape away and let ourselves take shape.

Surely this is the way we must go if we are to find ourselves, know self-respect, accept our fate. Fitness can be our formula, if not for greatness, at least for the self-knowledge necessary to live a full life. Which is the most all of us, great or small, can expect.

The weakest among us can become some kind of athlete, but only the strongest can survive as spectators. Only the hardiest can withstand the perils of inertia, inactivity and immobility. Only the most resilient can cope with the squandering of time, the deterioration of fitness, the loss of creativity, the frustration of the emotions, and the dulling of the moral sense that can afflict the dedicated spectator.

Physiologists have suggested that only those who can pass the most rigorous physical examination can safely follow the sedentary life. Man was not made to remain at rest. Inactivity is completely unnatural to the body. What follows is a breakdown of the equilibrium. When the beneficial effects of activity on the heart and circulation and indeed on all the body's systems are absent, everything measurable begins to go awry.

Up go the girth of the waist and the body weight. Up go the blood pressure and the heart rate. Up go the cholesterol and the triglycerides. Up goes everything you would like to go down, and down goes everything you would like to go up. Down go the vital capacity and oxygen consumption. Down go flexibility and efficiency, stamina and strength. Fitness fast becomes a memory.

And if the body goes, can the mind be far behind? The intellect must surely harden as fast as the arteries. Creativity depends on action. Trust no thought arrived at sitting down.

The seated spectator is not a thinker; he is a knower. Unlike the athlete who is still seeking his experience, who leaves himself open to truth, the spectator has closed the ring. His thinking has become a rigid knowing. He has enclosed himself in bias and partisanship and prejudice.

He imagines himself self-sufficient and has ceased to grow. And it is growth he needs most to handle the emotions thrust upon him, emotions he cannot act out in any satisfactory way. Because he is, you see, too far from the athlete and participation in the effort that is the athlete's release, the athlete's catharsis.

He is watching people who have everything he wants and cannot get. They are having all the fun. The fun of playing, the fun of winning, even the fun of losing. They are experiencing the exhaustion that is the quickest way to fraternity and equality, the exhaustion that permits you to be not only a good winner but a good loser.

Because he cannot experience what the athlete is experiencing, the fan is seldom a good loser. The emphasis on winning is therefore much more of a problem for the spectator than for the athlete. And the fan, in losing and being filled with emotions that have no healthy outlets, is likely to take it out on his neighbor, the nearest inanimate object, the umpire, the stadium, or the game itself.

It is easier to dry out a drunk, take someone off hard drugs, or watch a three-pack-a-day smoker quit cold turkey than to live with a fan during a long losing streak.

And should a spectator pass all these physical and mental and emotional tests, he still has another supreme challenge to his integrity. He is part of a crowd, part of a mob. He is one of those the coach in *The Games* called "the nothingmen, those oafs in the stands filling their bellies." And when someone is in a crowd, out go his individual standards of conduct and morality. He acts in concert with his fellow spectators and descends two rungs on the evolutionary ladder. He slips backward down the development tree.

From the moment you become a spectator, everything is downhill. It is a life that ends before the cheering and the shouting die.

5. Becoming

*My fitness program was never a fitness
program. It was a campaign, a revolution, a
conversion. I was determined to find myself.
And, in the process, found my body and the soul
that went with it.*

I PROPOSE TO YOU that human enterprises succeed because they
are absolutely rational or because they are just as absolutely absurd. Science is a success, but then so is religion. Knowledge
succeeds, but so does faith. We usually act when something can
be proven. But we act with equal frequency when it cannot.
"Credo quia absurdum," said Saint Paul.

Just so are there two types of successful fitness programs.
One is rational, practical, physiological; the other nonrational,
mystical and psychological. One is obligatory; the other volun-
tary. One aimed at changing the person to fit the life style; the
other aimed at changing the life style to fit the person. One is
utilitarian; the other creative. One is work; the other play.

The first is successful because it is concerned with the result;
the other because it is concerned with the process.

In one instance, the exercising person is satisfied with Dr.
Cooper's minimal daily requirements; in the other, he is dissatisfied with his own maximum daily capabilities. In the first, there
is a purpose, the product, which is fitness, but little or no meaning in how it is attained. In the second, there is meaning in every
movement, but no purpose beyond the action itself; fitness is

merely a byproduct. The first pursues an ambition; the second pursues a dream.

The first program is for unfit, out-of-shape people with their backs to the wall. They know what they want to do, but are no longer able to do or enjoy it. They have finally and irrevocably had enough of how they feel and look and live out their lives. They are now ready to repent of past physical sins. Willing to obey the Ten Commandments of fitness. Anxious to follow the path of rectitude, provided vigor and energy lie at the other end.

You would think that such sensible decisions come easily. Nothing could be further from the truth. People just do not do things because they are good for them. And are even less inclined to do so when they enjoy doing the opposite. People accept the rational, practical, physiological only when it dawns on them that life any other way is a waste. Only then will they agree to a program which to them is a mindless, inconvenient and boring use of their time.

The other program is for unhappy people who find that it is life that is mindless, inconvenient and boring. Common-sense programs are of no help here. Only something that is nonrational, mystical and psychological can benefit them. Only something that is spontaneous and creative and playful will be effective. These people are looking for no less than an alternate way of living. Looking for a leisure-time activity to involve them completely and give them a new life style. Looking to become a true believer, to be struck like Paul on the road to Damascus with a new passion to replace the old one.

That passion of profession or career had changed, as Jung predicted, first to becoming a duty and now to being a burden. Life had become, as James Michener suggested, a falling away, a gradual surrender of the dream. What is left? "To live one's days," writes Bill Bradley, "never able to recapture the feeling of those few years of intensified youth."

Such pessimism is unwarranted. This fifty-eight-year-old man who has rediscovered play and sports can attest to that. It was simply enough for me to ask the question "You have one life to live. How do you want to live it?" and then come up with an absurd answer: "As a distance runner." With that decision, I awakened that passion, relived my dream, recaptured my youth. I re-entered my life through re-entering my body.

And so my fitness program succeeded because it was absurd. It was nonsense for someone my age to decide to become an athlete. Purely preposterous to concentrate the intensity and involvement that I once felt for the life of a physician into the life of the distance runner. Ridiculous to make running my vocation and medicine my avocation. But then my fitness program was never a fitness program. It was a campaign, a revolution, a conversion. I was determined to find myself. And, in the process, found my body and the soul that went with it.

For me, medicine was an illusion that had failed. I was seeking a new world, where I could live and create my own drama, and not play with the meaning of life. I found it in running.

So when you see a jogger out on the roads, you can never be quite sure what is going on in his or her head. Whether the reason for running is reasoned and practical and altogether a matter of just getting it done. Or, on the other hand, whether this child-like foolishness is the focal center of the runner's day. And running is the answer to the crucial question: How do you want to live the rest of your life?

A Canadian observer, John Sansom, has come up with a new solution to the physical-fitness problem. Religion. He suggests that we need more than a commitment to physical fitness for its own sake. We have to act on our religious beliefs (or a belief in a practically achievable Utopia) that regard bodily fitness as an essential part of life style directed toward a single all-important goal.

Will this be the answer? Jogging to eight-o'clock Mass? Cycling to temple? Doing circuit training before the Unitarian services?

I think not.

Every man is religious. Every man is already acting out his compelling beliefs. Religion is not something you belong to, or accept, or think. It is something you do. And you do it every waking minute of every day. Religion is the way you manifest whatever is urgent and imperative in your relationship to yourself and your universe, to your fellow man and to your Creator. Every act is a religious act.

That act may begin in dogma, but it ends in the deed of a unique, unprecedented and nonrecurrent individual. Religion or agnosticism or atheism may speak authoritatively to us about our bodies, but, whatever our persuasion, we will practice it only according to our inner compulsions and outer design. We are made for happiness and joy ("To miss the joy," said Stevenson, "is to miss all"), but we must pursue it in different ways. Fitness may not be one of them.

My design is thin and linear. I am a nervous, shy noncombatant who has no feeling for people. I do not hunger and thirst after justice. I find no happiness in carnival, no joy in community. I am one with the writers on *The New Yorker* whom Brendan Gill described. They touched each other only by accident, were secretive about everything, and never introduced anyone properly.

I am an intellectual. This does not mean I am intelligent, but that ideas are more important to me than people. My world lies inside of me, as it does with most people with my slight build. And that world and its completion depends on my physical fitness. In the perfection of my body lies my own perfection.

Fitness is my life; it is indispensable. I have no alternative, no choice, but to act out this inner drive that seems entirely right for me.

A majority of my readers will, I suspect, never feel that necessity, that urgency. The happiness, the joy they are born for, can be attained without it. They belong to one of the other two great races of men. Races with fundamentally different bodies and different temperaments, different life styles, and different religious expression.

The first of these races are strong, muscular people who are aggressive and insensitive to pain, both in themselves and in others. They find fulfillment in action, and seek to control people and events and things. Once athletic, they no longer need their bodies for their eyeball-to-eyeball confrontations. Where once they settled arguments with their fists, they now use their irresistible energy and moral courage. Physical fitness is no longer a priority.

The middle third are the round, pleasant people who love to have their arms around each other. They are generous and affable and quite close to being fat. Their bodies are for eating and drinking and company and family gatherings. Kierkegaard, another loner, once described such a man: "The ideal Christian is happily married, looks like a cheerful grocer, and is respected by his neighbors." For this race, fitness is irrelevant.

So I won't talk to you about fitness if you promise not to give me the kiss of peace or a membership blank to the Holy Name Society.

I gave a lecture on physical fitness recently at the Carrier Clinic, a psychiatric institution near Princeton. In the discussion that followed, one of the staff asked me, "Will jogging prolong your life?" I looked at him, my colleague in medical orthodoxy, and answered, "Will psychiatry?"

The answer was unpremeditated. A backlash against being required to answer a question I consider both irrelevant and immaterial. What runner cares whether running will prolong his life?

Will it? I don't know and I don't particularly care. On the other hand, running certainly does something to my body. But what exactly does it do? A few years back, I decided to find out. I went to a local community college for a fitness test. My maximum oxygen capacity, it turned out, was fifty-four volumes percent, considered excellent for a twenty-eight-year-old.

Apparently, running has given me an exceptional level of fitness. But what else? Has it prolonged my life? Pure absurdity. My physiology may be that of a twenty-eight-year-old, but I still have a fifty-eight-year-old body. I have my vigor, both physical and psychic, but the body ages relentlessly. My hairline recedes. My eyesight diminishes. And no one can persuade me that I have, at this date, a twenty-eight-year-old heart or blood vessels.

Yet something good is happening. Checking out as a twenty-eight-year-old must mean something. It does. It means that despite my years I am still an athlete. That running has gotten me to my lean body weight and to my personal cardiopulmonary best. Taken me to my physical peak. Because of my running, I am living at the top of my physical powers.

Now, to some that may mean that life will also be prolonged. Not to me. We are born, I suspect, with a built-in longevity quotient, which we can diminish but not increase. We are born, it seems to me, with an appointed time when noise will develop in the signals sent by our messenger RNA. When the song the molecules sing will no longer be heard by the cells. Disease, disintegration and death follow.

We can apparently hasten the process, but not retard it. Medical progress has gone through its finest hour and has had little impact on our life span. It is interesting that the Italian painters of the Renaissance had a life span of sixty-seven years, only a few less than medicine can produce in this nuclear age.

So let us forget about longevity. Get away from the idea of prolonging life. Let us realize the truth of Thurber's dictum "There is no safety in numbers—or in anything else." Despite exercise, diet and abstention from all the vices, we will die in our appointed time. That should not concern. It is what happens from now until then that is important.

Now rephrase that question. "Can running, or any strenuous form of play, improve my life?" This allows an answer. An answer which is clearly affirmative, if only because running concentrates on positives rather than negatives, emphasizes doing rather than not doing, and above all makes the person responsible for what he is doing.

The medical profession would like nothing better than to have all of us acting responsibly, taking a part in our own fate. The scientists think they can do better only if we do better. "The next major advance in the health of the American people," says Dr. John Knowles of the Rockefeller Foundation, "will result only from what the individual is willing to do for himself."

When I run, I am willing to accept that responsibility. But I also discover that to be responsible implies the ability to respond. To take care of my body, I must be able to listen to it, and to hear what it says.

In this continuing dialogue between me, the runner, and my body, I become more and more healthy-minded. I become eager for more training, more discipline, more self-control, seeking inside of me the person George Leonard called the ultimate athlete. All the while knowing, as Leonard suggests, that I am playing the ultimate game, which is life.

And in life, you remember, it is not how long you lived, but how you played the game.

A daily jogger has written to me in frustration because medical science has failed to come up with conclusive proof that jogging will prevent heart disease. Why jog, he asks, if there is no definite evidence that jogging will thwart a heart attack?

The answer, it seems to me, is that we should do so for more important and urgent and compelling reasons. We jog, play tennis, cycle, swim, hike, hunt, ride horses, or whatever because they have to do with the quality of our lives than the quantity. "I know only two things," a student said to Rollo May. "One, I will be dead someday; two, I am not dead now. The only question is what I shall do between those points."

Sport and play and exercise are essential to that doing, that being, that becoming. They are concerned with physiology, not disease; with health, not heart attacks; with fitness, not the lessening of hypertension, strokes or other human ills.

Sport and play and exercise are therefore vital to the process of maximizing ourselves and reaching the top of our physical powers.

We should not underestimate the importance of this in the full life. Training the body was an essential part of Plato's prescription for education. Education, he said, should train the body and mind as one. Only then can the body which is the source of energy and initiative be put in harmony with the mind which is reason. "The body," wrote Ortega, "is the tutor and the policeman of the spirit." It is the fit body, the body at the height of its powers, the body with range and daring matched with maturity that is the best teacher, the best disciplinarian.

Jogging or whatever our sport is, therefore, is the way we move from actuality toward our potential, toward becoming all we can be. At the same time it will fill us with uneasiness, with what Gabriel Marcel called inquietude, the recognition that there is work to be done to fulfill our lives. And it allows us to see, as Theodore Roszak has recently suggested, that our most solemn, and pressing, and primary problem is not "original sin" but "original splendor," the knowledge of our potential godlikeness. "We grow sick," writes Roszak, "with the guilt of having lived below our authentic level."

Can we reach this level or even attempt to reach it without sport and play and exercise? Can we hope to have the necessary energy and reason, the harmony and imagination without training and disciplining and enjoying our bodies? That is for each of us to decide.

For myself, the usual arguments for exercise are pathetic representations when placed beside this holistic approach to the human condition. "My troubles are two," sang the poet Housman. "The brains in my head. The heart in my breast." It is the day-to-day living with these troubles that makes us realize the importance of health and fitness. Not perhaps with making it easier. In fact, it makes living more demanding. The athletic individual can be more conscious of choice, more aware of the dangers of freedom, more awake to what the French call *difficulté d'être*.

Each of us must face this difficulty in being every conscious moment. And it is for each of us to discover how best we can handle this encounter. And here it comes down to whether you are an Aristotelian who sees the law outside himself or a Platonist who would look for it within. Should you wait for proof, or act out what your internal message tells you?

The message I get from consulting myself is clear. First I ran from instinct. Later I was forced to exercise in Phys. Ed. Even later I came to run and exercise because it was prescribed by authorities. But finally I have come to run because it is the right and true and just thing for me to do. In the process I may be helping my arteries and heart and circulation as well, but that is not my concern.

My true aim now is a state of fitness prior to and unrelated to sickness or disease. My true task, to live at my authentic level. My true goal, to reach my original splendor.

Run for my life. You had better believe it.

6. Playing

*Run only if you must. If running is an
imperative that comes from inside you and not
from your doctor. Otherwise, heed the inner
calling to your own Play. Listen if you can to
the person you were and are and can be. Then
do what you do best and feel best at. Something
you would do for nothing. Something that gives
you security and self-acceptance and a feeling
of completion; even moments when you are
fused with your universe and your Creator.
When you find it, build your life around it.*

SHAKESPEARE WAS WRONG. To play or not to play: that is the real question. Anyone with a sense of humor can see that life is a joke, not a tragedy. It is also a riddle and, like all riddles, has an obvious answer: play, not suicide.

Think about it for a minute. Is there a better way than play to handle "the slings and arrows of outrageous fortune," or take up arms against a "sea of troubles"? You take these things seriously and you end up with Hamlet—or the Nixon Gang, who came back from World War II, wrote Wilfred Sheed, "talking about dollars the way others talked about God and sex."

Neither of these ways works. Neither will bring us what we are supposed to be looking for, "the peace the world cannot give." That is also part of the riddle. You can have peace without the world, if you opt for death. Or the world without peace if you decide for doing and having and achieving. Only in play can you have both. In play, you realize simultaneously the supreme importance and utter insignificance of what you are doing. And accept the paradox of pursuing what at once is essential and inconsequential.

Play, then, is the answer to the puzzle of our existence. The stage for our excesses and exuberances. Violence and dissent are part of its joy. Territory is defended with every ounce of our strength and determination, and moments later we are embracing our opponents and delighting in the game that took place.

Play is where life lives. Where the game is the game. At its borders, we slip into heresy. Become serious. Lose our sense of humor. Fail to see the incongruities of everything we hold to be important. Right and wrong become problematical. Money, power, position become ends. The game becomes winning. And we lose the good life and the good things that play provides.

Some of those good things are physical grace, psychological ease and personal integrity. Some of the best are the peak experiences, when you have a sense of oneness with yourself and nature. These are truly times of peace the world cannot give. It may be that the hereafter will have them in constant supply. I hope so. But while we are in the here and now, play is the place to find them. The place where we are constantly being and becoming ourselves.

Philosophers have hinted at this over the centuries. Now the theologians are taking a hard look at the thought that we must become as little children to enter the Kingdom. If so, there is nothing more characteristic about children than their love of play. No one comes into this world a Puritan. If there is anything children care less about, it is work and money and power and what we call achievement.

We watch and envy as they answer the call "Come and play."

What happens to our play on our way to becoming adults? Downgraded by the intellectuals, dismissed by the economists, put aside by the psychologists, it was left to the teachers to deliver the *coup de grâce*. ''Physical education'' was born and turned what was joy into boredom, fun into drudgery, pleasure into work. What might have led us into Eden led us into a blind alley instead. And simply changed our view of the universe.

A universe where we are to play and enjoy ourselves and our God is one thing; a universe that is a large, forbidding place where we have to fight for everything we get is quite another. A universe where it is either ''us'' or ''them'' will certainly make us seek peace in another world. Life under those circumstances is just as Samuel Beckett described it. ''A terminal illness.''

Play, of course, says otherwise. You may already have found that out. If you are doing something you would do for nothing, then you are on your way to salvation. And if you could drop it in a minute and forget the outcome, you are even further along. And if, while you are doing it, you are transported into another existence, there is no need for you to worry about the future.

When Dean Caldwell and Warren Harding reached the top of El Capitan a few years back, the nation breathed a sigh of relief and turned to other matters. Why anyone would spend twenty-seven perilous days climbing 3,400 feet of perpendicular rock is beyond the comprehension of even ordinary humans, much less those of us who get vertigo hanging curtains.

''Why climb mountains?'' is a question which, it turns out, cannot be satisfactorily answered even by mountain climbers. Everyone, course, attempts an answer. But all freely admit that the whole truth is not there. The whole truth, they imply, cannot be captured.

Participants in the ''blood sports'' are equally unsure. Forget about Hemingway's moment of truth. It doesn't even enter into novelist James Michener's explanation of why he ran with the bulls at Pamplona. Two men met death within feet of him. Yet he made himself go back a second and a third day. Why did he and the crowds with the rolled-up newspapers (to touch the bull—and claim the touch) come to Pamplona?

Because, Michener claims, throughout history a certain kind of man has wanted to test himself against the most demanding experience in his culture. Michener characterizes this motive as idiotic, jejeune, unrewarding and senseless. But notes that you frequently find that it is the best men who insist on taking the risks. "In our age," he says, "you can climb Everest, fly to the moon, or run with the bulls of Pamplona."

For those of us who are "endlessly catching trains," the thought of testing ourselves against the most demanding experience in our culture can be a new and exciting idea. But the streets of Pamplona are as distant to us as the Sea of Tranquility, and even the mention of Everest causes nausea. Paradoxically our intuitive urge to expand ourselves, to test our limits, is blocked by our instinctive reaction that the way of Michener and his Spanish friends is not our way.

What our instincts (and athletes and sports psychologists) tell us is that sports and athletics will show us how to satisfy the main urges of this generation: to possess one's experience rather than be possessed by it, to live one's own life rather than be lived by it—in fine, to become all you are. Up until now that has always meant your brain. No more.

"As Prometheus (sometimes called the Greek Christ) sought to stretch the capacity of mankind," writes West Coast psychologist Wilfred Mitchell, "so do athletics."

One who has found sport stretching his capacity is Joe Henderson, the running editor of *Runners' World*. Henderson feels he can't answer the why-I-run question any better than others. But he tries. "I write," he says, "because the thoughts inside have to be put in more visible form. I run because it's inside pushing to get out."

Running is a total experience. That which some of us do best just as others find their satisfactions and fulfillment in skiing, mountain climbing, bicycling, snorkeling, pitching or what have you.

The experience is one that proceeds from one level to another. It can be merely physical fitness (which is like taking up painting to improve the strength of your arm). Or distraction: "I think" said Tug McGraw, "the reason I like baseball so much is because when I come into a game in the bottom of the ninth, bases loaded, none out, and a one-run lead, it takes my mind off all us screwed-up people." Or religious: "Surfing is a spiritual experience," says Michael Hynson, one of the world's top surfers. "When you become united with a wave, you lose your identity on one level and make contact with it again on a higher plane."

At one end of the spectrum you find a former college cross-country runner stating that the "opportunity to encounter and deal with pain is one of the aspects that makes the running experience ultimately so satisfactory." At the other, you hear Dick Cavett, a dedicated snorkeler, report, "Snorkeling is a rebirth. You just hang there in liquid space like an irresponsible fetus. For me it combines the best features of sport, sleep and religion."

This quiet revolution is spreading over the land. The rarity of the true dropouts should not fool us. For each ski-bum who belongs to the mountains there are thousands who already know that's where they come alive. For every runner who tours the world running marathons, there are thousands who run to hear leaves and listen to rain and look to the day when it all is suddenly as easy as a bird in flight.

For them, sport is not a test but a therapy; not a trial but a reward; not a question but an answer.

The first and basic commandment for health and longevity is the following: Pursue your own perfection. No one will have difficulty with this dogma. But as usual with dogma, we begin to have dissensions when the theologians start interpreting it. Then we become schismatics and heretics and start religions of our own. In health, the main problems with orthodoxy are with the word "exercise."

I am ready to start a new religion, the first law of which is, "Play regularly." An hour's play a day makes a man whole and healthy and long-lived. A man's exercise must be play, or it will do him little good. It may even, as we see regularly in the press, kill him.

I have scientific support for my position. Recent studies in both England and Ireland have shown that hard physical work did not change the coronary-risk factors or heart disease in more than thirty thousand men. However, in the same group, hard physical activity during leisure time was accompanied by a significant reduction in risk factors and heart attacks. Not by hard work, but by swimming and running and heavy gardening, and by tennis and squash and handball, and other forms of play, these men achieved health and a long life.

So it is not effort that reduces heart attacks and degenerative disease. If it were only effort, then effort on the job would do the trick. So it is not running, but running that is play, that is necessary. Exercise that is work is worthless. But exercise that is play will give you health and long life.

Exercise that is not play accentuates rather than heals the split between body and spirit. Exercise that is drudgery, labor, something done only for the final result is a waste of time. If I hated to run and ran only for longevity and was killed by a truck after five years at the sport, I would have a right to shake my fist at Providence, or at the doctor who advised it.

It is not the runner, but those impersonating the runner, who is at hazard. Those with the "hurry sickness." Those aggressively involved with achieving more and more with less and less time. Those who are always competing with or challenging other people. "Only the sick man and the ambitious," wrote Ortega, "are in a hurry." It is these people who use jogging to escape from death who find it taking them to their appointment in Samarra.

What, then, should you do? Run only if you must. If running is an imperative that comes from inside you and not from your doctor. Otherwise, heed the inner calling to your own play. Listen if you can to the person you were and are and can be. Then do what you do best and feel best at. Something you would do for nothing. Something that gives you security and self-acceptance and a feeling of completion; even moments when you are fused with your universe and your Creator. When you find it, build your life around it.

"Therein lies perfection," said Marcus Aurelius, "to live out each day as one's last." That is why I run and will always run. I have built my day and my life around it.

There is no better test for play than the desire to be doing it when you die.

as yes is to if, love is to yes

—E. E. CUMMINGS

If sport had a feast day, it would be Christmas. It is the day that speaks to man the player. Homo ludens is what Johan Huizinga called him. To differentiate from Homo sapiens, man the thinker, and Homo faber, man the maker.

Christmas tells us once again that play is a proper activity of man. It reminds us that fun is something philosophers cannot explain or understand, and insists that life is a game in which all can be successful.

A lot of this is not new. Plato in his *Laws* says, "Life must be lived as play, playing certain games, singing and dancing." This idea was also prominent during the Renaissance. But those enemies of man and his body, moral zeal and intellectuality, moved in during the Reformation, and with them a decline in play.

The nineteenth century and the Industrial Revolution were even worse. "All Europe," writes Huizinga, "donned the boiler suit." Utilitarianism, efficiency and educational aspirations almost wrecked the play spirit.

But there is hope. We still have the poets, the children, the athletes. And sports.

The intellectuals who look at sport start with the assumption that it must serve something that is not sport. They see its useful functions of discharging surplus energy and providing relaxation, training for fitness and compensation for other deficiencies. What they don't see is that play is a primary category of life which resists all analysis.

Play, then, is a nonrational activity. A supralogical nonrational activity in which the beauty of the human body in motion can reach its zenith. Just as the supralogical feast of Christmas confirms man's unique value and destiny. So the intellectuals are probably as upset with play as the theologians are with Christmas. Men having fun is as mystical and supralogical as the Word made flesh.

Fortunately, mysticism doesn't come hard for the common man. "History unanimously attests," wrote G. K. Chesterton, the master of paradox and therefore the master of Christmas, "that it is only mysticism which stands the smallest chance of being understood by the people."

Philosopher Jean Houston has observed, "We tend to think of the Faustian man, the one who fabricates, manipulates, seduces and ends up destroying. But the new image will be man the creator, the artist, the player."

The first Christians told us all that. The game plan had been changed. When the angel said, "Rejoice, be not afraid. I bring you good news of great joy," we knew that everything was going to be different. The world, which had moved from "if" to "yes," was now moving on to love.

The game would be for everyone. And the arena would be the world. And the good news is that man will eventually triumph. All of us for this once are going to be on the winning team. And not only that. All of us can be great players.

The first Christmas says with Shakespeare, "What a piece of work is man. How noble in reason! How finite in faculties! In form and moving, how express and admirable!"

Homo ludens knows this. Oh, what pieces of work are Muhammad Ali, Jimmy Connors, O. J. Simpson and Kareem Jabbar! No sports fan needs to be educated about man's potential. Or the irrational elements that go into the intensity of the game. Or about the community of the crowd.

The sports fan knows all this and suspects that there is nothing more spiritual than the human body. Knows that nowhere is every man given his dignity as he is on the playing field. And instinctively feels that somewhere here is the news of the first Christmas.

Those of us weary and discouraged by the front-page tragedies caused by Homo sapiens and the ecological disasters of Homo faber can turn for uplift to the sports pages and know that there every day is Christmas. A Christmas foretold in the Book of Proverbs:

"I was with Him forming all things, and was delighted every day, playing before Him at all times; playing in the world. And my delights were to be with the children of men."

Who speaks for play? These days, almost everyone. The physiologists and the physicians, the psychologists and the psychiatrists, the economists and the sociologists all champion play.

Play and sports and the use of the body are becoming respectable. Play is good for losing weight and reducing our risk factors. For relieving stress and returning us to work relaxed. Play maintains our health and promotes our longevity. Compensates for needs not met at work, and provides a harmless way to vent antisocial emotions. Play, the experts say, is a necessity in a leisure society.

But these acceptable and respectable reasons for play are not the real reason we must play. The reason for play is much more radical than the scientists and thinkers presume. The reason for play is to be found in our reason for being. And, therefore, with the problem of God.

The problem of God has moved from the ancient question "Does God exist?" past the medieval inquiry, "What are his attributes?'' to our present dilemma, "Why did He create the world?'' Our difficulty now is the inability to explain the existence of the world and therefore ourselves. We are unable to define our purpose, to show how we serve, to demonstrate our usefulness.

The best answer, it seems to me, is to consider Calvin's thought that the world is *"theatrum gloria Dei."* We are here, therefore, to glorify God. And that we do this by glorifying the God who is Himself a player. Who created in joy, in play, in sport.

Calvin, the Sunday bocce player, may not have thought of it this way, but it does answer today's question. We are in this world to give glory to God and rejoice in our own and God's existence. And we do this in play.

Children, who are athletes and poets and saints and scientists all in one, do this naturally. They seldom question themselves about purpose. Rarely wonder whether or not they are useful. Practically never consider service and respectability. These latest arrivals from Paradise are nevertheless examples of pure unity of heart and soul and brain united with a body which is almost always in action. And that action is play.

What the child lacks is wisdom. Undirected action is not enough. When we become adults, we realize this. "Fight, do not pray," advised Plutinus. "Play, do not pray," we might say. But first we must know our fight, our action, our play. The child does not yet know the role he plays in his own drama. We must find that without losing the gift childhood provides, the gift of play. Without becoming what Erikson defines as an adult: "a commodity-producing and commodity-exchanging being."

The aim of education is to avoid this. It is to help the child become an adult but at the same time to find the secret of allowing the adult to remain a child. We should be children grown but children grown wise and discovering the significance of our peculiar union of flesh and spirit. Children grown wise and knowing that the answer to the question "What are we doing here?" is "I am."

The center of that existence is my play. From it springs all other activity. Sport and play are the stuff bodies are made of. They are also the stuff that makes the person and the self. My running enables me, as Norman O. Brown wrote, "to live instead of making history, to enjoy instead of paying back old scores, to enter the state of Being which is the goal of Becoming."

True, running does not fill my day. But it influences the rest of what I do and how I do it. From it comes my role and the style in which I play it. In it I find myself and my design. I start in play, use myself increasingly, and end in joy.

You may notice that play can be painful and strenuous and dangerous. It can demand endurance and suffering and perseverance. It can ask the most that a person can give. It presupposes an absence of greed and vanity and the appetites that remind us we are mortal. Play, you see, can be more difficult than work, and no easy task for an adult.

It is, however, worth every effort. What better to be than a player in the hands of a playful God?

I love them all. Love every Buck, every Celt. Love Kareem and Oscar and Mickey Davis; Perry and Warner and Bobby Dandridge. Love Cowens and JoJo and John Havlicek; Silas and Chaney and Baby Face Nelson. I love Tom Heinsohn and Larry Costello. I love them all. Because these men, doing what they do best and doing it superbly well, proved to me that sport is the eighth art. Made me realize how precious is the thing they do, how priceless is the thing we watch.

No one can say after watching the Buck–Celtic playoff that sport is an inconsequential thing. That play is simply recreation for the players, a diversion for the spectators. Huizinga, who said that the imperishable need of man is to live in beauty, went on to say, "There is no satisfying that need except to play."

And this was beauty and play at its best. The fascinating Kareem who is so good at what he does, you are put off by the ease and simplicity with which he makes the most difficult look easy.

And Robertson, the complete basketball player, with his slow-motion fakes. Oscar lives in another time frame, where he can wait and wait and wait some more; and finally comes the release of that soft shot tracing a perfect parabola to the net. The Bucks were without Lucius Allen, but they had Dandridge with his quick hands, the menacing Warner, and Mickey Davis looking like some kind of mad king who had come off the throne to play with his jesters and by royal fiat had declared that all his wildly impossible shots would go in.

Against them, the Celtics had brought champions of equal strength and speed and skill. The tireless Havlicek, who was everywhere he was expected to be and everywhere he wasn't expected as well. And Nelson, the Knick Killer spelling Silas after his incredible leaps under the enemy basket. And forever joined in the battle was the bullyboy Cowens, who could be as soft as silk from the outside.

And making the team move through space in patterns as intricate as Balanchine's were imperturbable White and Chaney, before the impulsive Westphal inscribed his signature on the final outcome.

It was, as Santayana said of athletics, "a great and continuous endeavor, a representation of all the primitive virtues and the fundamental gifts of man." It was also a work of art. It certainly satisfied the first half of Santayana's definition of art: "manual knack and professional tradition." We are unlikely to see the manual knack and professional tradition displayed by the Bucks and the Celts surpassed by anyone but the greats in art and music and dance.

Santayana further defined art as having a contemplative side which he described as pure intuition of essence. I am not sure what he meant by that, although I suspect it has to do with knowing the inner meaning of what you are doing. I also suspect that the Bucks and the Celts were doing whatever Santayana was trying to describe.

It is usually true that philosophers try desperately to put into words what is familiar experience to the man in the street. "The poet," said Emerson, "is in the right attitude. He is believing. The philosopher, after some struggle, has only reasons for believing."

I am a believer. What I saw during those games was good and beautiful and therefore important. I may get an argument from those who are more likely to spend their afternoons on Madison Avenue than at Madison Square Garden, who see their art in the Met and not in the Mets, who find their joy in colors and shapes and nature, not in knack and tradition and essence.

Still, I can take heart from something Hilton Kramer said about Ansel Adams' exhibit. "For myself," wrote Kramer, "the look on the face of Georgia O'Keefe—in the 1937 photograph—is worth all the views of Yosemite Valley ever committed to film."

And I'll take the look on the face of Oscar Robertson, or any other Buck or Celtic.

Mr. Kramer has told us what we always knew. That we really know a lot about art. Primarily because we know what we like and what brings us joy. Pure joy, said Santayana, when blind is called pleasure, when centered on some sensible object is called beauty, and when diffused over the thought of a benevolent future is called happiness.

It is possible that sport and play do all these things. That having found our sport, as the Bucks and the Celts have found theirs, we will feel its pleasure, know its beauty and live happily ever after.

But that is philosophers' talk. Let them try to explain what I already feel. I love them all. Every Buck, every Celt.

7. Learning

*"Thank you, God, for school!" Somewhere, an
astounded Creator clapped his hands. One of
His creatures has understood His creation. Had
realized he was born to be a success in a
successful universe. Had discovered what a
wonderful thing it is to be a human being. Had
found himself lovable and his friends and
teacher loving.*

I REACHED MY PEAK in creativity when I was five. I could draw
and paint and sculpt. I could sing and dance and act. I possessed
my body completely. And with it became completely absorbed
in a life that was good and beautiful and joyful.

I examined and tested and explored. I could not bear to
watch. My every day was filled with the creativity that Rollo
May defined: "the encounter of an intensely conscious human
being with his world."

I do not confuse creativity with talent. I never had talent. Few
do. But I was aware and responded and I responded totally. And
I had what in older people is called purpose or dedication. At
five, I was creative and authentic. At five, I did it my way. At
five, I was like most five-year-olds, a genius without talent.

That genius came from energy and effort and taking risks. I
would not know for years that Thoreau had commended arduous
work for the artist. "Hard, steady and engrossing labor," he
said, "is invaluable to the literary man."

And I would not read until even later that the Greeks had no word for "art" or "artist." That they never separated, any more than I did, the useful from the beautiful. For them, either a thing was useful and therefore beautiful or it was sacred and therefore beautiful.

The five-year-old does not yet know sin, but he may well know what is sacred. Poetry and painting and music are, according to Blake, "three powers in man of conversing with Paradise." The five-year-old sees that Paradise correctly, not in technology but in the fairy story, in the great myths that control and guide our lives. And myth is meaning divined rather than defined, implicit rather than explicit.

At five I had that intuitive, instinctive faith that my cosmos, my family and the world were good and true and beautiful. That somehow I had always been and always would be. And I knew in a way of a five-year-old that I had worth and dignity and individuality. Later, when I read Nietzsche's statement that these are not given to us by nature but are tasks which we must somehow solve, I knew him to be wrong. We all had them once.

We lost them when we substituted watching for doing. When we saw the lack of perfection as a reason not to participate. When we became specialists and learned to ignore what was the province of other people.

For me, this meant no further interest in how things worked, in construction and making things, in crafts of any kind. I lost control of my life and in time became helpless in front of any malfunctioning machine. Now, if left to my own devices, I could not house or feed or clothe myself. Were I a castaway on a desert island, I would not know how to apply the efforts of all the scientists since the time of Archimedes. I would have to live as if they never existed. As if their talent and the products of their intense encounter with the world had never occurred.

And this all because my encounter, my absorption, my purpose and my interest and intensity had never occurred. I had changed from a genius without talent into the worst of all possible beings, a consumer.

The consumer is passivity objectified. Where the five-year-old finds the day too short, the consumer finds the day too long. I had lost the absorption of the five-year-old and gained boredom. I had lost my self-respect and gained self-doubt. Being middle-class, I had neither the need to use myself physically to survive, which poverty imposes, nor the absolute freedom to complete myself physically that wealth allows the aristocrat.

The five-year-old is just such an aristocrat. He seeks his own truth, his own perfection, his own excellence without care for the expense. He could well be a millionaire in his lack of concern for money and the family bank account.

But the five-year-old is more than an aristocrat; he is the worker Thoreau commended. He is the artist the Greeks saw no need to define. He is the athlete we all wish to be. And the saint we will never be. Every five-year-old is a success, just as every consumer is a failure.

The road back for a fifty-nine-year-old consumer is a long one. But there must be untapped resources of enthusiasm and energy and purpose deep in me somewhere. Somewhere I have the same creativity I had when I was five. I suspect that it is hidden under my clean, neatly folded and seldom-used soul.

In the kindergarten class my daughter teaches, it is customary for the children to say a short prayer before the juice and cookies. They take their daily turn expressing gratitude or directing requests to their Creator. Last week, a pupil who has been a constant joy to her took his opportunity and exclaimed, "Thank you, God, for school!"

Somewhere, an astounded Creator clapped his hands. One of his creatures had understood His creation. Had realized he was born to be a success in a successful universe. Had discovered what a wonderful thing it is to be a human being. Had found himself lovable and his friends and teacher loving. And was using his tools, his sight, smell, touch, taste, hearing and intellect for creation, growth and self-discovery.

"Thank you, God, for school!" How I envy him that prayer. That sense of knowing who he is, and, even more, the sense of knowing why he is. His awareness of his infinite potential. School can do that. School is simply the unfolding of ourselves to our consciousness, a harmonious growth of our person and personality in our environment. And for us adults, this is attained in leisure.

What is school for the student, wrote philosopher Paul Weiss, is leisure for the mature. A time when we devote ourselves to detecting who we are and what we can do; a time to understand the world and how it works; a time to loaf and invite the imagination to full activity; a time to exhaust ourselves in play and dance and celebration.

"Mortals are most like gods," wrote one Greek commentator, "when they are happy, which means when they are rejoicing, celebrating festivals, pursuing philosophy, and joining in music."

Others from Aristotle to Cardinal Newman to Eric Hoffer have said much the same thing. The Greek word *schole* means leisure. Newman's writings on the university originated the idea of the liberal arts, studies undertaken for their own sake and enjoyment. Hoffer suggested dividing the state of California in half: northern California for those who wanted to go to school for the rest of their lives; southern California for those who preferred to work and support them.

These ideas have not done well in the marketplace. School has become more and more vocational, a place where one learns his life's work, then settles down to a quiet existence and a restful and eternal reward in heaven.

Leisure has become recreation time which revitalizes the worker, allowing him to return to work and higher productivity. Instead of being ends in themselves, school and leisure have become means to a designated "good life."

When one fools Mother Nature that way, terrible things are bound to happen, and they have happened. Our failure to see life for the great playful game it is has resulted in serious physical, psychological and spiritual disease. The world, since my day in school, has passed through three periods the psychiatrists are now calling the Age of Repression, the Age of Anxiety and our present era, the Age of Boredom.

If all the words spoken between the psychiatrists and the patients afflicted with these ailments were laid end to end, they would reach to the outermost galaxy. But not quite to their Creator.

To reach Him, and cure ourselves, we must return to the wonder of childhood; to the intensity of play; to the love of ourselves and our bodies, to growth and creation and self-discovery. We must return to school and leisure.

Only in leisure, that occasionally disorderly and disorganized pursuit of my being, of finding my thing and doing it, can I mature, can I become a man. Without it, life makes no sense. Without it, death is intolerable. Without it, I will never in this life or the next know who I am and who I could become. Without leisure, I will not be perfected.

But what about work? Isn't that an ever present necessity? It is, and somehow it has to be dealt with. There will come a time when technology will merge with art, when work will become play. Until then, work must be approached with a sense of humor, an understanding of how it can be used to make us more human than less.

To do this, we need the perspective otherwise available only to poets and philosophers and to children saying their prayers in kindergarten.

A juice-and-cookies break might be the first step.

I don't know if anyone ever said, "You can take the boy out of the city, but you can't take the city out of the boy." No matter. It's true. I've always felt the pull. When the kids are grown, I used to say, we'll go back to the city to live. Partly because that meant living where, as Paolo Soleri says, the institutions that make our civilization survive and develop. Living in what Peter Goldmark calls "our main learning device." Living with, in Henry James's phrase, "accessibility to experience."

But the city is, or was, more than that. In my time, it was an asphalt playground. Now they call it an asphalt jungle, but in those days it was a giant all-weather playground stretching block by block from Van Cortlandt to Bay Ridge.

The playground city is linear. And the games of the linear city are linear. The baselines straight along the curbs in boxball, or diagonal in stickball, banked off the curbs and ranging from sewer to sewer. And the final enclosures made by chalk, an indispensable item for growing up in the city. Not just for baselines and bases and out-of-bounds, but also for the box scores, which set each afternoon's contest in history, if only until the next rainstorm.

The squares and diamonds and box scores marked the mathematical precision of the city games. We learned that there was a certain dignity in losing by ten or fifteen runs, as long as it was recorded on the street next to home plate, inning by inning. We had rules for every eventuality. Many called, for some obscure reason, Hindus, which gave you a replay of your time at bat.

One thing alone was unforgivable: losing the ball over the roof. We learned what the city was to forget, that control comes before power.

In those days, the automobiles had not yet taken over the city. It was possible then to have a playing field of two sewers without a car parked its entire length. Few cars would ever drive through the street to interrupt the play. But later they marched onto our block and sat there twenty-four hours a day. If one left, another took up the vigil. Beneath them, the football fields, the hockey fields, the boxball and stickball fields lay unused. And the city died. Killed by Ford and Chrysler and General Motors.

Now we are being told by Barry Tarshis, in *The Asphalt Ath-*

lete, that the city is still a playground. But he is not writing about our street, our block, the home of our platoon. He is writing about schoolyard playgrounds.

Now, playgrounds are all right, but they are a compromise. They are neutral ground. There is no sense of belonging there. Your block was your block. Your block was your territory. No playground could duplicate its singularity.

One might as well try to substitute Shea Stadium for Ebbets Field. We knew our block. Knew how to play the caroms off the brownstone fronts and the stoops and the areaways. Knew which steps to get pointers in stoop ball. Knew where to push the ball past the third baseman in boxball so it would go down some basement steps for a double.

Our block was like no other. We knew it and ourselves. And we watched the seasons pass as surely as any country kid in Iowa. Touch football, which was really "association," then roller-skate hockey, the cycle went. Then came spring, and the Spalding High Bouncers would appear, and with them boxball and stoop ball and the game of them all, stickball.

In stickball, no matter what your ability, there was an occasional miracle when broom met "Spaldeen" and the ball would go high and far up the block for an unbelievable distance. It would be a memory never quite erased by past or subsequent failures. In all our games, this held true. Strength and power were almost never dominant. Grace and control and anticipation made the play in the city games. It was a world in which every bounce was true and the short hop came easy even for the tyro.

There are some who say that this city of the short hop and the three-sewer home run will never come again. That this city I knew as a boy is not only dead, but deservedly so. Many believe with theologian Jacques Ellul that the city is "a specific evil, independent of its inhabitants." And see no hope for better.

"Let there be no confusion," says Ellul. "There is no use expecting a New Jerusalem on earth."

I disagree. Mainly because the boy in me provides hope.

The city, I grant, is lying moribund—maintained like some person kept alive by machines after his heart and brain have given up the ghost. But it is dying because architects and politicians and ordinary citizens have forgotten that the city must primarily be a playground. And a playground is just what it isn't. "In my neighborhood," writes Joseph Lyford of the Fund for Peace, "every adult is a dead child."

Those children will continue to die until the block again becomes the block. The block without cars. The block with neighbors who know each other and walk to shops and work and school. The block where seasons will be marked by the games that its children play.

The block will be the measure of the new city, perhaps of the world. Arnold Toynbee thinks so. The new city, he says, will be a world of streets and houses. We will have an immense number of units on the scale of those planned by Doxiadis for Karachi, or the "quadros" designed by Costa for Brasília. Then once more we can be children and neighbors and men and women on our own block.

When that day comes, I'll be an expert. I know just the length and heft you need in a broomstick and where to get a Spalding High Bouncer. And don't worry about the chalk. I always carry some, just in case.

If I were a college president, I would recruit athletes, not scholars. I would give grants-in-aid for sports, not for academic achievement. The scales in education have been tipped too much in favor of the intellectual. It is time to raise our level of consciousness about the importance of sport and play.

Scholars will make their way whether we support them or not. We live in a knowledge society and they are the elite. But there are clouds in the future. The computer has an unrivaled intelligence quotient, and those it won't replace are coming to see their positions as white-collar facsimiles of the blue-collar assembly line.

Society needs a few geniuses, if you believe Bucky Fuller, or thousands of mediocrities, if you support the hypothesis of Ortega. In any case, most of us should be educated in the good life and how to attain it.

In that, the athlete provides a much better model than the scholar. The athlete restores our common sense about the common man. He revitalizes old truths and instructs us in the old virtues. However modest his intellectual attainments, he is a whole person, integrated and fully functioning. And in his highly visible pursuit of a highly visible perfection, he illustrates the age-old advice to become the person you are. Simply by being totally himself, the athlete makes a statement that has profound philosophical, psychological, physiological and spiritual implications.

Philosophically, the athlete gives us back our bodies. No matter what the Cartesians say in the classrooms, the playing fields tell us we do not have bodies, we are our bodies. "I run, therefore I am," says the distance runner. Man is a totality, says the athlete, and forces us to deal with that truth.

Psychologically, the athlete affirms the necessity of play. I should say reaffirms. We always knew the necessity of play. We knew it from the Scriptures and Plato and the Renaissance educators who gave athletes an equal share of the curriculum with the classics and ethics.

But somehow we forgot about play and sacrificed it and sport to the demands of our overgrown material civilization. We made play a means, not an end. Athletes show us that sport and play are essential to the good life. To consider their function as simply the cultivation of bodily vigor with a view to longevity is, as Santayana said, "to be a barbarian."

Physiologically, however, the athlete's vigor and longevity are immediately apparent. The athlete provides us with a new normal man. He shows us that those we previously considered normal were spectators heading for a premature old age. Normal man is man at the top of his powers, man reaching his maximal metabolic and cardiopulmonary steady state.

From the athlete, we learn that health is not merely the absence of disease, any more than sanctity is the absence of sin. Health, the athlete tells us, is a positive quality, a life force, a vital characteristic clearly recognizable in those who have it.

The athletes, then, can be a tremendous force for good on campus. We may not be able to teach virtue, but it is no small thing to demonstrate it. Nor is it inconsequential to have excellence in any form in clear view. Education, said William James, is a process by which we are able to distinguish what is first-rate from what isn't. Sport, more often than not, shows us the elements of what is first-rate.

It does this because it is the long-sought moral equivalent of war, not as an outlet of aggression and violence, but as an arena where man finds the best that is in him, a theater that reveals courage and endurance and dedication to a purpose, our love for our fellows and levels of energies we never knew we possessed. And where we see, if only for moments, man as he is supposed to be.

In these moments, the athlete makes a contribution not only to his classmates singly, but also to the entire college community. Because then, in these great spectator events, he provides celebration and adds to the myths that help us survive.

And the greatest of these is that man is born to be a success. We believe that only when we see him at play.

DEAR MARK,

Your father tells me you are worried about giving up time from your studies in order to run cross country. You wonder whether devotion to a sport might endanger your college career. Whether running and learning are compatible.

I can assure you they are. For you and me and others like us, running is the way we learn. For us, in fact, there is no better way to insure academic success than by running an hour or so daily. I discovered this in college, as I am sure you will. My marks paralleled my running. When I was running well and enjoying it, I studied with interest and profit and this was reflected in my grades.

But education is much more than that and so is running. Part of education is learning the fundamentals. Getting the tools for your life's work. But the more important part is to see life as a whole and the world as a whole and to come to your full potential as a complete human being. "We are not," says Pascal. "We hope to be." Education is the way we start toward that fulfillment. By taking what we are told, what we hear and what we read, and then experiencing it. By testing it through our body and mind and soul and by thus filtering out our own truth, our own reality.

We are taught collectively; we educate ourselves individually. Education, said Socrates, was the winning of knowledge out of yourself. Yet the activity of the classroom and the lecture hall is to homogenize people. To present every one with the same facts, the same data, the same information, even the same truth. What we must do is take it elsewhere as a dog does a bone to worry it until we get to the marrow.

This activity starts with the body. A healthy, well-working body. A body that is all it can be. Which implies dedication, desire, hard work, discipline. And requires a self-renewing motivation for physical activity that occurs only in play. The body desires play just as the mind desires truth and the soul desires good.

For you and me, running is our play, so we are well started. And because running operates at all levels, during our hour run the road is at once a gymnasium, a laboratory, a classroom, even a temple. In this gymnasium, we find fitness. And with it, our own uniqueness. We do not need to be told that each one of us is like no one else before or after in this universe. And in that hour on the roads, we so use our bodies that we actually become our bodies. And in them see the possibilities of other perfection.

The road becomes a laboratory where we subject what we have been taught to the test of this visible, experienced universe. Where we use our own senses to evaluate the texbooks. And thereby give them new meaning.

But more than anything, that hour on the roads is for ideas and principles, for meditation and contemplation. We runners think in congruities and incongruities. We do not remember through organization, but by relationships, and we have to wait for these to glide by. We cannot force our brain to our bidding. Running is the key to this lock. Somehow in the relaxation, the letting go, we arrive at a state which Heraclitus described as "listening to the essence of things." We open ourselves up to the world.

And what of the soul? This hour allows, as does no place else, the freedom of seeing yourself as you are. Where better to examine your life, or your conscience, or to say your prayers? In that hour, every vice, every weakness, every shortcoming is seen and accepted. There is no confession you would withhold from yourself.

And yet you can accept yourself as you are, because at that very moment you see doors open and glimpse possibilities for yourself you never imagined. And you know you are indeed finite and imperfect, but you are also, like David, fearfully and wonderfully made.

Because of moments like these, moments of sudden illumination which come effortlessly and without trouble, this will become the most valuable hour of your day, and a most necessary part of your education. The educated man who does not move through the countryside with his own thoughts as his companions is in danger of never making the real discovery. Who he is.

All the best,
Doc

If you would learn how to defraud the consumer, observe the educators. They imprison their audience; set up delusionary goals called success and happiness; sell inadequate means called science and the humanities; and disparage their competitors the body and the spirit. And when they fail, they blame the pupils, not the teachers. Blame us, not themselves.

In the final analysis, however, their indictment is correct. We stand guilty as charged. Not because we have failed as scholars, but because we have failed as people. Because our education has not led to our own self-development, our own self-fulfillment. That is our own responsibility. As with everything else in life, if you would be educated, you must do it yourself.

Fortunately, the natural course of the human mind is from credulity to skepticism. And there comes a time in every person's education when, as Emerson wrote, he arrives at the conviction that envy is ignorance, and imitation is suicide. "When none but he knows what that is which he can do, nor does he know until he has tried."

Yale's Kingman Brewster, in an introduction to *Dink Stover at Yale*, described this growth as a progression from arrogance to self-doubt, to self-pity, to rediscovery and finally to mature ambition. For Blake it was the succession of innocence, experience, rebellion, and finally Vision. When our view of man is limited, when we see ourselves as IQ's, SAT's, or Graduate Record Exams, we end this journey early. Even our best intellectuals, as Robert Coles has confessed of himself, can end in arrogance. Some are becalmed in doubt, others unable to move beyond self-pity. For more than a few, rebellion is enough.

The necessity is to see ourselves totally. To know that we also have a physical and aesthetic intelligence. Without them the IQ is just another pretty face. Education proceeds only when we realize that the body and the mind are indissolubly one. When we are our bodies, and play and sport are integrated in our minute-to-minute pursuit of our perfection.

Only the athlete in us knows this. Only the athlete, as philosopher Paul Weiss points out, pushes himself toward the state where he so accepts his body he cannot without difficulty distinguish himself from it. Sports, writes Weiss, are a superb occasion for enabling young men to be perfected; there is no better agency for helping them mature.

Nonathletic educators reject this truth. They would educate us in their own image. In Dink Stover's day that meant, as his friend Bockhurst said, "developing the memory at the expense of the imagination." Now, if the Yale alumni are to be believed, it is an even more fundamental error. At their fall convocation the highest per capita income producers among American college graduates complained that the body had been sacrificed to that success.

These men have come to know the frustrations of false ambitions. There are, after all, at any one time only five or six supremely intelligent people on earth, those half dozen whose discoveries could pay, as Bucky Fuller claims, to educate all the rest of us. We are, Yale graduates included, only deckhands. "Not one man in a million," wrote C. P. Snow, "granted all the training in the world and with total dedication, would be likely to make a significant contribution to theoretical physics."

The last men of thought to make a difference, according to Kenneth Clark, were Freud and Marx. A tiny few, therefore, actually merit education as potential contributors to society. The rest of us are entitled simply by being our unique selves. We deserve to be included in what William James called the stringent never-ending search for wisdom and freedom.

Yet the educators would close us out with our board scores. Check our SATs for verbal and math and decide whether or not we are educable. It is easier to teach those who need not be taught. Easier not to be threatened by a completely different kind of intelligence. Easier to label as primitive what may be the future and not the past.

Picasso had trouble with arithmetic. Terry Bradshaw, someone said, has a twelve-cent brain. Intelligence is never mentioned in the Bible. Nor is it, we are told, the hallmark of a poet. We are carnal creatures with an incarnate God. The artist, and athlete, the saint and the poet know that. The educators alone remain ignorant.

The people they are defrauding may be themselves.

Graduates of Downstate Medical School, families, friends and faculty:

Your dean said it was an honor to have me as a commencement speaker. That you were about to hear from a distinguished cardiologist, philosopher and an expert on fitness. That remains to be seen. But those are not the reasons I am here. The real reasons are quite simple. Your student body president, who extended the invitation, said they were looking for an alumnus, someone who would keep people from falling asleep, and they had no money. He hoped that would not matter. It didn't. At fifty-seven, I am willing to talk to anyone who will listen.

I will not deny I am a cardiologist. But I don't consider that important. Like most specialists, I am not intelligent enough to be a family practitioner. And of all the specialties, cardiology is the simplest and the safest for someone who is ambivalent and indecisive. In common with most heart specialists, I am a Hamlet who is always wondering what to do. Fortunately, the patient improves or is even cured during the soliloquy.

I also admit to being a self-taught philosopher. There is no other way for us physicians, for surely we must be the worst-educated of professionals. We go through medical school in college to prove we can cope with medical school in medical school. We are never taught the humanities or their importance. Scientists, you see, need know nothing about yesterday. It is already incorporated in today's technology.

But to be human, to be a person, you must start with the Book of Genesis and work forward. You must always be on the alert to find the giants, the writers, the thinkers, the saints, the athletes, who speak to you. Those who reflect your instincts, your temperament, your body, your mind, your tastes.

I do plead guilty to being fit. But only because at forty-four I became bored with medicine. When I applied for the faculty at Rutgers Medical School, citing that boredom was my only qualification, the application was rejected. I then turned to a higher ambition. To become a forty-four-year-old miler. And, in an absolute, unreasonable, single-minded dedication to that absurd project, discovered my body, my play, my vision and eventually a new life. I found my truth.

I stand here now hoping to transmit some of that truth. But even more, I don't want to lie to you. "The old lie to the young," said Thornton Wilder. And never more than in commencement addresses. All over this land at this time of the year, there are speakers talking about hard work. Of the need for continuing study. Of the necessity of becoming men and women. They are urging graduates to succeed, to give service, to dedicate their lives to others.

I am here as an advocate for other values. I am here to speak not for work, but for play. Not for the mind, but the body. Not for becoming a man or a woman, but remaining a child.

I am here to tell you that in your success will be the seeds of your failure. That in giving service, you will eventually do a disservice to yourself and your family and your patients. That in your dedication to others, you may die without actually have lived.

My experience has taught me that you must first and always seek the person you are. And this becoming unfolds through the intensity with which you use your body, through your absorption in play, and through the acceptance of the discipline needed to be an athlete. At all times, you must protect your Self. Maintain a childlike wonder. Acquire if you can the ability to be careless, to disregard appearances, to relax and laugh at the world.

If you are to succeed, you must always be on the alert. Establish priorities. Keep one hour a day inviolate. A full sixty minutes in which you retire from God, country, family and practice. And there must be one day a week that is yours alone. Learn self-esteem, self-acceptance. Know that you can be a hero.

It won't be easy. There are people out there waiting to kill you with their demands. They will want an eighteen-hour day. Then a twenty-four-hour day. A thirty-six-hour day if possible. The song tells you, "They will kill you if you let them. Don't let them. You have a friend."

But you have no friends. Those who call you by your first

name are the worst. They will call you any time, day or night, and especially on your day off.

You are your only friend. The only protector of your body and its beauty. The only defender of your play and its delights. The only guardian of your childhood and its dreams. The only dramatist and actor in your unique, never-to-be-repeated living of your life.

Rise to that challenge. Live your own life. Success is not something that can be measured or worn on a watch or hung on the wall. It is not the esteem of colleagues, or the admiration of the community, or the appreciation of patients. Success is the certain knowledge that you have become yourself, the person you were meant to be from all time.

That should be reward enough. But best of all is the fun while you are doing it. And, at the very least, you will heal yourself.

8. Excelling

*"Williams," wrote Updike, "is the classic
player on a hot August weekday when the only
thing at stake is the tissue-thin difference
between a thing done well and a thing done ill.
Because he was one of those who always cared,
who care about themselves and their art."*

AT MY AGE, I am no longer intimidated by the opinion of others. I no longer respond when told what book to read, what movie to see, what side to take in the Middle East, or why I need an antiperspirant. And I have had it up to here with being told I shouldn't enjoy the things I do enjoy. With people who are trying to give me guilt feelings because sports are a major part of my life.

But this is a new age. A time when we should be trying to communicate with each other. Explaining man to man. Explaining those of us who are really into sports to those who are not. Those who could watch football or some substitute fifty-two weeks a year to those who say if you've seen one game you've seen them all. And for the sake of that communication, it's time to set the record straight on sports being boring, repetitious, a waste of time, and a meaningless pastime to which serious things are in danger of being sacrificed.

Boredom, like beauty, is in the mind of the beholder. "There is no such thing as an uninteresting subject," said Chesterton.

101

"The only thing that can exist is an uninterested person." That puts the critics in the dock. If you are not interested in football, it's because you don't understand it. Be bored, you pundits, but know it to be your own inadequacy. If you don't enjoy the Super Bowl, it's your fault, not the game's.

That, of course, works both ways. I may have difficulty comprehending the grasp that music has on its enthusiasts, but I see that as a deficiency in myself, not the music lovers. When a musician tells me Beethoven's Opus 132 is not simply an hour of music but of universal truth, is in fact a flood of beauty and wisdom, I envy him. I don't label him a nut.

And being a city kid, I may be slow to appreciate the impact of nature on those raised differently, but, again, I regret that failure. And when Pablo Casals said, as he did on his ninety-fifth birthday, "I pass hours looking at a tree or a flower. And sometimes I cry at their beauty," I don't think age had finally gotten to old Pablo. I cry for myself.

And if like many scientists I have trouble grasping the meaning of poetry, I see that as a measure of my want of imagination, not the poet's. When a critic like Randall Jarrell writes, "If you ask me, 'What can I do to understand Auden or Dylan Thomas or whomever the latest poet is?' I can only reply, 'You must be born again.' " Then and only then can I estimate the effort it takes to know, really know, what makes other people come alive. What brings them joy.

It is that effort that the cool, dispassionate uninvolved critics won't make. So for them the Super Bowl is three hours of yawns. But what of the fans, the losing fans who feel pain; and the winners, who are stirred to frenzy? Does the boredom of the critics make their emotion less legitimate?

Now, some would think that pain is the opposite of joy. It isn't. Numbness, apathy, lack of feeling and caring are. Caring is the operative word, the central emotion of the fan. It is by a nice coincidence a very theological word. I must care. The players must care. Together, like actors and audience, we must make each other care. Together, we make athletics, as the philosopher George Santayana said, a physical drama in which all the moral and emotional interests of man are involved. "Watching a football game," he wrote, "the whole soul is stirred by a spectacle that represents the basis of life."

No need to tell me that, or the average fan. No need to tell the players either. To what vocation do men bring such effort, such ability, such excellence?

All share to some degree the skills and virtues of Ted Williams. A player who brought to the plate, John Updike wrote, a competence that crowds the throat with joy.

"Williams," wrote Updike, "is the classic player on a hot August weekday when the only thing at stake is the tissue-thin difference between a thing done well and a thing done ill. Because he was one of those who always cared, who care about themselves and their art."

That is why sport is never boring, never repetitious. Why Santayana, a Harvard professor, could take time to write an essay replying to those who asked him, "Why do you go to games; why do you waste your time upon the bleachers?"

Politicians may say it, theologians may write it, Americans may even believe it, but it has taken sport to prove that race, creed, color and country of national origin are only incidental qualities of a human being. It is of little moment in sport whether you are black or white, Catholic or Protestant, whether you are Italian or German, Israeli or Arab.

Sport eliminates these divisions and substitutes new ones. It demonstrates that we are divided by more fundamental differences which cannot be transcended. Sport shows that mankind is divided into three basic groups, and that these groups have identifying physical and physiological and psychological characteristics.

This is not a new concept to philosophers and theologians. They are continually trying to reconcile the unity of our goal with the variety of ways of attaining it. The *Bhagavad Gita,* for instance, outlined three paths to union with God: the way of works, the way of knowledge, and the way of devotion. Which path a person took was determined by his essential nature, his constitution and his temperament.

In sport, it is the football player who works out his salvation through works. He is the man of action. His body, his personality, his temperament demand it. And his zeal and enthusiasm and courage give us a glimpse of why these same men occupied with lesser loyalties like race and creed and country completely disrupt the world.

Unfortunately, adherence to such causes can be easily manufactured. This is another lesson derived from sport. Fans are made by such incidentals as what high school they attend, what town they live in or what college they graduated from. Sherif, the social psychologist, used a boys' camp to show how easily loyalties and friendships could be developed and destroyed simply by rearranging team rosters. The exaggerated importance of such superficial attachments is a phenomenon which is highly visible in any sports-minded community.

This passionate identification is also highly visible in the international community where these direct, bold, adventurous men act in the name of patriotic interests of various countries. They are, however, identical, except for the flag they wave and the cause they support. Like Sherif's campers, if moved to another country, another continent, they would joyfully fall in to fight their former friends. And meanwhile, the rest of us suffer and wonder what to do about these militants. Wonder how to enlist these marvelously courageous and dedicated people to a higher cause.

It has always been this way. The world looking for some way to harness and utilize this energy. "Civilization," wrote Aldous Huxley, "is a complex of religious, legal and educational devices for preventing these extremely muscular individuals from doing too much mischief, and diverting their irrepressible energies into socially desirable channels." William James spoke in much the same vein. He sought a moral equivalent of war. Some demanding activity, some cause of peaceful nature that would occupy these people, and turn them from destructive pursuits.

James saw war as a source, however unacceptable, of many good things like fitness, manliness and instances of the highest sacrifice man can make. It provided for many the way to perfection.

It is instructive that the Catholic Church in attempting to perfect her adherents gave them a choice of Orders corresponding to these divisions of man, including the man of action. One could join a meditative order like the Trappists, or fulfill himself in the ritual of liturgy of Benedictines, or go out and change the world with the Dominicans. In the Church, they did not let incidentals of birth and geography get cluttered up with more fundamental differences.

Similarly, sport does not care whether you are a Democrat or Republican, capitalist or Communist. Sport goes to the essence. It reminds me of an encounter group I once attended. In the first exercise, the person next to me asked me again and again, "Who are you?" When I answered successively with the conventional identifications and relationships, my neighbor kept repeating, "Thank you, but who are you?"

Eventually, you get down to basics that have nothing to do with flags or slogans, political campaigns or fund-raising dinners, where you come from or what you do for a living.

Such exercises do not give solutions. But they do show how shallow and trivial most of our allegiances are. The answer to "Thank you, but who are you?" is available to any athlete who has found his sport.

A world record always reassures me that author Teilhard de Chardin was right. A 3:49.4 mile convinces me "that man is still moving along his evolutionary trajectory." The breaching of another physical barrier makes me certain that "like a multistage rocket, mankind is now visibly starting a fresh forward leap."

I can see in this external perfection, this economy of energy and space, a sign of internal perfection, an indication we are getting better and better. We are, as Teilhard said, seeking not simply to enjoy more or know more, but to be more. And evolving in love toward the perfection of man and the universe. The Omega Point. The divine milieu.

This is not a popular view with the experts. Not many see man as essential to God's plan. Not many more see any hope for the future. One prominent exception is the athletes. While everyone around is crying doom, the athletes are caught up in Teilhard's "continually accelerating vortex of self-totalization." They are telling us that nothing can prevent man—the species— from growing still greater, as long as he preserves in his heart the passion for growth.

And there is nowhere better to watch that growth than the mile run. The runner has three great challenges, and the greatest of these is the mile. The others are the dash and the marathon. Taken together, they comprise all of exercise physiology. They correspond to the three major sources of muscular energy, and they call on man in his various guises as body, mind and spirit.

The dash is raw speed powered by high-energy phosphates. The marathon is the unerring test of endurance and the use of oxygen. But the mile is all these, plus a third force, anerobic metabolism, the use of sugar in the absence of oxygen, and the ability to clear the body of lactic acid.

The dash is pure body; the marathon is pure mind. The mile is body, mind and spirit. "The mile remains the classic distance," wrote Paul Gallico, "because it calls for brains and rare judgment as well as speed, condition and courage." And its searching third quarter requires the leap of faith that what you are doing is worth the effort.

What better place, then, to observe mankind evolving, to look for the ultimate in human performance?

John Walker, the current ultimate, is the athletic descendant of another outstanding New Zealander, Peter Snell. At six feet, one and a half inches and 185 pounds, Walker compares to

Snell's five feet, ten and a half inches and 175 pounds. Like Snell, he is a four-hundred-meter man coming up to the mile. And like Snell, he is driving the smaller man into longer races.

His record run was unbelievably easy. But so are most world records. When they come, they appear easy, expected, even inevitable. But why they happen still confounds our traditional scientists. Despite the detailed and accurate statistics of track and field, the scientists consistently underestimate the human body and its potential.

They do, of course, figure in factors of better food, better training and better equipment. What they fail to calculate is the human factor, the multitudes of people engaged in this struggle who are constantly producing better individuals and better community. They do not see that man is a process, not a product.

Genes and numbers and passion for growth will produce not only new records, but also a new world. The mile, then, is a minor but very evident part of this common enterprise. From it, we can take heart that "far from reaching his ceiling or even slipping back, man is at this moment advancing with full vigor."

Teilhard and John Walker and every athlete who has put on a track shoe, indeed all those who have tried to become the best they could be, keep telling us this. We have yet to see the true marvels of mankind and the universe.

"Man is so made," wrote La Fontaine, "that whenever anything fires his soul, impossibilities vanish." No one in our lifetime has shown this more clearly than Vince Lombardi. Lombardi was a practical demonstration of the power of emotion, will and, finally, prayer and meditation to unleash the untapped energies of man.

I suspect that not a few intellectuals are distressed by the fact that a football coach and his players should provide such an example of the unlimited capacities of man. (When *Commonweal*, a liberal Catholic weekly, put down pro football and the Super Bowl a few years back, an irate reader wrote that Lombardi was forming at Green Bay one of the few truly Christian communities in the country.) But others now recognize sports as one of man's major endeavors.

Among them is philosopher Paul Weiss, who classifies sports with politics, art and religion as relating to issues of fundamental importance. Weiss might also agree that no political leader, artist or even religious figure has had the positive impact of Vincent Lombardi on the nation's thinking.

The impact was partly the result of the fundamental importance of sport that Weiss mentions. The personality, character and beliefs of Vincent Lombardi did the rest.

What is the source of immediacy and vitality of sport? Denison, in his *Lives of Children,* writes of the look of children in games: "the brightness of their faces, the vivacity of their faces, the swiftness of their intention, the accuracy and drollery of their observations." Add to these priceless qualities the miracles of dexterity (occasionally performed ourselves) and the achievement in becoming all we are; that is what sports in all about.

Becoming all you are was the Lombardi credo. Religion is not something you believe; it is something you do. For Lombardi, born into a world of Original Sin, a world of imperfect men to be endured while en route to heaven, that religion became one of the perfectability of community, and the overwhelming importance of the present. Football was not merely important to living the good life. It was the good life.

No more revealing story about this conjunction of life and football has been told about him than the one about Leroy Caffey loafing on a play in a practice session. "Caffey," said Lombardi, "if you cheat in practice, you will cheat in a game." This is where most coaches would stop, but Lombardi went on: "And if you cheat in a game, you will cheat for the rest of your life. And I will not have it."

The failure to live up to potential was the supreme tragedy to Lombardi. Like the New Theologians, he preached the importance of the body. And he saw the Good News that God loves men no matter what they do as making the short passage through time and life crucial. Death, writes Leslie Dewart, is the termination of the possibilities open to human nature and life. For Lombardi, those possibilities had to be tried and improved and worked on every waking moment. Let death and heaven and hell take care of themselves.

So Lombardi was a disciplinarian, but not for discipline as discipline. Sonny Jurgensen, for instance, said Lombardi was the first coach who didn't mention his weight. He merely told him that he expected Jurgensen to be ready to play his best. To give one hundred percent, to love one hundred percent, Lombardi found, was impossible without a discipline that was more than discipline. It was a belief. That sort of belief which is commitment without reservation. It was a commitment without reservation that Lombardi demanded and got both from himself and from his players.

How did he do it? Others—Lombardi was not the first—had these ideas. Held these beliefs. Sought to motivate men. Why was Lombardi successful?

Many of his friends and associates, players and politicians, have tried to tell us who and what Vincent Lombardi was. But when the final word is written and the last story of his dedication to football is told, the one thing that will stand out about Vincent Lombardi will be his vocation.

Not the restricted sense of vocation as a football coach, but his vocation as a man. The vocation that theologians define as the strong sense that one's life and responsibilities must always tend toward evoking a sense of God's presence for one's self and one's fellow man. And it comes only to a man of prayer.

It was this third element, prayer, that made Vincent Lombardi a man of great emotions and great willpower, able to do the impossible. Also to be, as Willie Davis said in his eulogy, "All the man there is."

Amen.

"Can you really see Christ as a professional football player?" a professor of philosophy asked me recently. We were discussing a criticism he had written of football and the men who play it. "Programmed violence," he called it. "The joke," he said, "was on those who cultivate the illusion of eternity in time, of perfection in trivial things, of camaraderie of violence, synthetic hatred and relentless dedication to bloody, competitive victory."

The joke, I suspect, is on the professor. He is in the ought-to-be of the intellect which is telling him weird things about what are essentially physical experiences. The football player is in the has-to-be, arising from the deepest regions of his being. He is following a call which is almost as mysterious to him as the game he plays is to the professor.

Yes, I can see Christ the football player. Just as I can see Christ the plumber, Christ the artist, or Christ the carpenter. The Good News he brought two millennia ago is that the body is holy, the world is sacred and nothing human is alien to Me. When He became Man, we became men. The message of Bethlehem was not simply that all men were created equal, but that all men were created unique. And they would succeed or fail in the way they fulfilled the possibilities of this uniqueness—the one authentic life each one should lead.

Unfortunately for the professor, this starts with the body, the temple of the Holy Ghost, as our professor of surgery used to say very carefully before he began his lectures. What do we in the intellectual pursuits really know about the body? What do we professionals with the clean white hands know of the world of Christ the linebacker? What would we know of the world of Chirst the plumber? Or of Christ the carpenter?

What do we know of the sound of a nail hit true, the smells of the different woods, the feel of the grain and the planed surfaces, the easy grip on the hammer and the smooth expert use of the saw? Cannot the carpenter find his eternity in contemplating his completed house, his perfection in apparently trivial things?

Undoubtedly, the waste of a mind is a terrible thing. The waste of a soul is worse. But it all begins with the waste of the body.

"Our first concern," says Carlos Castenada, whose experiences with the Mexican sorcerer Don Juan have made him a folk hero, "should be with ourselves. I can like my fellow man only when I am at the top of my vigor and not depressed. To be in this condition, I must keep my body trim."

This care of body, says Castenada, must be impeccable, because the body is an awareness with which we know the world and ourselves. This is not too far from the thought of C. G. Jung. The great psychiatrist felt that there were a number of separate centers in the body, called chakras, each capable of human thought. A Taos Indian chief had once told him that white men were covered with wrinkles because they were crazy. And they were crazy, the chief said, because they thought only with their heads.

Of course, in our present culture, the head is paramount. Success, which is money and fame, comes easiest to the brain worker. People are graded to the extent they use their hands (blue collar) or their minds (white collar). In our system, professors of philosophy are light-years ahead of pro football players in status.

But isn't the linebacker the one who is living authentically in his own world, his body impeccably tuned in, believing in himself and what he is doing? "Work," wrote Mark Twain, "is anything a body has to do. Play is anything a body doesn't have to do." By those standards, the professor might be a slave and the football player a free man.

The unlived life is the real threat. And because we don't understand ourselves and our prejudices, we are in danger. How can I find the has-to-be deep inside of me if I am already persuaded by my society that working with my hands is second-class work? How can I follow my vocation if that is a vocation supposedly fit only for the uneducated?

"Have we at last," I asked the professor, "found in football the one occupation of the twenty-eight thousand open to man that the Lord would not have for his own?"

The truth is, we know many jobs fit for the Lord, but not his children. It happens whenever genius and talent are replaced by that worst of heresies—good taste.

When I was fifty-two and no longer interested, I learned the secret of all hitting games. While watching a TV program about racquet ball, I suddenly grasped the principles of hitting a ball. I saw the basic physics of translating my power into an object's velocity. I knew at that moment how to hit a ball, any ball.

Who at that age, seeing how it should be done, would not mourn over a lost youth? Who would not dream of three-sewer stickball home runs, or a tennis game of serve and volley and smash, or even using an eight iron for the second shot on a par-four hole? Who would not want to relive his life as a hitter?

I wouldn't, for one. At fifty-two, I had learned the real secret of all hitters. They are born and not made. And I was not one of them. Technique is essential, but it cannot stand alone. No amount of timing and rhythm and biomechanics will make a hitter out of a person lacking the physical and mental and emotional equipment.

The hitter is born with the hitter's physique, and the hitter's psyche. Technique will not make a hitter out of a nonhitter. It will merely make the hitter a better hitter.

TV also told me this: Close observation of baseball players, golfers and tennis players revealed a common structural characteristic. Power. Their muscularity is evident from all angles. No one makes it in those sports who is not that type of person. The number of golfers who are ex–football players or who could easily be taken for ex–football players alerted me to this. Even apparently slender athletes have an underlying bone structure that belies their slight build. Fred Patek, for instance, the vest-pocket shortstop of the Kansas City Royals, has arms as big as my thighs. And his wrists are enormous.

There is where the hitter is to be found. The wrists give him away. They are the evidence of his power and his willingness to use it. If you become a wrist watcher, you can pick out the natural athlete, the person with the potential to succeed in these competitive sports.

You will also be able to recognize those with the potential to succeed in this competitive personal life. Those who will bring to their job or profession or career that same aggressive, energetic and direct approach.

Some, like Patek, are deceptive. To see them in clothes, you wouldn't imagine the inner strength they have, the courage and willingness to mix it up. But one glance at the wrist and you know you are prey facing a predator.

I am a wrist watcher myself. When you have the thin, delicate wrists of a nonhitter, noncombatant in life, you have to be. So when I check my fellow man, I check his wrists, Other aspects may change. The waist may enlarge and recede. The double chin come and go. But the wrist is unchanging. And it tells me about the inner man and how he is going to respond. I know then who comes to each day tough and ready for whatever comes.

With the proper technique, I could impersonate this hitter, but I would never be one. At fifty-two, I realize this. My philosophy has ripened, as Aristotle had predicted so precisely, at the age of fifty-one. I passed the crisis that comes to all men who find that their machismo must lie in other, presumably less masculine activities. Who find that they are not designed for confrontation and assertive action.

I passed the crisis that comes when you realize that Rollo May was wrong when he said the myth of competition was dead. (Arthur Miller's *Death of a Salesman,* said May, showed that competition was outmoded and that cooperation would be the new myth of our lives.)

I suspect that May's wrists are no bigger than mine, and that he would like to think competition is finished. The way I see it, competition is alive and well and flourishing in sports and in corporate America. And no one is going to make it to the top without the wrists to do it.

Some critics have called sports the religion of America. I think not. Religion is an unprovable assumption about the experienced universe. It requires a construct too comprehensive for sports to provide. But there is a good case to be made that sports is the basis of our present culture, providing common values that men of all religions can live by.

For a culture to be passed along, Santayana wrote, it is not necessary that people read certain books, but simply that all people read the same books. And if by books we mean the literature of the day, then sports has indeed become the basis of our culture.

The literature of this day is journalism, and the authors of this day are journalists, whether they are called novelists or playwrights or essayists or reporters. Our daily reading is journalism because our novels and plays and essays and newspaper scores are clearly reports on the personal observations of actual events and people, even if more times than not the people observed are the authors themselves.

And the heavyweights in these writing fields are writers to whom sports are always important, or sometimes the whole ball game. Mailer, Marianne Moore, Updike, Roth and Dickey, to name a few, have found in sports the analogies to explain what happens elsewhere in life.

When Mailer had his fiftieth birthday party and Fifth Estate fiasco at the Four Seasons, he said the failure was not without some compensation; he could now write intimately, he said, "of the after-sensation of being called out on strikes in the last of the seventh when there are men on base and you never take your bat off your shoulder."

The game was just as important to Miss Moore, who wrote in her review of George Plimpton's *Out of His League* that the book should earn Plimpton the triple crown for poetry, biography and drama. And also as important to Updike, who wrote: "A game can gather to itself awesome dimensions of subtlety and transcendental significance."

The root of this subtlety and transcendence is the body. We proceed to these almost mystical heights through a reality common to us all. The body is where all religion, all culture, all literature must start. The body is where all writers must start, and few do.

"Literature does its best to maintain," wrote Virginia Woolf, "that its concern is the mind; that the body is a sheet of glass through which the soul looks straight and clear, and (the body) is null and negligible and nonexistent. On the contrary, the opposite is true. All day, all night, the body intervenes."

Writers who know sports and play never make that mistake. And having started with this deep regard for the body, they are able to go off in diverse and wonderful ways to praise men and their games. They have shown again the old truth: The deeper the belief, the more various the ways it can be expressed.

"Marianne Moore, Pulitzer Prize winning poet and a baseball fan extraordinary," read the wire service report last weekend, "died yesterday at her Manhattan home. She was 84."

The ex–left fielder of the Carlisle High School girls' baseball team, poet laureate of the Brooklyn Dodgers, and watcher of three television sets in season had, in one of her favorite expressions, "run out of room."

The teacher of Jim Thorpe, lover of Bach and Elston Howard, Stravinsky and Floyd Patterson, admirer of birds, animals and athletes, had taken her penetrating vision to another and because of her presence more lively and interesting place.

And I had lost one of my saints.

She had appeared, as saints usually do, when she was needed. Needed to provide acceptance and to champion the faith, the myth, the guiding fiction of my life. Not only to give it social and intellectual respectability, but also to give me assurance that the truth I dream is true.

Back in the thirties, the attack was, "Religion is the opiate of the people." And I was there when Peter Viereck said, "Anti-

Catholicism is the anti-Semitism of the intellectuals." In those days, my saint was G. K. Chesterton, a man of talent, wit and humor who took on and defeated all comers. Chesterton, the master of the paradox, was the right person at the right time not merely because he was a thinker and writer equal to any of his opponents, but because he spoke what the common man felt. What we felt but could not express.

"The common man," he once wrote, "may be as gross as Shakespeare, or as garrulous as Homer; if he is religious, he talks almost as much about hell as Dante; if he is worldly, he talks nearly as much about drink as Dickens." And we can now add, if he is philosophical, he will think as much about baseball as Marianne Moore.

Miss Moore was the saint I needed for sports. The answer to "sport is the opiate of the people." Her genius was in observation. She saw everything vital and fresh and new as if for the first time. Her interest was in the common things in life. She did not write on eternal things or infinity. "I'll talk about them," she said, "when I understand them," and she wrote about Jackie Robinson and Campy and Big Newk instead.

She became a baseball fan at the age of sixty-six. A friend had taken her to a Dodger game and there she caught the fever. Not from a spectacular play, a memorable catch or a clutch hit, but from a conference on the mound.

It was the sight of Roy Campanella out there calming Karl Spooner down, the big mitt resting on his hip, his mask pushed back on his head and his earnest look—zest, she called it—and how he imparted encouragement with a pat on Spooner's rump, that captured the poet, who appreciated not only the skills but the emotions as well.

Marianne Moore knew the skills ("I don't know how to account for a person," she said, "who could be indifferent to these miracles of dexterity"). And although her favorites were Howard and Campanella, because they were strong, lumbering quarterbacking catchers, she also liked what she called the precision positions, third base, pitcher and first base.

She knew what they were trying to do. When Mike Burke asked her to throw out the first ball in 1969, she told a reporter that she had been instructed to throw it high for the benefit of the photographers. "But," she said, "I'm going to keep it low and outside where you're supposed to."

Earlier this poet, whose work is said by T. S. Eliot to form part of the small body of durable poetry of our time, whose poems were praised by Ezra Pound and pilfered by W. H. Auden, wrote in her poem "Baseball and Writing": "Your arm too true at first can learn to catch the corners, even trouble Mickey Mantle. They crowd him and curve him and aim for the knees."

Her poems were like that. Never the fat one down the middle. She worked the corners. No rookie from Tidewater was she. Reading her is going against the speed of Koufax, the accuracy of Seaver, and the assortment of Preacher Roe.

"Pitching," she said, "is a large subject." And so is her poetry. Full of sliders, slips and slants, but marvelous in its compression, its control.

To her, it was like baseball. You can never tell with either, she wrote, how it will go or what you will do; generating excitement, a fever in the victim—pitcher, catcher, fielder, batter. Athletes for her were exemplars of art ("You cannot see art off in a corner," she said, "and hope for it to have vitality, reality and substance"). And she and the athletes had this in common, that they see as opportunity what others feel as menace.

So the artist-athlete carves out his own drama, provides the pauses, determines the action on the field. He is not choreographed by Balanchine or playing someone else's music or reciting some playwright's lines. He is there, forcing his own identity on the game.

He is also contributing some no-nonsense virtues that Miss Moore always admired. Like patience, courage, loyalty and independence. And perhaps some of what she saw in the athlete, in this case Floyd Patterson, what she called "the age-old formula for results in any kind of work, profession, art or recreation—powerful feeling and the talent to use it."

Baseball gained stature from the stature of this admirer. Intellectuals might marvel that a "poet of extraordinary discrimination, precision and restraint" (Randall Jarrell), who "like Poe, Hawthorne and Henry James had a passionate predilection for the genuine" (R. P. Blackmur), would concern herself with baseball. Yet when she was leaving for Boston to receive her Doctor of Letters from Harvard ("By finding joy in earth and sky," read the citation, "she has stirred our hearts"), she remarked sadly that her schedule would not include the Red Sox game at Fenway Park.

Now this saint is dead. This kind, gracious, unpredictable woman is gone. But not before she had given the lance to "sport is the opiate of the people;" not before she had taught us the importance of the physical, and the attention we must give to every moment, every object, every animal, every human in what he says and does.

"Whatever you do," she said before she left, "do it with all your might."

I'll try, Miss Moore, I'll try.

9. Running

*The best most of us can do is to be a Poet an
hour a day. Take the hour when we run or
tennis or golf or garden; take that hour away
from being serious adults and become serious
beginners.*

EVERY MILE I RUN is my first. Every hour on the roads a new
beginning. Every day I put on my running clothes, I am born
again. Seeing things as if for the first time, seeing the familiar as
unfamiliar, the common as uncommon. Doing what Goethe said
was the hardest thing of all, seeing with my own eyes that which
is spread before me. Bringing to that running, that play, the attitude of the child, the perception of a poet. Being a beginner with
a beginner's mind, a beginner's heart, a beginner's body.

There is no other way to run, no other way to live. Otherwise
my runs become dull, uninspired interludes. The running becomes routine, becomes part of the humdrum apathy and indifference which the poet John Hall Wheelock called a shield between us and reality. It becomes a chore, becomes habit. And
habit kills awareness and separates us from ourselves.

My awareness begins with my body, my beginner's body.
Each day I discover how to breathe. Taste the air. Feel it move
through my lungs. I learn to exhale totally and groan and grunt,
marking my passage through the fields and trees like some animal.

Each day I search out how to run. Feeling the thrust of the hamstrings. Letting the foot drop below the knee. Arriving at the form the child adopts naturally. The body, a little stronger perhaps, certainly more durable, must come upon these ideas as fresh as if newly thought. And then concentrate on this beginning and bring to it the beginner's joy in doing this tremendously simple yet tremendously complex thing so well.

From then on it becomes more and more difficult. It is relatively easy to return to basics with the body. But to have a beginner's heart and mind is a different matter. To take sight and smell, hearing and touch and become a new Adam in a new Eden is tough going even for a poet. Even for those who live more and participate more in their own existence. And yet like them I must listen and discover forgotten knowledge. Must respond to everything around me and inside me as well.

Poets do this naturally. A really good poet, wrote James Dickey, is like an engine with the governor off. And it's no good for people to say that life should not mean that much to a poet. The really good poet, said Dickey, has no choice; that's the way he is.

The best most of us can do is to be a poet an hour a day. Take the hour when we run or tennis or golf or garden; take that hour away from being a serious adult and become serious beginners. Take an hour away from what Shelley called a life of error, ignorance and strife, and introduce love and beauty and delight.

Those good things began in my beginning. When I was not afraid to respond to my feeling. Before I was taught not to cry. Before I learned that humor had a time and a place and deep emotions had best be concealed, that passion be left unfelt.

When I run I go back to those better days. Now no emotion is foreign to me. I express myself totally. My body and heart and mind interact and open me to the infinite possibilities only a beginner can envision. And I relive that moment in the beginning of things when, as Yeats said, we understand more perfectly than we understand until all is finished.

And what of that finish? "It is development, improvement and completion that means the deterioration of the creativeness," wrote Berdyaev, the Russian theologian, "the cooling down of the creative fire, decay, old age."

I will have none of that. So each day I take to the roads as a beginner, a child, a poet. Seeking the innocence of the beginner, the wonder of the child and the vision of the poet. Hoping for a new appreciation of the landscape, a new perspective of my inner world, some new insights on life, a new response to existence and myself.

There are times, more often than the good times, when I fail. I never do pierce the shield. I return with a shopping list of things to do tomorrow. The miraculous has gone unseen. The message has gone unheard. I have had one of those loveless days on a lovely day for love.

Still, there is always the chance I'll have beginner's luck. And this run, this hour, this day, may begin in delight and end in wisdom.

I am a noonday runner. In the past, and still from time to time, I have run in the morning or evening. But almost always these days, I run in the early afternoon.

You might think this choice of when to run simply a matter of convenience. Of fitting it in when time becomes available. Most people believe that running is running, regardless of when it is done. But I know this is not so. There is a time, as Ecclesiastes wrote, for every purpose under heaven. There is a time for running. Mine is midday. I run at midday because I must. I run at midday because my body and soul tell me to.

My body is at its best in early afternoon. My circulation rhythms at their crest. Like the sun, my energy is at its zenith, my fields of force at maximum. Whatever I do, I do best at this time of day.

But midday has more than physiological importance. When I run at noon, I run at the sixth hour. I run at an hour that has significance that goes back through the history of the race. An hour that reminds me I am participating in an ever-recurring mystery, seeking and making a self I will never fully know. An hour that brings me back to myth and ritual and a feeling for the holy.

In the sixth hour, I am in a time that is recurrent and symbolic. A time that Eliade wrote of as circular, reversible and recoverable. A time that tells me I am a child of the universe born for more than is visible in this world.

Daybreak and sunset have similar implications. The morning run speaks for rebirth and the new life. Just as morning prayers praise the Lord, sing the earth, tell of renewed purpose. And the evening run is for those who have fought the good fight and now desire only the peace an hour's run at a slow, steady pace will give them. When I run in these closing stages of the day, I am a philosopher. I accept life, death, the self, what I have done. I am content.

From this perspective, the morning run is my youth. Running in the morning is to wear the bright morning face. It is for health and fitness and making the team. It is accepting discipline, obeying duty and acquiring self-control.

Midday is adult. The run is in pursuit of goals, the making of the self, the looking for something to leave behind. You must say it is in the Catholic traditon, linking goodness to beauty and proportion and achievement.

If so, the evening run is toward the East, toward that ancient acceptance of things as they are. That mature wisdom with which we see a world that has order and sense. And we know, as Erikson said, that our one and only life cycle was something that had to be and, by necessity, permitted of no substitutions.

One thing we runners know. There is no substitute for running. No matter what age we are. No matter what time we do it.

My fight is not with age. Running has won that battle for me. Running is my fountain of youth, my elixir of life. It will keep me young forever. When I run, I know there is no need to grow old. I know that my running, my play, will conquer time.

And there on the roads, I can pursue my perfection for the rest of my days, and finally, as his wife said of Kazantzakis dead at seventy-four, be mowed down in the first flower of my youth.

The fight, then, is never with age; it is with boredom, with routine, with the danger of not living at all. Then life will stop, growth will cease, learning will come to an end. You no longer become who you are. You begin to kill time or live it without thought or purpose. Everything that is happiness, all that is excitement, whatever you know of joy and delight, will evaporate. Life will be reduced to a slow progression of days and weeks and months. Time will become an enemy instead of an ally.

When I run, I avoid all this. I enter a world where time stops, where now is a fair sample of eternity. Where I am filled with excitement and joy and delight, even with the intensity and inner fire and never-ending search for self of a Kazantzakis. I enter a state that will be man's most congenial environment.

"Play, games, jests, culture, we affirm," wrote Plato, "are the most serious things in life." And for the most serious of all reasons, what Kierkegaard called "choosing one's self." Or, to use Plato's thought again, to recapture our original state of perfection.

But isn't that perfection, or at least the bodily part of it, only resident in youth? Not if you persist in your sport, persevere in your play. True, we delight in our bodies in our youth and envy the young as we grow old. But this need not be.

We can continue to keep our bodies in beauty and competence until death claims us. We should know that the fit die young in body as well as in mind and heart. That, like Kazantzakis, whatever their age they will be mowed down in the first flower of their youth.

Running has made me young again. I run now as I did at twenty. I have the same health, the same vigor, the same sensations of power and grace. And I have the strength and speed and endurance of those years younger than me. Not because I am exceptional, but because I do what I do with my whole self. My running is an incitement to energy. It is an outpouring from the very center of my being. It is a vital force that takes me to the peak of my powers and there opens me to myself and to the world and to others.

Running gives me a body and mind and heart willing to follow my own vision, to break the mold, to choose a new course, even perhaps to become the hero that Ortega said we all carry within us. This is a lifelong task. A lifelong of saying, as did Ortega, "That's not it, that's not it." And therefore a life that must be very young and eager and full of enthusiasm, full of sport and play, full of running.

If you would not age, you must make everything you do touched with play, play of the body, of thought, of emotions. If you do, you will belong to that special class of people who find joy and happiness in every act, in every moment. Those to whom leisure is the one thing valuable. Those whom Ruskin called "the proudly idle."

My running and your play may be idleness to those of another mind. But it is the self-awareness, the consciousness, the intensity, that is important, however inconsequential the activity. "Come into the kitchen," said Heraclitus. "The gods are there, too." And out on the roads, and whenever you play, there is fitness and self-discovery and the persons we were destined to be. There is the theater where we can write and act out our own dreams. Having first, of course, gotten down to bone and muscle, and then come to some understanding of the unique once-in-an-eternity person each one of us is.

Running reminds me that any age man is still the marvel of creation. With the passage of time, there is little deterioration of our physical or psychic powers, little worth thinking that is lost. The only important issue, as Rollo May tells us, is not whether a person is twenty or forty or sixty, but whether he fulfills his own capacity of self-conscious choice at his own particular level.

That's a game the playful person almost always wins.

Is running an art and the runner an artist? The best answer is that of Picasso. When asked, "What is art?" he replied, "What is not?"

So running is an art along with everything else we do. When I run, I know this to be true. Running is my art and I am an artist however ordinary my performance. Running is for me what the dance is to others. The oldest and highest of the arts. My ancestors ran before they danced. And it is running, not dance, that gives me a perfect conformity of form and matter.

Running also fulfills Herbert Read's definition. Art, he stated, is an escape from chaos; movement ordained in numbers; mass confined by measure; matter seeking the rhythm of life. You could almost believe Read was watching runners while he wrote.

Where better to escape chaos and find order? Where more is movement numbered, in steps, in breaths, in minutes, in miles? Where more sharply is space and mass defined; the runner lean, the road unending? Where else, for me at least, to seek the rhythms of life, to listen to the body, to hear it speak of my soul?

And because body becomes soul, soul becomes body, running is a total experience. It is art and more than art. In itself it provides the thinking and abstractions that precede other arts. "I need hours to read and think about what I've read, to synthesize and be alone," one painter said. "The time spent at the canvas is minor compared with that."

The runner, on the other hand, is always at his canvas. He is always observing, feeling, analyzing, meditating. Always in the process of raiding the preconscious that stores past preconceptions. The preconscious that stubbornly refuses to illuminate the present with what we experienced in the past. And beyond and before it the runner explores his instincts and emotions and even dips into what can only be called mystical states.

Where the runner fails is as an artist. He may be able to express these feelings, these insights, and perhaps does, but no one sees them. He fails in the prime function of the artist, to transmit the understanding of the emotions he has experienced. The spectator sees little of this inner life. Even the poet, tuned to see life at various levels, sees the runner in almost one plane.

"Alone he emerges / Emerges and passes / alone, sufficient." Loneness, motion, sufficiency is the runner. The world knows no more about him.

In time this will change. Running is an old art but only newly resurrected. We are still learning how to develop a total response. In traffic I may be as expressionless as Buster Keaton, but on lonely roads and in empty woods the inner man is becoming visible. There I respond to grass and dirt and fallen leaves. My running is part of sun and shadow, wind at my face, wind at my back. If you saw me, you would see elation, mastery, struggle, defeat and despair. There I reveal sorrow and anger, resentment and fear; fear of dogs and men and high places, fear of the dark and of being lost and alone.

But what matters whether we can be understood by someone else? By someone who is not a runner? Not certainly to induce them to try it themselves. But rather to encourage them to seek their own art, to become their own artists. To listen for that inner voice calling them to their own way of being in this world. To what they must be.

The runner knows this necessity. I know that although I am free to be anything I choose, I must be a runner. Ortega put it this way: "You are able to be whatever you want to be; but only if you choose this or that specific pattern you will be what you have to be."

When I run, all that Ortega says falls into place. I have found my specific pattern, heard the voice that calls me, found my art, my medium to experience and interpret life. Nor do I worry that running will be inadequate to the task. I know the truth of what William James once said of a young man learning about himself and his instincts and emotions: "Sport came to the rescue and completed his education where real things were lacking."

The distance runner is the least of all athletes. His sport the least of all sports. That he does it at all, either well or ill, implies that he can do nothing else. He has by the process of elimination come to the level of his competence, which is little more than survival.

Nor does he survive in ways we might admire. By challenging his environment, for instance, for conquering his enemies. He performs no feats of skill or strength or agility. He is no Crusoe who would build a new house, a new town, a new city, even a new civilization. He does nothing more than this: bring his body to the performance of a minor art, and attain an inconsequential type of perfection.

And being the least of all athletes, he appears to be the least of all men. A lonely figure on a lonely road, he seems to have no past, no future, and to be living in a present that has no rational meaning.

He performs with perverse intensity an action which has no marketable value. And is completely engaged in what is not only impractical, but even unintelligible to his fellows.

Still, this apparently witless and homeless creature, this most ordinary, most commonplace, this least of all men, has a message. A message we all carry, but sometimes fail to hear.

The distance runner is a prophet. Like the poet, he is the antenna of the race. Like the poet, he does what he does with his whole being. And like the poet, he gives thanks for his "fabulous possessions, his body and fiery soul." Like the poet, he sees himself as a question to himself. And seeks the answer by seeking to be, by creating himself. And again like the poet, he suggests that each one of us has this revelation, this Truth; and that we must find it through our bodies, through experience, and always in the present.

Most of us think of religion as something out of the past that promises something about the future. We ignore the primacy of the present. We forget that the opposite of the present is not past or future; it is absence.

The distance runner who accepts the past in the person he is, and sees the future as promise rather than threat, is completely and utterly in the present. He is absorbed in his encounter with the everyday world. He is mysteriously reconciling the separations of body and mind, of pain and pleasure, of the conscious and the unconscious. He is repairing the rent, and healing the wound in his divided self. He has found a way to make the ordinary extraordinary; the commonplace, unique; the everyday, eternal.

What he does begins in play, moves through suffering and ends in delight. And tells us that we must do the same. That we who began in play as children and move toward a heaven where we will have nothing to do but play will find our revelation and ourselves only in play.

The distance runner has found his play. And with it, he purifies his body. He does not, as the early Fathers suggested, kill his body because it kills him. He accepts it and perfects it and then seeks out suffering, and finds beyond the suffering the whole man. Not at first, of course. At first he explores the possibilities of letting the suffering pass. Of trying every diversion to remove the pain. But in the end, he grasps it and holds it and welcomes it.

This may be an odd way to find the meaning of life. And the distance runner is certainly an odd person to be demonstrating it. But the meaning of life is beyond reason. Genius upon genius has told us so.

The meaning of life is found in revelation, a revelation that is present in each one of us. To be found where our blood and flesh whisper to our unconscious. The distance runner, the least of all athletes, the least of all men, is continually taking his daily encounter with his universe on that inward journey.

Consider your body, he tells us. Not in the memory of past

pleasure. Or in anticipation of a glorious future. But for this present moment when you might indeed be in Paradise.

As soon as the race results are in the paper, the usual comment I hear in the hospital corridors is, "I see you let a girl beat you." The statement is wrong on all counts. Wrong in what it says. Wrong in what it implies.

For one thing, she is not a girl, but a woman. Anyone who has had their consciousness raised knows better than to call a woman a girl. You use "girl" where if it were male you'd use "boy." And it is about time everyone learned that. Further, she is not only a woman but a runner, and a good one. Women runners can be more than just competent. They have less percent body fat than most men. Their maximum oxygen uptake can be amazingly high. And their slow and fast twitch muscle fiber ratios are identical to men runners' in other events.

I have discovered in races and in training that women runners have the same spectrum men have, from very good to very bad. I have been beaten regularly by the best and have had some head-to-head struggles with those not quite good. And I have trained with some whose cruising speed left me speechless and gasping to keep with them. So there is no question of letting a woman beat you. Some do. Some don't. As with all runners, it depends on who is best that particular day.

But mostly I am upset with that statement because it implies that there is something wrong about women in sports and particularly in men's sports. There is the suggestion that the whole thing is somehow unnatural.

And in the sense of the orthodox, it is. In becoming a runner, the woman gives up her appearance of completeness. She becomes less and less of a mystery. She relinquishes her power, the intimidation of being a woman. Running removes what Ortega called her "perpetual self-concealment." And in this surrender, she finds who she actually is and reveals that self to others. The woman who comes to know herself to be truly a runner has discovered not only her body, but her soul as well.

People who see only the differences between men and women do not understand this. Their herd-thinking cannot conceive that sport has something to offer women, who, after all, need nothing but children, church and kitchen. They cannot imagine any benefits from men–women competition. And their emphasis on the biological and social perpetuates the war of the sexes.

The truth is that sports, and that includes men running against women, may well be the salvation of the man–women relationship, the answer to our marriage problem, the solution of the eternal discord between what is masculine and what is feminine.

You may find this theory farfetched. But consider this first and primary thought: Nature works for the herd. She has us breed toward the middle. Opposites are attracted to opposites, and produce the average, the mediocre, the commonplace. "The decisive factor in a nation's history," wrote Ortega, "is the common man." Our herd's future, the future of the race, has always depended on its innumerable mediocre men.

This is fine biologically and even socially, but not psychologically. Each of us wants to be an individual, a thoroughbred, whether it be a quarter horse or a Clydesdale. The herd would have us marry for what we lack. We should marry for what we see of ourselves in others. Our aim should be, as Plato said, to find our other half.

This cannot be done unless each is revealed, body and soul, to the other. And where better can this be done than in sports? In those arenas where a person finds his or her moment of truth. Knows what she or he has been from all time. And, in that knowing, reveals it to others.

Nature would rather avoid this revelation. Rather the woman remained a mystery. Rather the masculine in women and the feminine in men went unrecognized. So men and women are attracted at an early age in the interests of forces that are unconcerned about their personal fulfillment. Originality, individuality, creativity and personality are sacrificed. And all of this has gone unnoticed because, as H. L. Mencken once said, a man can be happy with any number of women. And Mencken could have added: women continue in situations that cry for vengeance on heaven.

But in our overpopulated world, the herd is no longer that important. Leisure and free time now make the psychological problems of such marriages more evident. In 1976 for the first time, divorces in the United States exceeded one million. Our affluence and forty-hour work week have allowed for communication. And, as Ogden Nash once wrote about your conscience, you should have a good communication or none at all.

Eventually, love, marriage, communication, good conversation or good silences depend on a total meeting with someone who is most like ourself. So that, as Berdyaev put it, we are "united in one androgynous image, overcoming our loneliness."

That, of course, is the ultimate. Creating union, knowing the other, overcoming loneliness, bringing together two solitudes.

Sport is the key to this undertaking. Athletes who know themselves in their body know when they differ from others. But even more, they know when they are alike. When they are simpatico.

When I see women running, I see a new world coming. Not perhaps for girls who are as soft and as pink as a nursery, but certainly for those who wear sweats and running shoes and train thirty miles a week.

10. Training

Nature, as T. H. Huxley has told us, never overlooks a mistake or makes the smallest allowance for ignorance.

IF YOU WANT to run a marathon you must train six miles a day. If you are looking for that natural high that distance runners talk about, you must do the same. And if you would prefer to die of something other than a heart attack, the daily six miles is physiological magic.

But know this: Disaster will pursue you to the very gates of heaven unless you do the Magic Six. These are exercises designed to counteract the bad effects of daily training—the muscle imbalance that contributes to overuse syndromes of foot, leg, knee, and low back. Without the Magic Six you will soon become an ex-runner, no longer able to accept five thousand footstrikes an hour on a hard flat surface with a foot constructed for sand or dirt.

Training overdevelops the prime movers, the muscles along the back of the leg, the thigh, and the low back; they become short and inflexible. The antagonists, the muscles on the front of the leg, the thigh, and the abdomen become relatively weak. The Magic Six are necessary to correct this strength–flexibility imbalance. Three stretch the prime movers; three strengthen the antagonists.

The first stretching exercise is the wall pushup for the calf muscles. Stand flatfooted about three feet from the wall. Lean in until it hurts to keep the knees locked, and the legs straight, and the feet flat. Hold for ten "elephants." (The time it takes to say "One elephant" is about one second.) Relax. Continue for one minute.

The second is the hamstring stretch. Put your straight leg, with knee locked, on a footstool, later a chair, and finally a table as you improve. Keep the other leg straight with knee locked. Bring your head to the knee of the extended leg or toward the knee until it hurts. Hold for ten elephants. Relax. Continue for one minute.

The final stretch exercise is the backover for the hamstrings and the low back. Lie on floor. Bring your straight legs over your head and try to touch the floor with your toes until it hurts. Hold for ten elephants. Relax by bringing your knees to your ears for ten elephants. Continue for one minute.

The first strengthening exercise is for the shin muscles. Sit on a table with your legs hanging down. Suspend a three- to five-pound weight over the toes of one foot. Flex the foot upward. Hold for six elephants. Relax. Continue for one minute.

For the quadriceps assume the same position with the weight. This time strengthen the leg, locking the knee. Hold for six elephants. Relax. Continue for one minute.

The final exercise is the bent-leg sit-up. Lie on the floor with your knees bent and your feet close to your buttocks. Come to a sitting position. Lie back. Repeat until you can't do any more or until you've reached twenty times.

It takes a little over six minutes to do the Magic Six. Done before and after running, this means just twelve minutes a day to keep you in muscle balance and counteract stress fractures and heel spurs and Achilles-tendinitis and shin splints and runner's knee and sciatica and all those other terrible things that happen to runners.

Is your second toe longer than your first toe?

If so and you are an athlete you are in for trouble. If you haven't already had it. The long-second/short-first toe, called Morton's foot, is probably the most disabling of the common congenital defects in the architecture of the foot which cause it to fail with overuse.

Until Dudley Morton noticed it, the long-second/short-first toe was considered no more important than a large nose or a square jaw. No one had thought about what constitutes a normal foot. Morton changed all of that. In 1935 he published his classic, *The Normal Foot*, which for the foot was what Harvey's *De Motu Cordis* three hundred years earlier was for the heart and circulation.

The function of foot, wrote Morton, depends on two factors:

1. Structural stability, supplied by the 26 bones and the 112 ligaments which bind these bones together. Any abnormality in the bony architecture or laxity of the ligaments, Morton said, can end in weak, painful and inefficient feet. Further, these bio-mechanical problems can cause more remote difficulties in the leg and the knee and even the groin and the low back.

2. Postural stability, maintained by the short muscles of the foot and the long muscles of the foot and the leg. Imbalance caused by a short heel cord or strong inflexible calf and thigh muscles, he claimed, puts additional stress on the foot and the arch.

The most frequent cause of structural instability in the foot is Morton's foot. It is a biomechanical absurdity. The two-millimeter or more shortening of the first metatarsal distorts the normal weight-bearing tripod: the heel, the head of the fifth and the head of the first metatarsal. The foot adapts by either (a) bearing most of the weight on the head of the second metatarsal, thereby causing a stress fracture; or (b) pronating the foot (rolling over the inside) and opening up a Pandora's box of overuse injuries.

The most prevalent of these injuries are evenly distributed among the foot (the heel spur), the leg (the stress fracture) and the knee (runner's knee, or chondromalacia).

If you are an athlete and have suffered from any of these illnesses it is possible, I could say probable, that no one has observed whether or not your second toe is longer than the first. Or whether you have any of the other more subtle structural flaws that can cause foot difficulties.

Morton's discovery has been forgotten. It was taught to one generation of physicians and then discredited. Many people had Morton's foot without symptoms. So when it appeared in those with complaints, it was thought a coincidence.

The truth was that people were just not using their feet that much. It wasn't until after World War II that athletes upped their practice time fivefold and the overuse syndromes of foot, leg, knee and back became the major concern of sports physicians. By that time Morton's book had disappeared from the libraries and the curriculum. And with it his theory of structural and postural strain which was the answer to these mysterious ailments.

For many who are on their feet very little, Morton's theories are just that. For the practicing athlete his theories can be the difference between being active and being on the injured list— indeed, the difference between being an athlete and being an ex-athlete. When the basketball player spends hours on the court daily, and the runner increases his mileage to fifty and sixty miles a week, and the tennis player makes it a twice-a-day thing, then we begin to hear about Butazolidine and cortisone shots and whirlpool treatments.

But we never hear about Morton's foot and structural stability and postural stability.

I wonder why.

"At this late date in the history of sport," writes Paul Weiss in his *Sport, a Philosophic Inquiry*, "we still do not know much about what an athlete ought to eat before he engages in a grueling contest." This ignorance, of course, extends further. At this late date in the history of mankind, we still do not know much about what any of us ought to eat before we engage in work or life, much less play. The human intestinal tract, its physiology, and its diseases remain a mystery.

Fortunately the experts are confessing their ignorance and thereby liberating us from relying on their diets and treatments. The cause of duodenal ulcer, states a recent editorial in *The Lancet*, a British medical journal, remains poorly understood, and "the logical basis of treatment completely escapes us." It also escapes the task forces on gastrointestinal research commissioned by the National Institutes of Health. The reports of these groups, assigned to various parts of the digestive system, come to one general conclusion: Most of our firmly held ideas about digestion and digestive diseases are either untrue or unproven.

What are we to do while the experts suck their thumbs? The best answer is to go back to the three rules of digestion known since antiquity:

1. Eat foods that agree with you.
2. Avoid foods that disagree with you.
3. Don't go to bed mad.

One thing the investigators are discovering is that the foods we said agreed with us agree with us. And the foods we said disagreed with us disagree with us. Their high-powered sophisticated technology is confirming what patients have told their doctors over the centuries: certain foods give them heartburn or indigestion or cramps or diarrhea, other foods do not. Only now the people in the laboratory are finally finding out why. Learning why certain people have trouble with certain foods and others don't. Why foods that should be good for you can cause wholesale trouble.

Milk is a prime example of a food that should be good for us but frequently isn't. Some people are allergic to milk, but many more cannot handle the milk sugar lactose because of an enzyme deficiency. It seems likely now that if you never liked milk you shouldn't drink it. It may be the perfect food but not for you.

Each of us has particular foods that we know are not for us. Foods that cause heartburn or a variety of gut symptoms. Each of us is, therefore, an experiment-of-one in finding out what foods we can handle and what foods we can't. There is no sense appealing to the books, or the experts. The body will not listen. Eventually we will get a scientific explanation for what is happening. For the time being we must accept the reality.

One such reality is that if we go to bed mad we are likely to wake up with a riled-up stomach. If I go to bed with fire in my eye, I will wake up with fire in my stomach. It is not only food but emotions that act on the intestinal tract.

When I become an athlete, emotion becomes even more important. Pre-game tension, pre-race apprehension, can stop the stomach from emptying. Food that would ordinarily get in and out in four hours may sit undigested for six or more. Then I add the effect of strenuous exercise which is to increase spasm and propulsion through the bowel. Emotion and exertion are why the athlete has one additional rule:

> 4. Always compete on an empty stomach and an empty colon.

Otherwise the athlete and his food are soon parted. He will either throw up or have diarrhea, or both.

Follow the rules, however, and you can come up with your own answer to your pre-event meal. Liquid or semiliquid, with little fat and not too much protein, so that it will be easily digested and quickly out of the stomach. And composed of foods you take every day and know you can handle.

Here, as in all things related to health and to well working and to functioning at our maximum, we must listen to our bodies. Fortunately the gastrointestinal tract speaks in a loud, clear and unmistakable voice. When we make a mistake we know it.

Even slow learners get the message if they lose their lunch or have to retire from the fray for a bowel movement.

Life is the great experiment. Each of us is an experiment of one—observer and subject—making choices, living with them, recording the effects. "Living," said the philosopher Ortega, "is nothing more than doing one thing instead of another."

But that doing must be total. We must live on the alert and perform at capacity. "From my point of view," Ortega declared, "it is immoral for a being not to make the most intense effort every instant of his life."

When these conditions of conscious choice and maximum effort apply, we find that nature has set up the best of experiments, simple and controlled, solving questions one at a time. When we study ourselves in motion, under stress, trying to be all we can be, then, and sometimes only then, our deficiencies become apparent in unmistakable ways. If we would be artist or scientist or philosopher or saint, we soon learn what makes us more human or mortal than those who succeed. But we learn even quickest when we are athletes.

And of all athletes, the endurance athlete—the distance runner, the swimmer, the cross-country skier—is the researcher's dream. When my mind and heart turned to the marathon, my body could do nothing but follow. I became willing to accept any schedule, any training, any diet in the promise of better times, in the hope of breaking the three-hour barrier. And so I became one of the observers and subjects in the great carbohydrate-loading experiment.

The program is simple. One week prior to the marathon you take a long run, preferably about ninety minutes. The following three days you limit your diet to meat, fish, cheese, and eggs, staying away from carbohydrates. During this time you continue training. The final three days you stop training and eat mainly carbohydrates.

This dietary sleight-of-hand first depletes the muscle sugar, or glycogen, then supersaturates the muscles with the same glycogen, which is the major source of energy in marathons. Original experiments in Sweden showed that work capacity could be increased anywhere from one hundred to three hundred percent. That means that running time in an eighteen-mile race could be improved as much as fifteen minutes. No wonder marathoners all over the world have become carbohydrate "loaders."

You can now see the great carbohydrate-loading experiment taking shape. Given these large numbers of runners training maximally and eating much the same diet, the variables are reduced to those inherent in each runner's muscular system, in his intricate metabolic and biochemical and enzymatic reactions. It is here where nature conducts the most instructive of experiments, where the lack of just one of thousands of enzymes can be shown to cause serious difficulty in body function.

And so it is with carbohydrate loading. For most of us the

results were marvelous. The last quarter of the run became less and less of a nightmare. If, perhaps, the three-hour barrier remained unbreached, at least the times were much faster. Paul Slovic's studies of carbohydrate loaders (*Nutrition Today*, 10:18, 1975) showed an average improvement of eight minutes and thirty seconds, which translates to twenty seconds, or one hundred yards, a mile.

However, nature had more to tell us. One of Slovic's loaders met disaster and ran one hour slower than his predicted time. Here and there we heard of other runners who had developed leg cramps or fatigue and had been forced to drop out very early in marathons.

What these unfortunates had in common was muscle breakdown and an increase in myoglobin in the blood sufficient in some instances to clog the kidneys and cause renal shutdown. These events are most likely set in motion by the first three days of low carbohydrate intake and continued training, rather than the three-day binge of carbohydrates that follows.

And so it goes. The marathoner who cannot load has discovered (as I did when I found I was tone deaf, and as all of us do in some fashion) that life is unfair. But he has also learned what everyone performing this great experiment of life must know. That nature, as T. H. Huxley has told us, never overlooks a mistake or makes the smallest allowance for ignorance.

The party line of the scientists is that we catch colds. We become infected with one of the numerous rhinoviruses and in short order come down with the familiar sore throat, cough and runny nose. And it will be only a matter of time, they assure us, until research will produce a vaccine or antibiotic and the common cold will be just a memory.

I don't believe it. The way I see it, the common cold will last as long as the common man. We have those rhinoviruses in our systems and always will. Usually they lie dormant, but when our defenses are lowered, then somehow the barriers are breached, the cold develops.

You don't catch colds. Everyone from Plato to our sainted aunts has told us that. They are caused by pride and stubbornness and arrogance, three qualities the Greeks put together in one word: *hubris*. As soon as we put ourselves over ordinary men, as soon as we aspire to be better and better, as soon as we risk going beyond our capabilities, just as soon do we risk what the Greeks called coryza and catarrh.

The runner who is a modern-day Greek knows this all too well. Like the Athenian, he is trying to live each day at the top of his powers. And always looking to the day when he will suddenly break through into a greater source of energy. A day when he will be filled with strength and speed and feel no fatigue. The runner knows with Sophocles, "The best is to live without disease;/To have that most sweet power to win each day the heart's desire."

But in reaching for this, in the training and the racing and, yes, in his pride and stubbornness and arrogance, the runner would be more than he actually is. And it is then that he begins to come apart, his defenses fold, the rhinovirus strikes, and he gets the common cold. And then, if only for a week, he agrees with another thought of Sophocles, "Never to have lived is best."

How to avoid this, how to reach for it all and not fall into the pit? Plato had some rules for athletes: Don't drink. Avoid Sicilian cooking. Stay away from Corinthian girl friends. Abstain from Attic confectionery. But giving up beer and pizza, groupies and chocolates is not the real answer. Plato knew that also. The athlete in training, he said, is a sheepy creature and the smallest deviation from his routine leads to illness.

The runner is aware that this deviation from routine is racing. It is in the race that he challenges himself to his limits. And instead of husbanding his strength and hunkering down, instead of waiting for spring and the fulfillment of his year, he tries to become everything he is right now in this Sunday race and next Sunday's race and the race after that. Few can resist the call to test themselves to the limit today, here, on these hills. Few runners are ruled by reason when autumn and cross-country are here.

And unfortunately when the running is going well, the runner must be most alert. He is on a collision course between his heart's desire and the common cold. He should know that just beyond this workout, if run too hard, or this race, if too demanding, lies disaster. And he must be prepared to break off when he loses his zest for training, or a race leaves him fatigued for days afterward.

Just recently I ran three very tough races in seven days, the last ten thousand meters over hills at Holmdel Park. According to my family I looked worse at the two-mile mark than I did finishing at Boston at the marathon. My son even had ideas of tackling me to get me out of the race. When I finished, I lay motionless for five minutes, asking for someone to take my shoes off.

That should have been it for the cross-country season. Unfortunately it wasn't. The National Masters Championship was the following week at Van Cortlandt Park, another grueling ten-thousand-meter run. I could already feel the rhinoviruses preparing to charge. There was nothing to do but rest. I took the whole week off, hoping I had one more race before the barricades came down. I did. I ran my best race of the year. The next day I came down with the cold.

The goal of the runner is not health. His objective is the fitness necessary for maximal performance. Health is something the runner goes through on the way to fitness. A way station he hardly notices in his pursuit of the twenty to thirty percent of capacity that lies untouched. And health, therefore, is what he risks in training to do his best. Because just beyond fitness and a personal record lies staleness, and with it fatigue and exhaustion and depression and despair.

I have gone through this sequence many times over the years. In reaching for my peak at distances from the mile to the marathon I have discovered that disaster is only a hard workout or an all-out race away. I have gone through the runner's version of being overtennised or overgolfed, of leaving my fight in the gym. I have become stale. I have reached that state where, as Lombardi once said about fumbles, "there is nothing to do but scream."

My task then is to reach this fine line; and not go over. To reach a state where training runs are what I live for and racing is the supreme experience; and not to go over the cliff that awaits just ahead.

In such a project in this exploration of my absolute limits, I would like as a motto that of another explorer, Roald Amundsen, "Leave nothing to chance." But the science is just not there. Staleness is something the physiologists know very little about. I must seek my own ways of knowing when I am in danger, when I must limit my training. When I must avoid races. When I must stop all activity and rest.

Over the years I have come to believe in two rules about training. The first: it is better to be undertrained than overtrained. The second: if things are going badly I am undoubtedly overtrained and need less work rather than more. This is in line with Bill Bowerman's belief that a bad race almost always indicates too much work. For this reason Bowerman has always recommended hard-day/easy-day schedules to avoid overtraining. Most runners and coaches, of course, take the opposite view. For them a bad race is an indication to double the training rather than cut it in half.

But must you wait for a bad race? Is there some way to guide yourself more precisely? Yes. First, by listening to your body. Second, by keeping a fitness index.

Your body is always trying to tell you where you are. Listen to it. Beware when you become tired and listless, when you lose interest in workouts and approach them as a chore rather than a pleasure. Back off when you become lightheaded on arising or notice an irregularity in your pulse. Slow down if you get a cold or sore throat or feel as if the "mono" is coming back. Be on the alert if you develop depression insomnia (ease in getting to sleep but repeated awakenings during the night) or remain unrefreshed after a night's sleep. Take it easy if your attention span diminishes and you can't concentrate. Listen well to these things. Your homeostasis, your equilibrium with training stress is breaking down.

The method of keeping a "fitness index" is simple and can be charted, which makes it more satisfactory to some than listening to your body. When you awake in the morning, lie in bed for five minutes, then take your pulse. To do this, grasp your Adam's apple between your thumb and your index finger. Then slide the fingers back about an inch or more until you feel the carotid arteries pulsating. Now count for sixty seconds. Also check your weight and breathing. Then chart. Do the same later in the day after training. Take your pulse immediately and then fifteen minutes later.

As you record these figures over the weeks you will chart your course through health to fitness. You will see a weekly improvement until you plateau out at your basic heart rate, usually around fifty per minute. Now you must be wary of any sudden rise. If the morning pulse is up ten or more beats, you have not recovered from the previous day's training. Practice therefore should be eliminated or curtailed until the pulse returns to normal.

Such attention to pulse taking may make a hypochondriac or a neurotic out of you. But more than likely the "fitness index" will give you better control of your running life rather than less. At present writing there is no better early-warning system for the proximity of overtraining. No better way to avoid staleness, the catastrophe on the other side of fitness.

The race should be the ultimate test of my running ability, the stopwatch the final judge, but I never really believe it. I always feel I could do better, that I have not yet exhausted the limits of talent and training. Most of all, I fear I have not given a full one hundred per cent.

So I went to Indiana to find out the truth, to spend a day with David Costill, Ph.D, in the Human Performance Laboratory at Ball State University in Muncie.

I had all the exercise physiology tests given our Olympic distance-running candidates earlier in Dallas—vital capacity, percent body fat, muscular strength, maximum oxygen intake, running efficiency, and a calf muscle biopsy. All this to tell what my potential is and whether I am running up to it.

I soon learned that to Costill and his crew, human performance meant maximum human performance. I hardly had time to rejoice over having only 5.3 percent body fat when I was being pushed to my limit and beyond. Every test was accompanied by a constant stream of encouragement to do more, to try harder. And every test was repeated until I was doing worse instead of better. They had to know they had pushed me as far as I could go.

A few hours later, while doing the maximal oxygen uptake test on the treadmill, I knew they had. I had first run a mile at an eight-minute pace, then one in seven minutes, and finally one at 6:40, which is approximately nine miles an hour. All with a short rest to towel off, get my breath, and then resume.

But now it was time for maximal effort. I had the electrodes for the electrocardiogram reapplied to my chest, the plastic helmet holding the oxygen apparatus readjusted, and the mouthpiece fitted. Then suddenly I was off at a 6:40 mile going up a four percent grade. They were to increase this grade to six percent after three minutes and then an additional two percent every two minutes until I couldn't go any farther. When I felt I had only thirty seconds of running left I was to give a hand signal.

The first half hour required a noticeable increase in effort, but I felt in command. It was hard work, but I was getting accustomed to the peculiarity of the treadmill, of staying in one place, and of always having people just feet away urging and cajoling and imploring me to do my best.

When they raised it to six percent, I knew I was reaching my limit. My legs began to get heavy. The helmet became cumbersome and started to flop around. The mouthpiece was a distraction. I was barely able to keep up. And then they raised the grade to eight percent.

A mounting wave of fatigue and pain went over my body. My chest and legs were in a relentlessly closing vise. More people had wandered in to watch my final agony. They began to take up the chant: "Push!" "Harder!" But the struggle between me and the machine was coming to a close. Six minutes into the test and one minute at the eight percent grade, I gave the hand signal.

I had waited too long. I was finished and still had thirty seconds and 130 yards to go on this infernal, unforgiving apparatus. It was an eternity in time, an infinity in space.

Fifteen seconds to go and there was Costill just inches away. "Hang on!" "Hang on!" Then ten seconds. How slowly time goes. Five seconds. How could five seconds last so long? Someone was counting: four, three, two, one. The treadmill stopped.

I took out the mouthpiece, gasping, "Oh, God! Oh, God!" The physiologists were poring over their figures. They were delighted. "He went over the hill," said one. I had peaked and gone down the other side, reached my maximum and gone past it. I had done what they wanted me to do.

The pain had receded. I sprawled out on a chair, content, trying to think of an equivalent maximum human performance.

"How soon," I asked, "can I see the baby?"

No one heard. They were on the way to prepare for my muscle biopsy.

11. Healing

*When I am ill I become a skeptic. What has
hitherto been a certainty becomes perhaps;
what was perhaps becomes maybe; and what
was maybe becomes probably not.*

THE JOGGER has three natural enemies: drivers, dogs and doctors. The first two are easily handled. Motorcars are part of the logical technology we have learned to live with. In fact, cannot live without. Running against traffic allows the runner to be in command. Anyone who is alert and agile should be able to stay alive.

Dogs are even less difficult. The dog is, after all, just another animal like ourselves who reacts to aggression, seizure of his turf and other inroads much the same way we do. He is simply more spontaneous and uninhibited in expressing his feelings. As the jogger becomes more runner, more body, more animal, he finds that a dog can be more a friend than an enemy.

Not so the doctor. Doctors are human. And to be human is not to be logical like a machine, or predictable like an animal. To be human is to be gullible, to have opinions that thereby become truths, and worst of all to become altruistic. And doctors are for the most part altruists. They are accepted into their profession because of their altruism, for their selfless dedication to their fellow human beings. And unfortunately when a man does a thoroughly stupid thing, as Oscar Wilde pointed out, it is usually done from the noblest of motives.

The jogger is continually having to cope with this nobility and stupidity. He is constantly reading stupid articles about the dangers of his sport, written by noble, high-minded physicians whose only desire is to help him.

Jogging has recently been described as one of the most wasteful and hazardous forms of exercise. And its followers have been told they can expect a myriad of illnesses ranging from hernias to ruptured discs, from sagging breasts to varicose veins.

What is the truth? Is jogging hazardous and wasteful? Or is it, as joggers insist, the most economical, least dangerous and most satisfying of physical-fitness programs? Do joggers get more hernias, back troubles, female pelvic problems and floating kidneys than nonjoggers? Or are these conditions a matter of individual susceptibility, deficiencies in the protoplasm from which we are constructed, and therefore independent of the running and jogging? Is the fifteen to sixty minutes a day spent jogging a danger to health? Or is what we do the rest of the day that is preventing our enjoyment of life and leading to disease and an early demise?

We joggers have one set of answers, the doctors another. Those who are uncommitted and undecided might do well to consider what jogging actually is. Better yet, they might try it.

Jogging or running is the most efficient and natural way for the body to move. When it is done correctly, the jogger flows through his environment using his largest and most powerful muscles. He is propelled along smoothly with the least of impact. The body from the hips up being used merely for balance. The abdominal muscles occupied only with breathing.

His footstrike is heel first, with the foot under the still bent knee. This keeps him from bouncing up and down, and his shoulders are thereby kept parallel to the ground. The overall effect is one of smoothness, a physical activity done at a pace at which the jogger can maintain a conversation with a companion, an activity without stress or strain.

When injuries come, and about two thirds of joggers report

injuries, they are due to weak feet and to muscles that become too tight and overdeveloped while their antagonist muscles are becoming too weak. Both problems, the one structural, the other postural, are easily corrected. The feet with arch supports, sometimes individually made. The muscle imbalance, with daily preventive exercises.

In seven years of writing a medical-advice column for runners, I have yet to hear from an injured runner who regretted his jogging. The jogger's main concern is the "dark night of the soul" he experiences while he is unable to run.

Those well-meaning articles about the dangers of jogging serve little purpose except to expose the inadequacy of orthodox medicine when faced with a human being trying to be all he or she can be. Nevertheless, the proper care for these "diseases of excellence" is available. What needs to be known is exactly where to find it.

Until the doctors do, they will remain one of the jogger's natural enemies. And, like cars and dogs, best be avoided.

One way for a doctor to acquire skill, said Plato, was to have knowledge of medical science and a wide acquaintance with disease. But the best way was to have experienced in addition all kinds of disease in his own person. And to this end, he thought that doctors should not be of altogether healthy constitution. Such a liability would not, of course, keep them or any Greek from being an athlete. Everyone in those days was urged to train both body and mind. And thereby to arrive at the proper harmony between energy and initiative on one hand and reason on the other.

Like it or not, I have followed the Platonic prescription. I am a runner-doctor with a defective constitution. And my diseases are a lengthening litany ranging from head to toe, from dandruff to athlete's foot. At one time or another something in every section of me has gone awry.

My respiratory tract, for instance, is noticeably defective. My sinuses refuse to empty. My Eustachian tube is forever closing off. My ears ring. My tonsils are out. And a postnasal drip is a constant companion.

My circulation is little better. My electrocardiogram is abnormal. I have peculiar heart sounds, a pulse that occasionally goes into a conga rhythm, and a worrisome ache in my chest when I think on these things.

All the while, there is hardly anything right going on in my abdomen. How could it with a hiatus hernia, a duodenal ulcer, an absent gall bladder, diverticulosis and two sizable inguinal hernias?

From my hips down, I am a battleground of the war between me and my running. Feet, legs, knees, and sciatic nerve all have been the sites of major skirmishes, and now exist relatively pain-free in an uneasy truce.

All of this has turned out to be, as Plato suggested, an extraordinary learning experience. And I now know, as every teacher should know, the truth of Ortega's statement "It is not desire that leads to knowledge but necessity." When illness strikes I suddenly develop an immediate and urgent need to learn, an interest in books that would delight my former teachers.

But with it comes also the almost certainty that there is no answer. And I approach this ready-made knowledge, as Ortega suggests, with caution and suspicion, even assuming in advance that what the book says is not true. I suspect, and often rightly, that my problem, my specific and unique and desperately important problem, has never been answered.

When I am ill I become a skeptic. What has hitherto been certainty becomes perhaps; what was perhaps becomes maybe; and what was maybe becomes probably not. I realize that most regimens for disease are proposed not because they are effective but because there must be a standard operating procedure for every illness. And in this process I discover that I need such things as disease and doubt, failure and defeat, to make me wise. Anyone can follow the book. Only someone who has fallen on his face and started over can write one.

Being an athlete introduces another decisive element. The runner-doctor knows that health has nothing to do with disease. Health has to do with functioning and wholeness and reaching your level of excellence. My health has to do with my life style, with moderation of the soul and the body. It is a matter of discipline of my total person. And my health can be maximized even when disease is present. There is, I find, a healthy way to live your disease. Disease may change or modify my excellence, but it does not remove excellence as a possibility.

Disease, then, is one of those bad experiences that turns information into knowledge and knowledge into wisdom. The bad experiences that make you love yourself and your body and the world. And make you know you are in a game that has to have a happy ending.

At the age of fifty-six, when faced with the choice between the book and the body, between reason and instinct, between learning and intuition, I go with doing what comes naturally. The experts, of course, advise otherwise. Human beings, they say, are born defenseless and must learn how to live in this world. And that will be by our wits, not our reflexes.

But when I get down to the basic questions of stress and survival, when, for instance, I am gasping for breath, it is my body, not the physiology text, that tells me the right thing to do. This act of inhaling and exhaling, an act which symbolizes life itself, has occupied the wise men since the beginning of recorded time; but none seemed to have analyzed it by pushing himself to his own limit, and beyond. I have.

I have spent twelve years in distance running. Twelve years in various states of air hunger. Twelve years of panting training and gasping races. Twelve years seeking how to get the most oxygen with the least amount of effort. Twelve years of going to the point where my only thought was self-preservation. Twelve years that qualify me for a bachelor's degree in respiration, a master's in labored breathing, and a doctorate in dyspnea.

What has it all taught me? What have I learned from the animal inside of me? That when man rose on his two feet when he stood upright, he forgot how to breathe. Belly-breathing, which is natural when we are on all fours, fades from memory when we become, as Milton wrote of Adam and Eve, "Godlike erect."

Yet belly-breathing, all the authorities agree, is the proper way to breathe. The white-coated wizards who deal in vital capacity and tidal volume and expiratory reserve all recommend the bellowslike action of the diaphragm for maximum oxygenation. Even those geniuses whose field is the human spirit have made this type of breathing an essential of the practice of yoga.

But as rapidly as they teach, just as rapidly their pupils forget. The masters have not understood why this fundamental and innate ability has been lost. They have not discovered that it is Man on all fours, Man prone, Man prostrate, who breathes correctly. I have. And I discover it anew at the end of every race.

Relieving that incredible postrace shortness of breath is the crucial experiment. When my respiratory rate goes to fifty a minute and it still isn't enough. When I am literally fighting for air and consciousness, I yield to impulses older than history and go down on my hands and knees. And finally find the position, the only right position, with my head and shoulders and hands on the ground. No longer Man "Godlike erect," but Man the supplicant. Only then do I have any confidence that I will someday rise to run again. Only then does the air on this planet become adequate.

It is this posture that makes me belly-breathe. Not education, or knowledge, or enlightenment, or wisdom. Once I start to lean forward, my belly goes out and my diaphragm comes down when I breathe in. And this is most likely the reason why people with asthma are better at swimming and cycling than at running; and why they often obtain relief by getting on all fours.

Posture has a remarkable effect on respiratory capacity.

Why this has remained a secret is no secret. Our researchers believe they are studying the new Adam. But they have accumulated vast amounts of data on a creature who is not the new

Adam and never will be. They are examining Man sedentary, in repose, and slowly deteriorating. They should be observing Man gasping and panting his way toward the day when he will truly be "Godlike erect."

If they do, they'll rewrite the book.

If, as Eric Hoffer claims, man's most useful occupation is play, then the care of the athlete must be medicine's most important duty. Yet the athlete who consults a physician often wonders what goes on in medical school. He begins to question the priority of disease and disaster; the emphasis on crisis and catastrophe. His own problems of health and preventive medicine, of maximum performance and day-to-day living, seem to have been ignored.

Physicians who handle emergencies with éclat, who dive fearlessly into abdomens for bleeding aneurysms, who think nothing of managing cardiac arrest and heart failure, who miraculously reassemble accident victims, are helpless when confronted by an ailing athlete. They are even less able to counsel the athlete and his never-ending questions about health.

Health is what makes the athlete medicine's most difficult patient. It is as simple and as complicated as that. Health, said Chesterton, is the mystical and mysterious balance of all things by which we stand up straight and endure. Athletes want that mystical balance by which they can do all things. They want that mysterious harmony of body and spirit which they have come to know as fitness and feel as an all-encompassing rightness. And because no one man can give them that, because no one man can specialize in health, which is to specialize in the universe, the athletes overwhelm any physician who presumes to treat them.

The athlete needs a medical team to treat him. A team composed not only of physicians but also of professionals from all the health-science fields. The physician educated in isolation from these colleagues is usually unaware of the contributions these people can make; and is unwilling to give them authority and autonomy in caring for patients. The physician still sees himself as a member of an elite group in which some members are more elite than others.

A recent poll taken by Professor Stephen Shortell of the University of Chicago makes this perfectly clear. Physicians who were asked to rate the status and prestige of 41 professional categories in the medical health field ranked no other professional group above any of the medical specialties. They gave first place to the thoracic surgeons and listed 22 more varieties of doctors before coming to dentists (24). The physicians seemed particularly ignorant of the importance of podiatrists (40), who were placed below nurse's aides (39), or osteopaths (37), who were given a niche just above practical nurses (38). The result is, as the British therapist James Cyriax points out, "huge numbers of relievable disorders in otherwise healthy people are not relieved, not because nothing can be done but [because] there is no one to apply knowledge already there for the asking."

Who is there, then, who will save us, the athletes and the potential athletes? Who is there to bring these specialists up and down the Shortell list together in one complete team dedicated to the nation's health?

I nominate the family practitioner. He is the one man who could orchestrate the whole of patient care, the one man who is close to patients and colleagues, the one man who could come to know the contributions of the other medical health-care professionals. The one generalist among all the specialists.

The physicians place the family practitioner (22) at the dividing line between their medical establishment and the professions they consider subordinate to them. I find it a happier concept to see this primary-care physician as the one man who can unite the medical profession and the others in the health sciences. He alone can go anywhere on this 41-category scale to get help. Freed from the ego problems of the experts whose reputations depend on success, he can advise and counsel and let others take on the onus of the specialist's infallibility.

In time such a man will come to resemble the athletes he treats, caring little for the status and prestige Professor Shortell would publicize. But simply seeking truth and accepting it wherever it appears, and turning medicine into play.

The athlete is medicine's most difficult patient. His pursuit of perfection is an unprecedented challenge to what Cannon called "homeostasis" and Claude Bernard termed the "internal milieu," the body's inner harmony with its external environment. His desire to run faster and jump higher and throw farther is causing injuries and illnesses the medical profession is unprepared to treat. And in his attempts to reach his potential he is aiming at goals not in the medical texts. And using methods that are at times unorthodox, and not infrequently heretical to medical dogma.

Yet the athlete is no different from the rest of us, except in degree. He is simply trying to get more out of himself than we are. By definition an athlete is someone who is trying to get the most out of his

(1) GENETIC ENDOWMENT
through
(2) TRAINING
in his
(3) ENVIRONMENT.

This is the prescription for maximal performance. It is also the equation which limits it. The athlete's difficulties start (as do ours) with the person he is. They begin with the stuff he is made of. His basic material. And the pattern he is cut from. His body type, his bone structure, the way he inhabits his body. All these things are crucial to his susceptibility to injury and illness. As are his peculiar differences in other functions, cardiac, pulmonary, metabolic. And his own unique response to stress. Each athlete has (as do we) a built-in weakness for certain diorders. Inherited defects in the germ plasm. His DNA and RNA carry the seeds to his destruction. Breeding and bloodlines do count.

He then takes this weakness, this susceptibility, and subjects himself to training, to stress which Selye defined as any demand for vital activity. Overtraining then becomes relative. It varies from person to person. Used correctly, training and stress lead to the ultimate in fitness. Used incorrectly, they lead to disaster. And the physician who must know the athlete's inherited strengths and weaknesses therefore must also know how he trains, and how much. How long he sleeps. How much he rests.

The physician cannot stop there. He must also know the athlete's environment. This includes anything taken into or externally affecting the body. Heat, cold, altitude, diet, drugs, the equipment he wears, the implements he uses. Nor can the social and psychological climate be ignored. Stress, we now know, is not only physical.

Let us consider these factors in the relatively simple matter of a leg injury in a distance runner.

Unless the doctor uses this holistic approach, genes, training, and environement, he is almost certain to have an ex–distance runner as a patient.

To begin with, the slightly built fine-boned runner frequently has been born with a Morton's foot (which is peculiarly prone to injury and to causing leg, knee and low-back problems). And he may also have minor but significant anomalies of the lumbosacral spine. The physician who does not look for these abnormalities and treat them will fail his patient.

In addition, the runner's training leads to tight, inflexible prime movers which cause even more stress on the Morton's foot and the low back. At the same time the antagonists are becoming relatively weak and are inclined to pull or become tender and swollen (shin splints). Hence the saying "When an athlete trains three things happen to his muscles, two of them bad."

But even having treated all these, the negative genetic endowment, and the imbalance induced by training, the physician may fail if he is unaware of the athlete's environment, in this case his shoes. The doctor who is unfamiliar with the inadequacy of most running shoes is treating his patient in the dark. A shoe with no shank and little shock absorption can lead to injury as certainly as the presence of Morton's Foot or the lack of remedial exercise.

This simple problem shows how the athlete's care calls for the integration of numerous specialties (in this case trainers, coaches, podiatrists, physiotherapists, osteopaths, orthopedic specialists and even shoemakers). As we get into other systems, cardiac, pulmonary and others, this interaction of exercise with health and disease becomes much more complicated.

The principle, however, remains the same. The material we are made of, and the stress our exercise and our life style and environment put upon it. Our genes and how we treat them produce our diseases. Or our personal bests.

This New Medicine is as old as Bernard and his "internal milieu." We were just put off the track by his contemporary Louis Pasteur and the discovery of germs, obviously the cause of all disease. It might be well to recall that on his deathbed Pasteur said, "Tell Claude he was right."

The prevention and treatment of athletic injuries could easily be considered human engineering. These injuries are caused and can be corrected by consideration of stress, strain and torque applied either acutely, as in trauma, or chronically, as in the overuse syndromes of the foot, leg, knee, thigh and low back.

Such overuse syndromes constitute the majority of athletic injuries in this country. Trauma may occupy the press, the medical journals and the TV screen, but the majority number of injured athletes participate in the noncontact sports.

Until recently, the ever-increasing demands of training were thought to cause these injuries. Hence the term "overuse." Stress fractures, both metatarsal and fibula, heel spur, Achilles tendinitis, posterior tibial tendinitis, shin splints, hamstring pulls, and sciatic neuritis, among others, were thought to be due to the enormous number of footstrikes occurring per hour of practice, be it track, tennis, basketball or soccer. This is calculated to be approximately five thousand footstrikes on each foot per hour.

However, it is now evident that the "overuse" is simply the precipitating agent. The overuse searches out any biomechanical weakness in the athlete and results in the symptoms.

This biomechanical instability can be either congenital or acquired, structural or postural. It is usually, as will become evident, both. The congenital or structural biomechanical weaknesses are:

1. *Weak feet*.

Here the untutored physician, like myself, should look for the Morton's foot or the eversion of heel. These indicate a neutral position of the foot which decompensates with each footstrike. The pronating or flattening foot sets up stresses and torques which cause near and distant injuries.

2. *Lumbosacral abnormalities*.

A high percentage of sciatic-pain patients have abnormal lumbosacral X rays.

3. *Leg-length discrepancy*.

This causes a variety of biomechanical adjustments which place stress on the foot and pelvis. Foot, leg, knee adductor and sciatic pain can result.

The acquired or postural biomechanical abnormalities have to do with muscle strength and/or flexibility imbalances. These relative muscular inadequacies come as a direct result of the volume of training. They can be divided into:

1. *Inflexibility of the prime movers*.

Tightness of the posterior tibials, gastrocs, soleus, hamstrings and ilio psoas. This inflexibility below the knee puts further stress on the inadequate foot and this feeds back to cause Achilles, calf and knee problems. Above the knee, this inflexibility causes forward rotation of the hips, lordosis and sciatic symptoms.

2. *Weakness of the antagonists.*

The anterior antigravity muscles, those of the anterior chamber, the quadriceps and the abdominals, are the critical structures involved. These weaknesses contribute to skin splints and other anterior-compartment syndromes, quadriceps pulls and lumbosacral-sciatic syndromes.

In analyzing overuse syndromes, the role of shoes and surface should also be recognized. Many athletic shoes have no support whatsoever through the shank and, therefore, should be avoided. Even wearing good shoes with proper supports, the runner with congenital and acquired susceptibility can be at hazard from the slant or camber of the road. This slant tends to pronate and stress the uppermost foot. Running against traffic stresses the right foot; running with traffic stresses the left.

Once the injury has been diagnosed, treatment must proceed along biomechanical lines.

1. Evaluation and correction of any biomechanical problem in the foot is a must. Faulty weight bearing on the first metatarsal must be corrected and the neutral position maintained.

2. Strength-flexibility must be evaluated and corrective exercises prescribed. (See Figure 1.)

3. Recommendations as to foot gear, surface, training methods and running style should be made.

4. Above all, treatment should be directed to the cause, not the effect. Heel spurs, Achilles tendinitis, shin splints, and chondromalacia, all point to a failure of the entire foot-leg continuum. Use of Butazolidine, steroid shots, and surgery have no place in the human engineering required in the treatment of overuse syndromes.

Treating overuse syndromes requires a thorough biomechanical analysis of the runner's foot, low back and musculoskeletal system and a knowledge of his training conditions. Unless the underlying biomechanical weaknesses are corrected, treatment will not succeed. Subsequently, a return to running will inevitably result in a return of symptoms. Pain-free running awaits proper analysis and appropriately integrated treatment.

Summary

Most athletic injuries of the lower extremity are not due to trauma, but to overuse. Underlying these illneses are: (1) congenital biomechanical instability of the foot and the low back, and (2) acquired biomechanical instability of the muscles. Additional environmental factors, including shoes and surface, contribute to the stresses producing symptoms. Treatment, to be successful, must take all these factors into account.

12. Racing

But even at the end there is strategy. It is not enough to have the speed. Not enough to give your all. That sprint, that giving, must be done at the right time, at the precise moment that allows no adequate response. It must be checkmate.

YOU MAY FIND it difficult to believe, but the distance runner is a one-man track team. The ambivalent, indecisive, forgetful, absent-minded, manually inept daydreamer is not merely a runner. He is also his own coach, manager and trainer; positions which he is incapable of handling. He is never quite sure what type of practice he should do; is liable to show up at a race a day late; and is always lacking some essential piece of equipment.

The runner fails as a coach, manager and trainer because he is a feeling, thinking, completely absorbed human being. The man you see running down the road is in a world of his own. He might at that very moment be taking a victory lap after winning the 1980 Marathon at Moscow. With such an exciting inner world, is it any wonder the runner forgets such things as shirts and shorts and starting times and first-aid supplies? And the only remedy for his dreamlike state is the ditty bag.

Into the ditty bag goes everything a runner might ever need, no matter what the emergency. Its supplies should be all-weather, all-seasons. Perennial and universal are the words for the ditty bag.

All this may seem ridiculous to you. What, you may ask, could a runner need besides the minimum he wears while running through towns? Until you've been through a season of road running, you could never guess how many things a runner needs and how these needs multiply.

Take shoelaces, for instance. Breaking a shoelace shortly before a race can cause a panic state equaled only by lining up your first deer. Paralysis, hope, despair, a sense of the time accelerating make for a moment you will never want to relive.

Tape is another item. For blisters and the blister-prone areas. If there is anything worse than running the last six miles of a marathon, it is running these last six miles with a blister. For this problem, ordinary tape won't do. It is too stiff. And Band-Aids tend to slide, which is worse. So Zonas tape is the tape to use.

Next is the Vaseline. To coat you when the wind-chill factor is in the twenties. And for the chafed areas. But tape your feet first. Once you have Vaseline on your hands, the tape becomes unmanageable.

Then come the gloves and the ski mask. There are days you just won't finish if you have to run without them.

And for the summer, there's the handkerchief. By using knots in the four corners, you can fashion a cap for the head and cut down on solar radiation. If you keep it wet during the race, it dissipates the heat on those August run days.

And don't forget the nail clipper and the felt pads to use as heel and arch supports. Or the pins for the number and an extra buck for the entry fee. And the nasal spray, the antacid tablets and the APC's. Remember also the ballpoint pen and the pad to record your place and number.

At one time or another, I have forgotten one, some or all of these essentials. In fact, I have arrived at a race with nothing at all. Not even my running gear. So now I have developed a foolproof solution. I put on my running clothes at home and then check out each article in my ditty bag.

I did that for the Heart Fund race in Jersey City. I dressed at home. No problem. Then I checked the bag. Money, pins, tape, Vaseline, ski mask, gloves, shoelaces, nail clippers, nasal spray, antacids, APC's, pen and pad, extra turtleneck sweater (in case it turned cold), the plastic wrapper that comes on clothes from the cleaners (in case it rained), the entry blank with the date and the starting time, some extra sugar cubes and a can of soda for after the race. All present and accounted for.

On the way up, I was relaxed, knowing I had prepared myself for any eventuality. But when I walked into the dressing room in the basement of the Stanley Theatre, I had the feeling I had forgotten something.

I had. The ditty bag.

In common with most distance runners, I have to get psyched up for practice, not for a meet. For athletes who go head to head with their opponents, the opposite seems true. They use the dominant emotions, hunger and rage and fear, to dominate their foes. From such extraordinary excitements come extraordinary efforts. I once heard a lineman relate how he would get into the right mood for a game by imagining his house had been burned down by the opposing tackle.

I have no need for such imaginings. Before I even park the car, I can feel the adrenalin flowing. The sight of runners warming up sends a rush through my bowels. The smell of the dressing room sets my pulse to racing. The track under my feet makes me break out in a cold sweat. And then comes the yawn that Darwin first described as the accompaniment of fear.

So I have no need to psych myself up for a race. Sight and sound and smell will do that unbidden. And this reaction must be curbed, not encouraged. I have no need for short-lived bursts of superhuman energy. My game is endurance. My object perfection. My race is a product of training, determination and reason. Strong emotions often contribute nothing but stupidity. It is the fired-up, psyched-up runner who runs the most irrationally placed races.

It would be equally irrational for me to view the other runners as my enemies. They are not. They are there to help me do my best; to make this event the culmination of all my training. Anger against them will only dissipate my energy; it will not increase it. I know this to be true, because I have experienced it.

Who, then, is the enemy? I have found my enemy and he is me. The runner's confrontation is with himself. And this confrontation begins and ends in practice. My struggle is not in my race with my friends, but in my day-to-day battle with myself. And for that battle I need all the emotions, the excitements, the feelings that others seek just prior to the big game.

In practicing, it is truly psych up or psych out. There, doubled and trebled, are all the difficulties I face in a race. There I must deal with doubt and discomfort and fear. Not once, but continually. There I reach the barrier where pain is at its worse. Not once, but repeatedly. There I must overcome the desire to quit, to break off, to leave until tomorrow. And do this daily.

And there in practice I must convince myself that there is no substitute for hard work and discipline, all the while looking for an excuse from this drudgery, an escape from this tedium. And I must believe that the payoff comes from this day-to-day commitment. Even while pushing further seems absurd and I am regretting the things given up and the time lost.

But where can one find emotions that support such punishment? When I park the car for practice, I feel no surge of adrenalin. The sight of the empty track does not cause the juices to flow. And when I get out on the track, I am filled with great reluctance rather than anticipation of things to come. Should I yawn, it would be from boredom rather than fear.

Yet there is an excitement in practice. Perhaps the greatest of all excitements. The discovery of who I am. Alone with myself and my stopwatch, I learn who I am. I find out what I can do. The race may subsequently confirm this, but it cannot deny it. I am first what I am in practice, and only after that what I am in a race.

Knowing that potential is there to be gained or lost can incite anyone to strong emotions. And there are times when I become my own Lombardi and I go to the whip. I turn my anger on myself. And on such occasions where I have described my character and my ancestry in words I have not used or even heard since leaving the Navy, I have finished practices I would have thought beyond my energy.

Whatever your game, you can always spot a pigeon. When I warm up for a road race I can usually tell at a glance the newcomers to the sport. When I am estimating how high I will finish, I find it reassuring to see groups of my fellow contestants sporting fancy sweat shirts, or dressed in all-white, or wearing their numbers on their backs. These are all signs of the pigeon.

An expensive warmup suit marks the runner as beginner. The suit is almost invariably a present from a friend in recognition of this new pursuit. But having arrived at this first race the recipient is immediately aware that the fashionable togs are out of place. Fortunately in due time the warmups are stolen and the runner quickly acquires some less obtrusive outerwear. And is on the way to becoming a veteran.

The all-white costume, plain white T-shirt and white shorts, is another giveaway of the neophyte runner. The all-whites indicate no previous experience. Plain white is the uniform of the embryo, the about-to-be-born. The runner in plain white is a maiden, has yet to break the novice.

There is a definite possibility that this is the runner's first race. And the chances are good that the distance will be too much, the race misjudged, or any one of a thousand things from shoes to shoelaces will go wrong in this first race.

If the number is pinned on the back it may not be the runner's first race, but I know it is the runner's first road race. And therefore I am dealing with a runner I can safely ignore if the distance is over five miles. I have occasionally been fooled by the fancy warmups and a few times by the all-whites, but never by the number on the back. It is an infallible sign of a tyro at road racing.

I recall years back when I arrived at a ten-mile race in Westport, Connecticut and noticed that every runner had his number on his back. I was suddenly struck with the thought that at forty-seven I was about to win my first road race. And win a trophy legitimately, not because of my 1918 birthday.

My certainty increased as the starting time approached. This was to be my day. Then five minutes before the gun was to go off (and they are always on time at Westport) my hopes were dashed. Eight members of the St. John's cross-country team arrived. They were shortly followed by Attila Mattray, one of New Jersey's best distance runners. He was visiting in the area, heard about the race and showed up.

I finished tenth behind the nine latecomers, but I beat all the others. The first law of distance runners, "Never worry about a runner who wears his number on his back," was put in the books that day.

But the pigeon remains a pigeon for only so long. The next race, the runner has the number where it belongs. The fancy warmups disappear, to be replaced by something less gaudy, less obtrusive. In a short time the runner becomes one of us, a T-shirt freak.

I have thirty or more T-shirts myself, and the longest preparation for any race is the selection of the shirt. These run from high school (a year I spent coaching) through college (old loyalties die hard) to clubs, those I've belonged to and others I run with in my travels. They are a record of road runs, some obscure, some famous, and of marathon after marathon. Some were won, most came with the entry fee. Whichever way, they were paid for in the race. Each one represents a racing experience.

The why of the selection I find difficult to explain. Somehow the T-shirt must go with my mood, the event, my fellow runners. But more often than not I try to be the runner who has come far. When I run in Central Park or at Van Cortlandt I wear my Oregon Road Runners shirt or the beautiful white nylon of the West Valley Track Club. Then when I run at Golden Gate

Park I wear the Jersey Shore Marathon or the classic running shirt of all time, the NYAC, the simple white with narrow shoulder straps and the red winged foot.

So by the T-shirt you know them. No longer rookies, no longer apprentices, the pigeons have becomes Hawks.

Now they are looking around for runners with fancy sweats, dressed in all-white with their numbers on the back.

I am not a runner who suffers in silence. When I am hurting, everyone around me knows it. If I am in pain during a race, and I almost always am, the runners in my vicinity are all too aware of it. And even alone on the roads when I feel distressed by hills or speed, I'm likely to fill the air with groans and sighs and Oh Gods.

One reason is that I have a pain threshold at the level of a firm handshake. I am hardly into a race, therefore, when the pain arrives and in quantity. I am like a novice nun who suddenly realizes she is not made out of the same stuff as Saint Teresa. Or a seminarian who now suspects he is not another Ignatius. But there is no going back.

So I feel the pain early and often. This is natural for me. It is equally natural for me to react to it. "Let the parts harmed by the pain give an opinion of it," wrote Marcus Aurelius. I agree. If I am my body and my body is in pain, let it speak. No animal would repress the wail, the groan. Why should I? Am I not first a good animal? Why not, then, do what is normal and natural?

I am also Irish. I come from a complaining race. We are civilized but not domesticated. Especially my people, the little black men from the bogs. Those who feel pain and sing those sad songs. Two generations of attempting to be gentry is not enough veneer to conceal what goes against our grain.

The result is what I am. A method runner. A runner who reacts totally, letting the pain become visible in my face, and audible over the countryside.

This is not the way I was taught. In my childhood my heroes

were those who withstood pain without flinching. The Spartan youth who uncomplaining allowed the rat to eat away his stomach. The Indian brave who impassively watched his own torture. Everywhere in my reading I was encouraged to be a stoic. Given as models those who were silent in the face of suffering, those who went to their deaths with a smile on their lips.

I have tried it that way and I can't handle it. When I come apart, the disintegration is total. I come apart all over. And with a loud noise. So I subscribe to Ken Doherty's holistic approach. The former Penn coach always espoused the idea of a total body-mind-spirit reaction. It takes extra energy, he stated, to maintain a passive expression when you're hurting inside. Don't do it, he said. Be yourself. Accept the pain, show it and then you will be able to use it in a positive way. You will be able to relax.

One of the great British runners, Gordon Pirie, was of the same mind. The stiff-upper-lip philosophy, he wrote, costs the runner and prevents him from reaching his greatest heights. Better to react completely and use it in the running. "The free relaxed runner shows in his face and gesture that it is torture and agony to give his last ounce of energy," he wrote. "How silly to pretend it is not."

Anyone who runs near me knows that I am in agony. Knows that I am ready to give my last ounce of energy. If indeed I haven't already done so. So disturbing is this to some that they have written to me complaining about the experience. Apparently they did not want to say anything during the race for fear I was actually about to collapse.

One colleague sent a note asking that I please not run within two hundred yards of him in the future. He also added the hope that I would desist from calling upon the Deity. Another, younger runner wrote that he had a phobia about running near me. "Your constant wheezing," he wrote, "drains my energy. I feel as if my lungs are a reserve tank for your breathing." Nor was that all. My sighs were shattering him. They contained, he felt, all the despair in the universe. "My mind quickly leaps," he wrote, "to why finish? Why race? Why are we here? Why exist? Please stay away from me."

I sympathize with them. It has to be disturbing to have an elderly man hanging on at your shoulder, using your pace, being carried along in your draft; all the while wheezing and groaning and sighing as if every breath will be his last, and continually asking his Creator to take notice of what is going on.

It has to be even more disturbing when this aged suffering soul noisily takes off in a long sustained sprint and beats you to the finish.

But then Percy Cerrutty could have told them that would happen. Conscious control, determined maintenance of proper style and decorum of facial expression was, he said, "a concept of weakly men."

You have to let it all hang out. Which is no problem for a thin little Irishman with a low pain threshold.

I am at my best nearing the finish of a race. Until then I am just another mediocre distance runner. Just one of the many run-of-the-mill competitors well back in the pack. Just one more old man trying to string together six-minute miles and not quite succeeding.

But with the finish in sight, all that changes. Now I am the equal of anyone. I am world class. I am unbeatable. Gray-haired and balding and starting to wrinkle, but world class. Gasping and wheezing and groaning, but unbeatable.

My running friends have come to know this. A few years back in a handicap race at Van Cortlandt Park, I sprinted the last three hundred yards to beat out someone straining at my shoulder. All I knew was that his name was Tom, because he had a number of people urging him to catch me. Afterward I discovered it was Tom Siggins, a Quantico Marine who only a year back had been captain of cross-country at Manhattan College. He came up later and said to me, "If I had known you wanted it that bad, Doc, I wouldn't have tried to catch you."

Wanting-it-that-bad comes from training. I was trained by a

coach of the Herb Elliot ("The only tactics I admire are those of do-or-die") school. He taught me to run one way. Give everything. Hold nothing back. The race you can walk away from was not worth running. It became easier to run myself into oblivion than face him after a race.

The ability to sprint, to kick it in, on the other hand, comes from breeding. I was born with half-miler's speed, and the half mile is still my best distance. With a quarter mile to go, I have the best part of my race still in front of me.

These two together, speed and the willingness to push myself to collapse, will win most of these last-minute duels. Other things being equal, the runner with the kick will beat his opponent. It allows me to run from behind, sit in the other man's draft, judge him for strength or fatigue, and decide when to make my move. It gives me control of the situation.

But even at the end there is strategy. It is not enough to have the speed. Not enough to give your all. That sprint, that giving, must be done at the right time, at the precise moment that allows no adequate response. It must be checkmate.

This last I have learned with age. A thousand races have taught me when and how to make my move, when to accelerate and in what manner. A thousand attempts to beat someone so far back neither of us will remember the next day where we finished have made me a grandmaster at this end game.

There are two primary bluffs in closing minutes. The first, that I am much more exhausted than I actually am. The second, that I am much less tired than I actually am.

The former I use in the fake-pass/late-sprint gambit. This is particularly effective against a strong, obviously fresh younger runner who is a sure bet to beat me.

I first make a tentative move to pass him. This must be done slowly, otherwise he may take off with a rush and I will be hanging on for dear life like a sailor with a harpooned whale. No, slowly does it, and with much audible travail and agony indicating this is about my last gasp.

I then let him draw away quite easily, thereby confirming I am no real threat even though I remain only a few steps behind. And then, with about thirty yards to go, I pull the trigger. I pass him as if shot from a gun. By the time he reacts, it is too late. When he does pass me again, I will be over the finish line.

The I'm-not-as-tired-as-you-are bluff works best on runners my own age. Here I make my breathing as quiet as possible, my footstrike almost unheard, and I pass them swiftly and with élan, exuding confidence. And I make my move earlier than they think sensible. The lead I gain is often enough to allow me to slow down briefly and then gather myself for another dash to the finish.

Once in the lead, I never look back. There is no greater spur to a tired runner who is about to give up and coast in than seeing this over-the-shoulder distress signal. So I never look back. I reach for the man in front of me no matter how impossible it seems for me to catch him.

Hills are great levelers. If there is anything that can cut a runner down to size, it is a reasonably long hill with a fairly steep grade. And particularly if it is placed near the end of a race. Hills make all men brothers. Coaches who use them for training swear by them. Runners who find them sources of suffering swear at them.

The runner's world, you see, is divided into two worlds: the world of the hills and the world of the flats. In the hills, the runner must move vertically as well as horizontally. It is a simple matter of physics. A body of known weight moving at a certain speed up a specific grade for a given distance. A simple matter of physics, but one that causes physiological results that can be close to unendurable.

The pay-as-you-go effort of the flat is transformed into the I'll-pay-you-later-if-only-I-survive struggle of climbing the hill. The runner working on oxygen he has not yet received arrives at the summit, his lungs bursting like a swimmer who has been held underwater; his leg muscles screaming for him to stop, his entire body a dead weight.

Such tortures are common. If the ecstasy of distance running is felt in those periods of rhythm and grace when everything is easy and flowing and natural, then certainly the agony of the sport is in the disrhythmic, graceless tortured movement up the hills. If the heaven of this distance running is in the moments when the runner and his running seem to reach toward infinity, then assuredly its hell or purgatory is in the hills that expose him as failing and inadequate and finite.

And if running on the flat is the world of those optimists that William James called the once-born, running the hills is for the twice-born, those of morbid mind who see and accept the evil in the world.

Some hills are, of course, worse than others. On the East Coast we have some well-known monsters. Heartbreak Hill in the Boston Marathon. Cemetery Hill at the four-mile mark of the five-mile course at Van Cortlandt Park. The final three hundred yards uphill to the Du Pont Hotel in the Caesar Rodney Half Marathon in Wilmington. And, closer to home, the last quarter mile at Garrett Mountain. There is hardly a major race that doesn't have a strategic hill to make the event memorable for the runner.

I have run all of these. And on them reached areas of pain unmatched at any other time in racing even in flat-out finishes or in marathons where I had to quit from exhaustion. But the worst hill of all was in a fifteen-mile race at Greenwich one August.

The heat and the mileage had taken their toll and I was nearing the finish when I reached this hill, which seemed the longest and steepest I have ever had to climb in a race. Going into the hill, I was some ten yards behind another competitor and well ahead of any pursuit. Up on top of the hill, a teammate yelled encouragement to me: "Go get him. You can get him."

Twenty yards up the hill, I had slowed perceptibly. The runner in front began to pull away. "Pick it up, pick it up," came the cry from the top. By now I was leaning forward, making groping movements with my hands but very little forward progress. My friend would not give up. "Keep moving," he yelled. "Keep moving."

It was no use. I was running in place. And now the others behind me were catching and passing me. The runner who was ahead of me had reached the crest and disappeared.

Then from the top of the hill came the best advice of the day: "Walk fast," he shouted. "Walk fast."

I did, and I passed two men who were running.

You frequently read that a runner would have done better if he only had someone to push him during a race. Perhaps so. But for me and probably most others the need is for a pull, not a push. I need someone to pull me along, to stretch me out. I do best following the pace, sitting in behind the leader. Running easiest drafting at another runner's shoulder. And then at the end I can always reach back for the little extra that is there if I look for it.

You might think that a mile is a mile whether you are in the lead or back in the pack. That the energy expenditure per quarter mile is the same for the leader as it is for those who follow in his wake. But you should know that leading a race costs. It costs in overcoming air resistance and, for most runners, costs in loss of efficiency. Running in front may be good for your ego but it is a severe drain on your physiology. Leading is a lonely and often stupid business. The leader should know that he requires more effort to do the job than those running behind him. They are shielded from air resistance by his body; and free from the tension and anxiety and mental effort of setting the pace.

The energy cost of air resistance has been investigated by the English physiologist L. G. C. Pugh, who found it to be on the order of 7.5 percent of the total energy cost at middle distance. Having established that, Pugh discovered that a runner by staying within a meter of the leader and directly behind him could eliminate eighty percent of this oxygen cost. This would give the second-place runner or someone back in the pack six percent advantage in utilizing his maximum oxygen uptake. A figure which further translates into as much as four seconds a lap and certainly not less than a second a lap.

So running in someone's lee pays off in ways a physiologist can measure. It also pays off in ways they have yet to measure but eventually will. In concentration, in relaxation, in rhythm, in harmony, in efficiency. When I follow a leader I no longer have to worry about pace. No longer have to concern myself with continual judgment and analysis of how fast I'm going. No longer have to worry about distance, the race, victory or defeat. That is all for the man in front. He is the stroke of this crew. The race is now his responsibility and I can simply key off him. Use him. And so I become lost in the running, lost in its rhythm, lost in its music. My mind and will are at rest. They leave my body alone, letting it do what years of training and conditioning have taught it to do so well.

I had this happen to me two years ago when I set a United States age-group record in the two-mile at Peddie School. You should know that except for that day I have never before or since in my fourteen years or so of running gone under eleven minutes for that distance. My only real competitor in the race knew it and set his pace accordingly. He ground out thirty-three seconds a lap on the Peddie ten-lap track hitting exactly 5:30-mile pace as if he had been programmed by a computer. And just three feet back I was in another world.

Given a pacemaker who had zeroed in on the perfect pace, I reached a state of blessedness that I have rarely equaled. I was for those minutes completely and utterly relaxed, unconcerned about the outcome, yet completely absorbed in what I was doing. I was in what has been described as a cocoon of concentration, absolutely involved, fully engaged in running. Not racing or winning but simply running. Everything was harmony and grace. Everything was pure. Effort had become effortless.

These things are much easier to experience than to describe. But at those times I think of running as Emerson did of poetry, that it was all written before time was. And I was trying to reach that original perfection. I was at the edge, to use Merton's phrase, of a great realization and was trying to get out and get lost in it.

And so it went. I felt incredibly fresh the whole race. And later it seemed to have been run without reference to real time or real space. Space and time had narrowed down to him and me and the running. It was almost as if I had taken some hallucinatory drug that altered my perceptions. Then there were only two laps to go. I gunned past him, increasing my lead with every stride. And finished still fresh in 10:53.

So there it was, my personal best by following the leader. Letting him do the work. Letting him pull me through that air. Letting him establish the pace. And all the while letting myself go. Letting myself get inside the running and become the running itself. Letting my body do what it does best.

Racing physiology is simple. Except for some early speed, the runner should find his maximum steady pace for that distance and hold to it. Racing tactics are even simpler. Follow the rule of the great Tom Courtney. He never took the lead, he said, unless he wanted to do something with it. Either to slow the pace down or speed it up.

The final answer to top performance, then, is evident. Find someone to set that pace for you. Then you can lock in behind him and run carefree until those last few yards when it is everyone for himself.

13. Winning

*I was moving in a sea of lactic acid, lifting legs
that no longer understood what made them
move. My breathing came in short, inadequate
gasps, but my body no longer cared. I had
broken through a barrier just as surely as I
broke through the tape at the finish.*

WHEN I WAS IN SCHOOL, I ran from the day classes began in
September until they closed the doors in June. Now I run from
the beginning of the year until its end. The Road Runners Club
schedule on the kitchen bulletin board has over 140 races extending from January to December.

So distance running is the sport for every day of my life.
There is no need to pack my gear until running starts again. It
begins every day. And every time of year is a time for running. I
love all of that ever-recurring cycle of the year.

But, like the lover who loves the girl he's near and clings to
the kiss he's close to and fancies the face he faces, the season I
love best is the one that's here. Soon I will see winter as Paradise, then spring as another Eden, and later summer as the
Promised Land. But for now, autumn is my season in heaven.

The October air does that. Crisp, clear, invigorating. Carrying
every sound. Demanding attention. And the weather perfect for
running. The runner is as sensitive to the weather as a Stradivar-
ius. And it is autumn that makes me go best. I am living the life

my youth had promised me. Living at the top of my powers. No wonder that Yeats, who saw spring as youth and summer as adolescence, saw autumn as manhood.

And autumn is heaven because there are races to do that best, to run at that peak, to manifest that manhood. And make no mistake, it is in action that we are in heaven.

Heaven is not quiet, said Yeats. There the lover still loves, but with greater passion; the rider still rides, but the horse goes like the wind; and the battle goes on. The runner still races.

And for now, in this forever that is autumn, cross-country is the best of all races. That is where I began. In autumn with cross-country. It was my first taste of running and it is good to taste it again.

Cross-country is free running at its best. Just me and the land. Me and that crisp air. Me and the leaves underfoot. Me and the silent hills. That's cross-country. Just me and the breathing and the leaves crunching underfoot on those silent hills. Nature has given up the ghost. Everything around me is dead or dying and I feel reborn. I am at my best.

And it is a best, a rebirth that I experience alone. Nature is the only spectator. In other seasons, in other races, there are people to cheer and encourage or just to watch. Curious onlookers. But not in cross-country. Within minutes, I am alone with my fellow runners. Minutes later and I am separated even from them. Yards ahead or yards behind, they are out of my line of thought, beyond the horizon of my mind.

I am alone on the back hills of Van Cortlandt. And the course which tested me as a teenager is testing me again. And again I suffer on hills that made me suffer when I was eighteen. Again I fly down hills I flew down in bygone years. And again I come out of those hills facing an all-out fight to the finish with any runner close to me.

And that was the way it was at Van Cortlandt last week. Nine miles, three times over those back hills. The first three-mile loop oddly the most painful. Then the second loop not quite as bad.

And finally the third time actually running at the hills and conquering them. So that when I came out on the flat, the man I had to beat was only thirty yards ahead.

Only in another autumn, in another season in heaven, will I relive that finish. An impossible quarter-mile sprint and then holding on to the man I had just beaten so I wouldn't fall down. Hearing his heart pounding against my ear and my own beating in unison. Knowing only that and a world suddenly filled with friends saying nice things to an aging man who felt ageless in autumn.

The note he put on our kitchen bulletin board finished Tim McLoone. It was there when I came down for breakfast Monday morning. "The Great Sheehan," it read, "is in trouble in the Takanassee handicap race tonight." It was signed "The Phantom."

McLoone the piano player had gone too far.

I had put up with losing three weeks in a row to this keyboard artist from a Fair Haven bistro. Had put up with the hordes of runners he had led across the line ahead of me. Had even put up with finishing so far back I was left out of the newspaper summaries, and people had asked me whether I had retired.

But the note was too much.

So, OK, he was an 8:53 two-miler at Harvard. That was two years ago, and any in-shape fifty-year-old worth his entry fee should be able to take a guy two years out of college at anything requiring skill, hard work and intelligence. Given weight for age, that is. And that was what I would be getting at Takanassee that night. McLoone, I thought, will get his comeuppance.

There was a time when all was different at Takanassee. The fields were small and incompetent. The runners a mediocre bunch of incoming high-school freshmen, out-of-condition upperclassmen and a few overweight collegians. In those good old days, I was usually in the first twenty and sometimes in the first ten. I was, I assure you, treated with respect.

Takanassee itself was part of an idyllic existence. The lake forms a three-quarter-mile loop which is rimmed by an asphalt road with just enough give to make it fast yet comfortable. The road has a sharp turn at the ocean end which gives you a quick glance at your pursuit without having to turn your head and letting them know you've about had it. And then after the fourth loop, the five thousand meters end with seven hundred yards of gradual downhill slope which has to be the best way to finish a race.

And don't forget the weather. The ocean is only yards away, so the evenings are cool. And when there is no wind and the air is dry and the sun is still bright in the west, it seems the best of all places to be. Maybe even more so when the race is over and you've run well and are still wet with sweat on the ride home. Then there's time to stop for a lemon ice and a dip at North End.

Into this Eden came the piano player and his friends, all 4:30 milers and sub-ten-minute two-milers. In came the guys who made running heartbreakingly easy, who cruise out of sight when your chest is bursting in an all-out effort. And for the first three weeks the only runners I passed had young spectators yelling, "Come on, Daddy" to them.

The time had come to convince McLoone that I had just been loafing up until now and was just about ready for a big one. But first I had to convince myself. Memories of other elders who had suddenly faded at age fifty-two raced through my mind. Was fifty-two the end of the trail? What was needed, obviously, was strong medicine.

First, the haircut. Streamlining your head has absolutely no effect on your speed in a five-thousand-meter race. Your brain says that—but not your gut. Your gut knows you are ten or twenty seconds faster right there. You know that. And McLoone would know it later, when he saw me. "That guy looks faster," he would say to himself. Then a shot of B_{12}. It always fakes a guy out to hear you've had a vitamin shot. He knows it won't help, but his gut doesn't. His gut says, "This cat has got to be stronger."

The real psych comes with the track shirt. My best is the "Caesar Rodney Half Marathon Wilmington, Del." shirt. Because just remembering you were able to finish that course does wonders for your morale. On this shirt I pinned my number saved from the Boston Marathon, and then I put on my racing Tigers. They were the same shoes, modified by the same Colombian shoemaker, that Mejía wore in winning the Boston.

I was ready. What was even better, I knew it and McLoone knew it.

There was a moment of apprehension at the line. The race director and handicapper had seen fit, in his wisdom, to give me a three-minute head start instead of the hoped-for four. But by this time I was completely psyched. I knew McLoone was through, and with three minutes I could beat anybody in the race.

And I did, except for two. A fourteen-year-old with a choirboy's face and the legs of an Apache messenger who had conned the handicapper out of six minutes, and a gutsy young redhead who started on the line with me and never gave me an inch. We kept picking up the larger handicap runners, and the little glimpses at the turn never showed a strong threat from the rear. Coming into the finish, I ran at the redhead. I was really hurting now, but knowing that the way to keep from getting caught from behind is to try to catch the fellow in front of you.

That was the race. The photographer took a picture of the first five finishers. We were weekly also-rans who had put together our best effort of the year. But no one had run really badly, and you could feel that warm Takanassee feeling settling over the pleasantly tired runners. And then McLoone came over and said some nice, extravagant things about my running.

It was the good old days all over again.

It was thirty-two degrees with a fifteen-mile-an-hour wind driving into our backs when we lined up for the start of the beach run. The beach stretched to the north, deserted for as far as the eye could see. The jetties were interrupting the white sand every two hundred yards or so, pushing ribbons of rock and concrete out into a blue ocean. The water was at low tide, calm and forty-five degrees, and there was a frigid wetness most of us would experience before the race was over.

Almost fifty runners waited for the gun, some drawn to the unusual event by the trophies and medals. Others addicted to the sport came like the gambler to the crooked roulette wheel, because it was the only game in town. A few of us who would be running our own race within the race came because sand and wind and ocean might bring another dimension to the running experience. That would be Bob Carlson, Tom Baum, Paul Kiell and myself.

Take Carlson, for instance. Carlson is the Brick Township mailman who has run the Pike's Peak Marathon, the most grueling race on the calendar, and can't wait to take a shot at Mount Washington, which he proudly declares "has the worst weather in the whole country."

Tom Baum is five years younger than Carlson and may yet outstrip him in seeking suffering. Baum, the director of the January 9 Jersey Shore Marathon, called me a few days before the beach race to predict that the event would be held in horrible weather. In a voice radiating joy he said, "I think we'll have a snowstorm with high winds and freezing temperatures. It will be an experience we will never forget."

The beach run was to be an experience that forty-three-year-old psychiatrist Paul Kiell would never forget. Kiell was to describe the race as a terrible dream all tied up with guilt and the ambivalence of weather we want to escape or be caught and punished. But that would come later.

At the start, he was off with the rest of us. The usual order of finish of this group was Carlson, Sheehan, Baum and Kiell, with an occasional change due to disordered physiology or lack of sleep. Carlson already had entered his excuse. Extra deliveries and the holiday drinks offered along his route had done him in.

What did him and the rest of us in was the sand.

I had once run at Ventnor and the sand was hard and packed, hard enough to use spikes and to maintain your usual form and speed. But this was the opposite. Soft and crumbling where it was dry. Soft and squishy where it was wet. On every step, we sank deeper and deeper into its yielding surface. Starting off with the usual rush, we found ourselves in distress and struggling within the first hundred yards.

Up ahead, Carlson, with his powerful, thrusting stride, was in early trouble, and soon he was left floundering in our wake. His style apparently unsuited for the mushy going. But the rest of us were having equal difficulty. We reached the mile mark, midway on the northward leg, and heard the time, 7:43, just two minutes slower than what we would expect for the effort, the breathing difficult, the legs heavy.

But on we slogged, running sometimes ankle deep in heavy, soggy sand at the water's edge, and then losing even that slim purchase on the sand rises built up on the south side of the jetties.

The intense effort was broken by the hard, sure step on the concrete, only to be followed by the tricky descent on the north side as we jumped from rock to rock. This usually ended in a final flatfooted jump to the level beach, forcing us to resume the running stride from a complete standstill. Frustration followed frustration.

And with this struggle came a new menace—Tom Baum. He suddenly appeared at my elbow and passed me as I turned for home. And with that shock came an additional one. Going north had been difficult, but now we would be going back against the wind and would have to climb the jetties instead of jumping off them.

Two miles to go and somewhere close behind us was Carlson, who had modified his stride, a discovery I had still to make. Kiell was farther back, deep in his dream of being chased. We all have that dream. In attempting to run, our legs feel heavy, we keep falling back and sliding, he said later.

Baum, all 170 pounds and six-foot-three of him, seemed to have had little difficulty guiding his size-thirteen shoes to adequate footing. It was taking me more and more effort to stay with him, and, with about a mile to go, he gradually began to draw away. I felt like a passenger on a boat watching another boat disappear upriver.

It was then I noticed his technique. He was running as if on a bicycle. His back was straight up and he was in a sitting position with his knees bent and rising up and down as if to follow the motion of the pedals. His size thirteens acted like snowshoes, with the result that his foot struck the sand for a minimum length of time, and while he was weight-bearing, the entire sole of his shoe was on the sand.

I mentally mounted my ten-speed bicycle, put it in low gear and went after him. Baum's ten-yard lead vanished, and I was on his shoulder as we climbed the last jetty.

After almost four miles, we had found out how to cope with our beach environment, found out how to live with the difficulties. The weather was no longer a physical thing. Our energy output had brought us to a humid tropical land. The wind we could no longer feel. The sand and its requirements had been met and defeated. But we refused to accept this as victory. There was the question of other energies, other insights as yet unknown to us, and whether we could escape to another level of consciousness.

So Tom Baum and I started to sprint on that unsprintable sand. Form and technique no longer mattered as we became the ache that was our legs and chest. The whole world was on that beach and getting smaller as we drove for the finish line. And for a long moment, the whole world was inside of us.

Then, once again, it was thirty-two degrees with a fifteen-mile-an-hour wind and we were hoping for the worst January 9 in history.

The Eastern Two-Mile Championship for fifty-and-over held on Cape May was no different from any other two-mile race I have ever run. The first mile was smooth and rhythmic, the second a painful agonizing effort to maintain the pace of the first mile.

I had run the first mile in 5:28, cruising along in the stead wake of New Zealander Bob Harmon, and both of us about fifty yards astern of Browning Ross, one-time king of the forty-and-overs, now in his first over-fifty race. But as we turned for home I began to feel the heaviness in the legs, the aching muscles and the breathing getting difficult.

And then as Harmon made his move to pull up on Ross, I was faced with the choice. Accept the challenge and maintain contact, or settle for a respectable third place. It was the moment that decided the race.

Some say races are decided beforehand. Depend on the runner's motivation. If so, I would be a loser. Prior to the start, I had conceded to Ross and Harmon and was hoping to beat the rest of the twenty-five-man field. But motivation, it seems to me, rarely stands up to pain. No matter how determined you are, that determination is conceived in a pain-free atmosphere. It has no relation to the real world that comes into being shortly after starting the second mile.

Still, if motivation enhances performance, task aversion, the psychological response to the discomforts of lactic-acid accumulation, the anticipation of future agonies, certainly diminishes it. Where motivation paints the future in unnaturally rosy hues, task aversion pictures it in somber grays and funereal blacks.

Task aversion is not new. Even the God-man asked that the cup might pass. We all have the tendency to give up. Army physiologist R. A. Kinsman reported that subjects working on a bicycle ergometer at fifty-six percent of aerobic capacity had quitting times ranging from one and a half to ninety-eight minutes.

When Harmon made his move, I was battling all three elements of fatigue: motivation, lactic acid and task aversion. If I went with Harmon, if I maintained contact, it would mean the escalation of effort in trying to catch the supposedly unbeatable Ross, and, even worse, the possibility of actually catching up to him and then having to sprint, God knows how, to the finish. What that would mean to my already suffering body was too cruel to contemplate.

But, cruel or not, I chose the race. And, having made the decision, concentrated on Harmon's shoes. And while I sat in behind him, using his draft, focusing my attention on his feet, narrowing the whole world to just him and me, we reached Ross and passed him.

Now the pain and the tension and the apprehension became unbearable. My great desire was not so much to slow down as to sprint. To sprint and get it over with, no matter how painful it might be.

And that was the way it was. With almost a full quarter to go, I took off. Not because I could stand the pain better than the other two, but because I couldn't. And because I wanted to control my own fate. Set my own pace and not accept theirs.

This much-too-early move took them by surprise and they waited, and that was fatal. By the time they came back at me, I was beyond catching because I was beyond pain.

I was moving in a sea of lactic acid, lifting legs that no longer understood what made them move. My breathing came in short, inadequate gasps, but my body no longer cared. I had broken through a barrier just as surely as I broke through the tape at the finish.

Fatigue, you see, does depend on motivation and lactic acid and task aversion, but it also depends on something else. Man's limits are not simply in his cells or even in his brain. You can measure lactic acid and stimulate brain areas with an electrode and make a person's arms and legs move. But there is no place in the brain where stimulation will cause a person to decide. No substance in his blood that will cause him to believe.

That choice, that act of faith, is made in the mind. And in answering the great question "Will you or won't you have it so?" we find the energy that conquers fatigue and conquers ourselves as well.

I am now fifty-nine years old, which is an awkward age to define. At fifty-nine, I am no longer middle-aged. I have, after all, no 118-year-old elders among my acquaintances. Yet I could hardly be called elderly.

An awkward age, then, to define, but a delightful one to live. I am aging from the neck up. Which means I am elderly enough to have attained a look of wisdom; middle-aged enough to have a body that allows me to do what I want; and a face that lets me get away with it.

You know that look. My hair is short and graying, the face is just skin and bones, the general impression of an ascetic who began the fight with the Devil in the garden, decided it wasn't worth it and walked away. My latest picture, in fact, looks a little like Teilhard de Chardin. The look of a man with ideas so heretical they bothered the Devil even more than they did the Pope. Preaching the perfectability of man might not get you banished from Rome, but it certainly would get you thrown out of hell. And the look, too, of a man who forgave God, and then his fellow men, and finally himself, and then was free.

Well, you know I am not yet old enough to look even remotely like that. But fifty-nine leaves quite a bit of time to go. Years that could be as exciting as any that have gone before.

What will always remain an excitement is the race. At fifty-nine, I am still the benchmark of performance for any number of runners. Over my fifteen years of running, I have consistently year in and year out been at the junction of the upper and middle thirds of runners finishing in a race. I have become the pass–fail mark for my fellow runners. If they beat me, they go home satisfied. If I beat them, they hope to do better next time. For my group, then, I am the top gun, the man they call out for a showdown.

I am no easy mark. I could give most readers of this book,

whatever their age, a five-minute head start and run them down in twenty or thirty minutes. I also have guts, which is simply the decision to stand pain.

Some think guts is sprinting at the end of a race. But guts is what got you there to begin with. Guts start in the back hills with six miles still to go and you're thinking of how you can get out of this race without anyone noticing. Guts begin when you still have forty minutes of torture left and you're already hurting more than you ever remember. Fortunately, guts seem to increase with age, rather than decrease. I may not want to wrestle with the Devil, but I am willing to wrestle with myself. And while I am beating myself, I usually beat others as well.

Newcomers are usually easy to handle, although I may have to pass them twice. The first time anyone is passed by someone my age, the natural reaction is disbelief and a sudden sprint to regain the lead. However, the next time I pass they usually give in, resigned to the fact that they are not yet ready to take the old man.

Some are injudicious enough to rile me up. This summer, I was passed at the halfway mark of a six-miler by someone who said, "I've been waiting to do this for three years." I passed him back about a mile down the road and now he'll wait another three years before he gets near me again.

Of course, I have that same effect on others, although I never say anything to upset anyone. This year, for instance, at Westport in a ten-miler, with about a mile to go, I closed in on a running friend, a twenty-five-year-old, whom I had never been near before in a race. With about two hundred yards to go, there were only fifteen yards and three runners between the two of us. As we entered the shopping plaza for the finish, the other three runners passed him and he did nothing. He was, as far as I could see, dead in the water. I cranked up, and with a hundred yards to go I blew past him. It was early, but it seemed safe. Did I neglect to tell you I am also dumb?

I was about ten yards ahead and apparently home free when I

heard this groaning, grunting animal coming up on me. He drew even and as I glanced over I could see him, wild-eyed, spittle all over his face, and his face the picture of agony. Then he was gone.

Later he told me he had recognized the bald head and there was no way I was going to beat him.

So it is not age that is threatened by youth, but the other way around. Youth is threatened by age. From where I sit the fifties look great, and I suspect the sixties will be even better. I may not yet look like Teilhard, but there's always this: I will never again look like my high-school picture.

14. Losing

I have seen death plain in a September surf,
and it was all wrong for me and I escaped. I
have seen death symbolically in a marathon and
know certainly that is the way I must end:
finally coming to a stop and falling apart, like
the wonderful one-horse shay.

LATER, after the hot tub had soaked some of the pain out of my legs, I hobbled to the bed and stretched out, enjoying being horizontal. Downstairs, John, our number-six son, put it to the rest of the family watching the Lakers–Bucks game. "If he's going to feel that bad," he asked, "why does he do it?"

Upstairs, I was asking myself the same question.

Why suffer this way? Why run marathons when nine out of ten of them end in a contest of the human will pushing the human body beyond endurance? This one had been no different. The first ten miles to Sea Bright had been a lark. Moving steadily along the coast with that strong south wind at my back was a fine way to spend a Sunday morning in January. Past Sea Bright, I had even picked up my pace, still feeling good and full of running.

The first hint of disaster came at the turnaround in Sandy Hook Park. The fifteen-mile-an-hour wind, hardly noticed as an ally, became a constant alien presence. Reducing my speed and increasing my effort, it would give me no respite for the next two hours. Still, the legs felt fresh, the breathing good and the form under control. Sea Bright reappeared and disappeared in my wake.

Then, as quickly as it takes to write this, the cramps came. They started in both calves, then spread to the thighs, cutting my stride in half and making each step a painful decision. It was ridiculous, I told myself, to even think of finishing with seven miles to go. No one who knew how I felt right now could expect me to finish.

But I kept going. My progress getting slower and slower as I tested a variety of running forms that might permit movement without torture. Nothing helped, but the thought of quitting gradually receded from my mind. When the pain was particularly bad, I would breathe, "Oh, God"; more a statement than a prayer. And I took to counting my steps. Counting by ones seemed the highest mental activity I could perform. It also reassured me that I was moving and would after 4,500 or thereabouts steps arrive at Convention Hall in Asbury Park.

Somehow in all this torment, Allenhurst came and went. Deal Lake appeared, then the Convention Hall and then three of the longest blocks in the world to the finish. Three hours and forty-five minutes after it started in ecstasy, the agony ended.

The marathon, I thought, as I lay there feeling warmer and healthier by the minute, is just not my race. True, I had not trained adequately for this one. Had not run over ten miles in one stretch since April and the last Boston. It was foolish to expect a good one on that amount of work. In the old days, maybe, but now, with age coming on and the desire dying, it might be best to let the marathon go.

There were times in the beginning when the marathon, any marathon, seemed an impossible dream. When any race over five miles was beyond my imagination. My goals were more immediate (a five-minute mile) and practical (physical fitness).

Subtly, insidiously, running became much more. Became, as exercise did for Oliver Alden, George Santayana's Last Puritan, a necessity. "To go a single day without two hours of rigorous outdoor exercise," wrote Santayana, "was now out of the question. It would have meant physical restlessness and discomfort indoors and the most horrible sensual moodiness in the inner man."

For Alden, the two hours of sculling or horseback riding brought him into genuine communication with nature such as he never found in either religion or poetry. And was able to turn him for the moment, Santayana declared, into the gladdest, the most perfect and yet the most independent of people.

Couldn't that "escape, that wordless religion," be enough? Why get into twenty-six-mile runs with the certainty of bone-weary fatigue and the possibility of the ignominy of walking to the finish line? Wasn't the marathon equivalent to Alden's Puritan ethic, from which he escaped only when rowing on the Charles or galloping his horse on a brisk New England day? Another mindless duty, another needless challenge, another unwanted privilege. All demanding success and achievement.

Downstairs, Kareem Jabbar was not looking to escape. He had engaged Wilt Chamberlain in hand-to-hand combat and was revealing what Fordham's Charley Yelverton once said was the principle of being an athlete—"the principle that makes you dig your guts out no matter what kind of game you're in."

I still don't know. "You can very well afford to dangle about enjoying the fresh air and admiring the sunset," the captain of the Harvard crew had told Alden, "but we've got to train. We're not in the crew to have a good time, but to win the Yale race."

But perhaps you could have both. Perhaps what I needed was more marathons, not fewer. Needed the pain, the torture, the indescribable fatigue of a marathon in February and another in March.

The Boston in April would be a breeze, another of those daily afternoon runs when you know who you are and where you're going. And I would come to the finish as I would come to my back door, warm and relaxed, still strong and full from running, enjoying the fresh air and admiring the sunset.

Now, where was that February entry blank?

You may have seen my name in the Shore Marathon summaries on Monday. It was there in the agate under "Other Area Finishers": "69, George Sheehan, Shore A.C., 3:18:32." Not bad, you might think. Not bad for place, with 235 starters. Not bad for time, about midway between my best (3:02) and my worst (3:33) serious efforts. You might think that. And you would be wrong.

Because it was a marathon without tears, without pain, without distinction. It was a marathon that I am ashamed of; a marathon I would like to forget. It was a marathon that proves there is a point where prudence becomes timidity, where caution becomes cowardice, where respect becomes fear.

The 26:22-mile distance tends to make all runners prudent, cautious and respectful. "Anyone," said the great Percy Cerutty, "can run twenty miles, but only a few can run the marathon." That extra six miles changes the game from penny-ante to table stakes. Your entire physical bankroll can dissolve in a matter of minutes.

We are not quite sure why this happens. Some physiologists suggest that at twenty miles the body exhausts its available sugar supplies and must switch over to another form of energy metabolism. Maybe so, but, whatever the cause, the runner knows that no matter how he feels at any particular stage of the race, disaster may be waiting for him at the twenty-mile mark. This makes the marathon a chancy and risky business, where the initial pace can be all-decisive. Too slow and you have a poor time; too fast and you may not finish. So those even more timid sometimes use the first seven miles to warm up, and thus change the marathon into an ordinary twenty-mile road run.

That is just what I inexcusably did. I had the mileage to go all out. Long runs with my Shore A.C. friends, and a fast ten-miler (sixty-two minutes) the week before when I beat them all. But within a mile after the start of the marathon, my quartet of friends were minutes ahead of me and my warmup pace. A pace I kept at not just for seven miles, but for the entire outward leg of 13.1 miles.

A mile and a half from the turnaround point, they passed me going the other direction, heading for home. Three miles and twenty-four minutes ahead of me, they were giving the race and the course and the weather (it was a perfect forty degrees and little wind) all they had. They had accepted the challenge. They were making themselves vulnerable, opening themselves to the possibility of great achievement or a wipeout.

Meanwhile I was sliding. That's what Ed Gentry, the get-through-the-day man in James Dickey's *Deliverance,* called it. "Sliding is living antifriction," he said. "It's finding a modest thing you can do and then greasing that thing. It is grooving with comfort."

But even groovers and sliders sometimes get religion. I did at the halfway point. The fact that I was back in 154th place may have helped a little. Provided some additional incentive. But whatever, I set out at full throttle for my colleagues up ahead. I went through Sea Bright like the Blue Comet and highballed through Long Branch passing seven or eight runners each mile.

With five miles to go, I caught struggling Paul Kiell (who was to finish in his best time ever and qualify for Boston), and a quarter mile from home I passed Gene Minor, now walking. Up ahead, Tom Baum had finished in 3:03 and Pat Barrett had become the tenth-fastest woman marathoner in the world with a 3:04.

The people at the finish line said some nice things to me. The time wasn't all that bad and I had run a hell of a last 13.1 miles. But I knew where I should have been. Up with Baum and Barrett, or walking. I had chosen the middle way, the way of the lukewarm. And afterward, when there were awards for almost everybody, I didn't wait around. I wanted no memento of that race.

On the way home, I recalled Nikos Kazantzakis, in *Report to*

Greco, asking his grandfather's ghost for a command. His grandfather answered, "Reach what you can, my child." But Kazantzakis refused that command and asked for a more difficult, "more Cretan" command. The ghost then thundered, "Reach for what you cannot."

I may put that slogan on my running shirt. If there is a better rule for a marathoner, I have yet to hear it. If you want to be all you can be, you have to expect a failure from time to time. Finding the limits of your ability will almost certainly end eventually in a walk to the finish line.

Which is why you can never tell from the agate who is a failure and who is a success; who is simply out there grooving and who is reaching what he cannot. Who is a twenty-miler and who is a marathoner.

Only God and the runner know that.

"Pain and wrong and death," wrote William James, "must be fairly met and overcome, or their sting remains unbroken." Prosperity is not enough, he said, if we expect to possess life excellently and meet best the secret demands of the universe.

Psychiatrist Viktor Frankl was another who spoke of the need to confront this "tragic triad of human existence": guilt for our past, pain in the present, and death in the future. These realities, they both warn us, must be neither ignored nor evaded, but squarely faced and conquered.

But where can this encounter be sought? Where can pain be found on demand? Where can we meet guilt head on and cleanse ourselves? Where can we experience death and then return?

The best answer, it seems to me, is sport. Sport is where an entire life can be compressed into a few hours. Where the emotions of a lifetime can be felt on the acre or two of ground. Where a person can suffer and die and rise again on six miles of trails through a New York City park.

Sport is a theater where sinner can turn saint, and a common man become an uncommon hero. Where the past and the future can fuse with the present. Sport is singularly able to give us peak experiences where we feel completely one with the world, where all conflicts are transcended as we finally become our own potential.

For me, these remarkable events occur almost every cross-country race. Every race begins in hope. Every start is filled with the joy that is hope in a physical form. I can feel it in my body and in those around me. It is a confidence, an anticipation, a unity which makes the race a celebration, a holiday.

Every race begins, then, in that optimistic state James called being "once-born," of treating evil by ignoring it. Two miles later, I am in the hills and I know differently. Life is no longer neat and cozy and comfortable. In the hills, it is short and painful and dangerous. My body is now crying for oxygen. And I have come to know pain that people otherwise know only in childbirth or disease or catastrophe. And I know it not once, but many times, because there is hill after hill after hill. And each more terrible than the last.

Once past, the hills are still in my body. Because the past is always incorporated into your body. Each cell contains the past. Either the hills and pain fairly met, or the hills and pain evaded. Either pain or guilt, but usually both. I am always sure I could have done better. Certain that somewhere I eased off and avoided the total commitment. Positive that I failed myself again, as I have done so often in the past. I come out of the hills filled with pain and guilt, looking for some way to make it worth the effort. Looking for a good place or a good time or a good finish.

And all around me, runners are doing the same. The race begun as a community in celebration is ending like an army in rout. Everywhere now it is friend against friend, as the quiet, tolerant nonaggressive runners become the tigers we are inside. Now there is a race for every place and the leader is the man in front of me, whether he is 45th or 86th or 203rd, just as long as I am one place behind.

And we go down that last stretch head and head, each demanding the other do more. Each giving until there is no more to give. Until there is nothing left but the "I." I am beyond pain and guilt. I am where I have never been or seen or touched in daily life. In those final yards, I am near the state described by the dying patients of Dr. Elizabeth Kubler-Ross, of floating out of the body and having a feeling of peace and wholeness. I feel just seconds away from being outside my body watching myself finish, just a moment away from the accomplishment of my task and the total peace that goes with it.

So there it is. Football, said Red Blaik, is the game most like life. What he meant, of course, was that life is the game most like football. Every athlete feels that way about his sport. He knows that sport is where he lives. Where he can best meet and overcome pain and wrong and death.

Life is just a place to spend time between races.

When death comes, we should have had time to fulfill the demands of Pythagoras: build a house, plant a tree, sire a son and write a book. There is the conventional wisdom about a subject where there is no conventional wisdom. Strike the Pythagorean bargain. The best revenge is to live long and well.

But what of the young who die? What of the athletes? How can we accept the deaths of the Israeli Olympians and of men like Brian Piccolo and Chuck Hughes? Is it possible that the athlete is better prepared for death than the rest of us? And for reasons more persuasive than "outrunning one's fame," which is the theme of Housman's poem "To an Athlete Dying Young"?

The answer, it seems to me, is yes. The athlete for very compelling reasons has found a way to live to his absolute limits and has reconciled himself to his own mortality; which is a way of saying the athlete has developed a sense of time, an acceptance of pain, an appreciation of relationships, and a happiness that so completes him that death becomes simply another experience.

The athlete's time emphasizes his mortality. Others of us may drive this thought from our minds. We do not like to think life is short and man corruptible, two obvious facts to the athlete. For him, as Ortega suggests, this fact compresses and intensifies his life, and gives it urgency, imminence and the need to do his best at every instant.

That instant, peculiarly enough, becomes one with the past and the present and the future. In each contest the athlete brings with him the sense of time which we associate with certain primitive people. Indians, for instance, who have only one word for past, present and future. An idea primitive yet so sophisticated as to be accepted by a great thinker like Einstein. Writing of a lifelong friend who had died, Einstein said, "He now has gone a little ahead of me. This is of little significance. For us believing physicists, the separation of the past, present and future has only the meaning of an illusion."

The athlete adds to this perception of time extending behind and ahead of him the realization that hardship and pain and discomfort must be met and overcome. Or else he will, as William James suggested, go through life suspecting that he is not really inside the game. That he lacks the great initiation. That initiation, meeting the terrible fatigue and exhaustion and suffering demanded in sports, can lead a man, thought James, to a profounder way of handling the gift of existence.

Many of us don't realize that gift of existance until it is already taken from us. Psychologist Abraham Maslow, who had suffered a severe coronary attack and almost died, spoke of his life thereafter as his postmortem life. "Everything," Maslow wrote, "gets doubly precious. You get stabbed by the very act of living, of walking and breathing and eating and having friends. Every single moment of every day is transformed."

Every moment of every day has been transformed for eight-year-old Jenny Bagwell, who received a kidney transplant from her mother. "Jenny," says her mother, "sees the flowers open their throats to sing in the morning. . . . She talks to the stars."

Maslow, now deceased, and Jenny alive and well and athletes

the world over live in close relationship to nature. They do not want to find out, as Thoreau feared, that they have not lived life at all. For them at least, damnation will not be an unused soul, as Bernanos suggested.

But, for all that, athletes would be incomplete if they weren't happy. This is, however, a characteristic of athletes and one way you can pick one out in a crowd. For them, everything else is work.

Yet this happiness is not simply pleasure, a sensual experience. Happiness is an energetic act, a real effort. Ortega, writing thirty years ago in an article printed in *Sports Illustrated* recently, made this point. Happiness, he declared, using hunting as a model, may include hardship and discomfort, but a man remains immersed in them, the whole present fills him completely, free from nostalgia and desire. Opposite to the life that annihilates itself and fails (the life of work), he builds a plan of life successful in itself, a life of delight and happiness.

Could Ortega be serious in suggesting that all this was possible with sports? No question. "What does a man do when he is free to do what he pleases?" he asks. And supplies the answer. "Raced horses, competed in physical exercises, gathered at parties and engaged in conversation."

The Ortegan proposition appeals to me. It has to do with being. The Pythagorean injunctions relate to having. The athlete becomes more and more as he has less and less. He is obsessed with being all he can be. And in the course of this becoming, he has already died the little deaths. Has learned how to accept the inevitable. Has even taught himself what death will be like when it comes.

For Olympians, death has no sting. They have had the great initiation.

Why mourn Peter Revson? He died doing what he did best. Died at thirty-five before the prudence of advancing years could prevent the full use of his skill. Died quickly and surely as the driver expects to die. Died happy as the philosophers say all men should die.

"When a man dies," wrote Charles Peguy, "he dies not from the disease alone. He dies from his whole life." For the Grand Prix driver to whom racing is his whole life, death in action is the true death. It was for Revson.

"I know Peter led the life he wanted to live," said his friend George Lysle. "He wanted to excel in his own way in his own universe." And Revson died at the height of his excellence. The race driver reaches his highest performance in his early thirties. Before that, he lacks the skills to be the complete driver. After that, he becomes too cautious.

And the event itself is to the driver almost nothing. "I'm not afraid of it [death] for myself," said Jackie Stewart. "I don't think any driver is, because it can't hurt for very long."

Stewart is typical of all topflight race drivers. They are willing to explore openly the possibilities of danger and death. The typical race driver, it has been found, is tough-minded, extraordinarily dominant, aggressive, with a high need to achieve.

Far from being a neurotic seeking death, the driver has a below-average need to feel guilt, blame himself or punish himself. He is a hard-nosed, unemotional, poised human being.

In a book Revson wrote before his death, he explained a tendency to see mistakes not as death-dealing but as something that is, as he says, "going to penalize me in a race. I'm going to lose time. I'm going to lose. Understand this: losing really hurts. To fail in a race is the most painful thing imaginable."

Revson put failing in a race above life itself. Ecclesiastes, who said the most—and the least—about death, would agree with him. Everything is vanity and chasing the wind, said Ecclesiastes. Driving race cars, running governments, amassing wealth, building cities: all this is vanity and chasing the wind.

But, said Ecclesiastes in an about-face, whatever you put your hand to, do it with all your might. He answers to life: It is not the inconsequential things that you do but how you do them that magnifies the Lord.

Doing is, of course, more obvious in those of the same temperament as those racing drivers. Men of action. They have no thought of death. They would die, if it had to come, *in medias res;* taken from life at maximum activity. But their fate is not to go over the guardrail at Indianapolis; they will be cut down by heart attacks or strokes, the hazards of the nonsports world.

A man, Peguy is telling us, is responsible for his own death. It should be in character. Done in one's own style. I have seen death plain in a September surf, and it was all wrong for me, and I escaped. And I have seen death symbolically in a marathon and know certainly that is the way I must end: finally coming to a stop and falling apart like the wonderful one-horse shay.

For people like me, with long histories as silent losers, there comes a time when there is just nothing left. There comes a time when death is welcomed; you just cannot take another step. And then, freed of both guilt and ambition, you can ride the bus back to the finish.

On occasions when I have done that in a marathon and passed runners struggling and suffering on the final miles, I viewed them as if I were already a member of the Church Triumphant, beyond such mortal interests.

The best we can do, it seems to me, is to die proper. There may be more to life than driving racing cars, or running governments, or amassing wealth, or building cities, or even running marathons. But not in this life. So we must pursue these vanities and chase the wind.

And do it with all our might, like Peter Revson.

15. Suffering

Not to yield says it all. The enduring, the surviving, does not stop with age. We may even grow more skillful at it as the years pass. So we do not envy youth. We ask no quarter of life. We accept no favors. We are men following virtue and knowledge.

FIFTEEN YEARS AGO, when I ran my first Boston Marathon, the race was little more than a club. We were 225 strong. But many of us were present only because of a dare or as a joke. Some were overweight and out of shape, attired in gym suits and tennis clothes. Others wore sneakers instead of running shoes. And, I recall, either that year or the next, a runner who led me all the way to Framingham wore a derby.

That first year at Boston, I finished ninety-sixth in three hours and seven minutes and because of this considered myself one of the top hundred marathoners in the country. Now, with nearly the same time, I am not even in the top five thousand. Back then, there were about seven marathons a year; now there are over two hundred. The Boston field has swelled to 2,200 and is kept manageable only by limiting entrants to those who have run under three hours the previous year. Women and men over forty are required to beat 3:30.

Where have all these people come from, and why do they do it? How did this mania arise, and what keeps it multiplying among the populace?

I can only answer for myself, and even my answer changes from day to day. For this day, then, I will tell you what I discovered in running. Then why I eventually came to run marathons. And finally, what the continuing fascination of the marathon is. Runners, you see, do not run one marathon. They run them again and again. They are much like surfers seeking the perfect wave.

Why I began running is no longer important. It is enough that it generated a desire to run. Then the running itself took over. Running became a self-renewing compulsion. The more I ran, the more I wanted to run.

One reason was the energy. "Become first a good animal," Emerson said. I did. I came to know my body and enjoy it. Things that previously exhausted me were no longer an effort. Where once I fell asleep in front of the TV set, I was up roaming the house looking for things to do. I was living on a different level of performance.

Then I discovered, or rediscovered, play. Running, I found, was fun. Running became an hour of play and enjoyment away from my daily routine. And in that hour of play I discovered, or rediscovered, myself. Finally, after forty-five years, I accepted the person I was.

It would seem that this should be enough—the fitness, the play, the self-acceptance. But it wasn't, and never will be. I wanted to be challenged, wanted to be tested, wanted to find my limits and then surpass them. Merely running and enjoying and creating were not enough.

From here on, I think more of the answers will be found in the philosophy of William James than anywhere else. However I phrase it, it comes down to one of the Jamesian expressions: "The nobler thing tastes better. The strenuous life is the one we seek."

James was not a writer for those who would simply cope, for those who would groove through life. He believed in effort. He thought the decisive thing about us was not intelligence, strength or wealth. Those are things we carry, he said. The real question posed to us is the effort we are willing to make.

And that available effort is always, he kept saying, much more than we suspect. We live far below the energy we have and therefore must learn how to tap these reservoirs of power. For this, he said, we need a "dynamogenic agent," a "moral equivalent of war." Like war, this would provide a theater of heroism, an arena where one could demonstrate courage and fortitude, a setting where one could be the best one would ever be.

For me and others like me, that is the marathon. We are all there in the works of William James. He is the psychologist who tells us we can be more than we are. The philosopher who appeals to everyone who values his own experience. The thinker who saw happiness in the struggle and found the meaning of life in the marriage of some unhabitual idea with some fidelity, courage and endurance. Which is as good a definition of a marathon as you are likely to find.

I tell you all this, and still you might not understand. What is so special, what is unique about this 26-mile-385-yard distance? Why this and not some other race?

The answer is the wall, the physiological breaking point that comes at the twenty-mile mark. Runners claim that at this mark the marathon is only half over, that the last six miles are equivalent to the twenty that went before. It is nearer the truth to say that the twenty-mile mark is where the marathon begins—there at the wall.

The miles that have gone before are just the foothills to this Everest. The wall is where the runner begins to come apart. Either as suddenly as it takes to write this sentence or slowly and inexorably as the final miles turn into a cauldron of pain.

Any reasonably fit runner can go a twenty-mile race. Were I to get up next Sunday and see in the *New York Times* that there was a twenty-mile race in Central Park, I would be likely to pack my gear and go. But if that same morning I discovered there was a marathon in town, I would draw a bye.

I would not be prepared to go that extra six miles, to handle the wall.

Exactly what happens there is not known, even to the experts. Is the exhaustion, the seeming impasse, due to low blood sugar or lactic-acid accumulation? Is it due, perhaps, to dehydration, or high body temperature? Is it the result of a loss of blood volume or, as many runners suspect, depletion of muscle glycogen?

No one seems quite sure. Whatever the reason, the runner's homeostasis, the equilibrium of his internal milieu, begins to break down. And the final six miles must be accomplished in some way unexplained by medical science. From the wall on, the runner goes it alone.

One exercise physiologist, Dr. David Costill, director of the Ball State University Human Performance Laboratory in Muncie, Indiana, ran the marathon as an experiment because he did not think the wall existed. When he came to that point, however, he said, "The sensations of exhaustion were unlike anything I had ever experienced. I could not run, walk or stand, and even found sitting a bit strenuous."

So there it is. It begins with running. Until one day you progress to where you want to be challenged by the marathon. And then you meet the wall. No matter how many times you attack it, you always think you can do better, find more energy, more fortitude, more courage, more endurance. You always think this time you will be the hero you were meant to be.

Fifteen years and fifty marathons later, that's the best explanation I know.

If you would be a marathon runner, study William James. Technique and training can safely be left to lesser teachers. You will soon find the proper shoes, know what to wear, how to eat, what exercises to do, how far to run. What you need most is to know it is possible, possible for you, possible for any common man.

And then you must learn it is not only possible, but necessary. And that there are ways to make what is possible and necessary, however difficult it appears, a source of joy and happiness.

James is the man who teaches this. He is the psychologist who speaks to all who would be more than they are. He is the philosopher who appeals to everyone who values his own experience. Everyone who suspects there is more to each one of us than meets the eye. He is the thinker who said that how to gain, how to keep, and how to recover happiness were the certain motive of all we do and are willing to endure.

James is the scientist who dealt in happiness. He went beyond science into the human heart, into those recesses where lie our values and ideals and with them the energies needed to accomplish them. For James, life was meant to be a struggle. Life, he said, was built on doing and suffering and creating. Its solid meaning was the same eternal thing—the marriage of some unhabitual idea with some fidelity, courage and endurance.

Sweat and effort and human nature strained to its utmost and on the rack, yet getting through alive, he wrote, are the sort of thing that inspires us.

"Man must be stretched," he wrote. "If not in one way, then another."

The marathon is one way. Running twenty-six miles is a feat that truly stretches a human being. At the twenty-mile mark, someone has said, the race is half over. Almost anyone can run twenty miles, but the last six are the equivalent of twenty more. Here the runner finds himself pushed to the absolute limit. And therefore needs to call on those hidden reserves, to use all the fidelity and courage and endurance he has.

Would James have considered the marathon an absurd waste of these energies, of these great human resources? I doubt it. Indeed, who better than James to speak to marathon runners? He always championed the life of sanctity or poverty or sport. He was always caught up with the athlete or the saint, whom he saw as the athlete of God. He always admired the ascetic way of life, which is no more, as the original Greek word would have it, than athletic training. "Asceticism," he stated, "is the profounder way of handling human existence."

This type of discipline, he thought, would allow us to live to our maximum. And find in ourselves unexpected heights of fortitude and heroism and the capability to endure suffering and hardship. To discover, if you will, the person we are. Reaching peaks we previously thought unattainable.

And how better to reach this state than by the rules of habit formation that James suggested? To lead life well and attend to the major things, we must, he said, make as much of our daily activity as possible simply habit. Otherwise we will consume both energy and time making decisions.

The marathoner who would be successful can learn how to get the correct habits from James. Put on the right course, his training will be no problem. The thirty to fifty miles a week he needs to run a respectable and suitably painful marathon will be a matter of course. He will suit up and get out on the roads without agonizing about wind or cold or weather. Or about more attractive things. Or the priorities of family or society.

Begin, said James, with firm resolve. Start with high hopes and a strong and decisive initiative. Do not permit exceptions, he warned. Unraveling a string is easier than winding it up. Practice must become an inviolate hour. Nothing should come between the runner and running.

Next, seize every opportunity to act in the direction of this habit. Further, do not talk about what you are going to do; do it. And finally, he said, keep the faculty of effort alive by a little gratuitous exercise each day.

The marathoner schooled by James comes to the Hopkinton Common on Patriots' Day at the height of his physical powers, willing to pay the price in pain and even agony the marathon demands. But James also wrote on other things that occupy the runner on the way to Boston: mystical states, the primacy of religion, and the problem of truth.

And in the end, when the race is half over, when there are six miles to go, because he is mind and soul as well as body, the runner will find new ways of looking at himself and his God. "Experience," said James, "is a process that continually gives us new material to digest."

And for the marathoner there is no greater experience than the marathon. And no better companion on that run than William James.

James Joyce took the ten years of Homer's *Odyssey* and compressed them into a Dublin day. He looked into the mind and heart and body of the hero Ulysses and created Leopold Bloom, who is everyman. And saw in the lotus-eaters, Cyclops, the gift of the winds, Circe, Hades, the Sirens and even the nymph Calypso, those inner and outer events that happen to everyone, every day. And then he put all of it into the waking-to-sleeping day of his Irish Jew. It takes eighteen hours.

The Boston Marathon does it in three.

Like many sports, the marathon is a microcosm of life. The marathoner can experience the drama of everyday existence so evident to the artist and poet. For him, all emotions are heightened. Agony and ecstasy become familiar feelings. The journey from Hopkinton to Boston, like the journey from Troy to Ithaca, reveals what happens to a man when he faces up to himself and the world around him. And why he succeeds or fails.

Ulysses succeeds not because he is a superior athlete, although he is. He can build a boat and sail it. He can wrestle, run and throw a discus. He can flay, skin, cut up, and cook an ox. But all these skills do not explain his eventual success. His secret is that he endures. He takes life as it comes and says yes.

This trait is so commonly displayed at Boston, it seems universal. I believe every human must have this capacity and could find it if he tried. And there is no better place to discover it than a marathon. For the truth is that every man in a marathon is a survivor or nothing, including the winner.

Winning is, in fact, unimportant. "Brief is the season of man's delight," sang Pindar in his ode to an Olympic winner. And many a winner has learned the truth that his laurel is indeed, as Housman wrote, a garland briefer than a girl's.

There is, then, no happy-ever-aftering for a marathoner, no matter what his age. Tomorrow is another race, another test, another challenge. And then there is another race, and another.

What, then, of Ulysses? Was he content to live as an aging and idle king? Others besides marathoners have thought not. Dante saw him calling on his old comrades, urging them to further adventures. "Consider your origin," he tells them. "You were not formed to live like brutes, but to follow virtue and knowledge."

Such pursuit would be in action. The Greeks developed the whole man. They saw no happiness in creature comforts, no wisdom in meditation.

We aging marathoners already know that. We learned it at Boston. And so, when Tennyson takes up Dante's idea and has Ulysses speak, we hear ourselves: "And though we are not now the strength which in old days moved earth and heaven, that which we are, we are—made weak by time and fate, but strong in will to strive, to seek, to find, and not to yield."

Not to yield says it all. The enduring, the surviving, does not stop with age. We may even grow more skillful at it as the years pass. So we do not envy youth. We ask no quarter of life. We accept no favors. We are men following virtue and knowledge.

"Though much has been taken," wrote Tennyson, "much abides." We will live and endure. We know, better than others, "how dull it is to pause, to make an end, to rust unburnished, not to shine in use."

I do not intend to pause, or rest, or rust. Descendant of Ulysses, brother of Bloom, I will survive.

There is no easier running for me than the first few miles of the Boston Marathon. I come to that race at my peak. I am lean and fit and ready. And the excitement of the day lights a fire. So I am almost pure energy when the gun goes off at high noon on the Hopkinton Common.

The start is all laughter and talking and wishing people well. The pace is a pleasure. Smooth and comfortable and little more than a trot. I move at a speed just above that of my warmup ("In the beginning always hold something back," Adolph Gruber, the Austrian Olympian, once told me). So these miles are like no others in any race.

Down the long hill out of Hopkinton and through Ashland and over the gentle slopes to Framingham, I coast along. The running is automatic. I feel nothing but the elation of being in this company. The miles pass as if I were watching them out of a train window.

But miles change, somewhere the holding back must end. I pass the ten-mile mark and enter Natick. The miles no longer effortless become an effort that comes easily. My style remains sure and smooth and economical. I increase my speed, but it is still well below the six-minute miles of those cruel ten- and twelve-milers in Central Park. I try for maximum efficiency. Careful to push off my toes and get those extra few inches a stride that make the difference in a three-hour run.

Soon I am at Wellesley, the halfway point. The miles again change. Now each mile is running at my best. It is now becoming hard work. Not disagreeable, but an exertion not previously felt. I am still surprisingly fresh and moving well. Better now than I have moved before or will move later. Still, the body is beginning to tell me this is no lark. No longer child's play. Not just a long run in the sun.

And now at the seventeen-mile mark come the Newtown Hills, a two-mile stretch which includes the four hills that make up the world-renowned Heartbreak Hill. I will take these on the grass divider behind the crowds that line the street.

The grass dampens the shock on my lower legs and thighs.

And I shift to shorter steps as a cyclist would shift to a lower gear to maintain the same work load. Even with grass and mini-steps, miles over hills are most difficult.

Quite suddenly, what in the beginning seemed like something I would accomplish with ease and even distinction comes down to survival. A question of whether or not I can keep moving. These two short miles seem interminable. And then, just as suddenly, I am at Boston College and it is, as the crowds insist, all downhill from there.

Downhill or not, we marathoners know that at Boston College the race is only half over. I am quite a different runner from the one who stood on the line at Hopkinton. The steady pace has used up my muscle glycogen, my precious fuel supply. The Newtown Hills have built up my lactic acid and the heaviness in my muscles. The downhills in the early going have inserted ice-picks in my thighs. My blood sugar is getting low. And although I have drunk everything in sight, I have not kept up with my fluid loss.

Descending the hill from Boston College, I feel these inner events for the first time. And I know again that the last six miles at Boston will be the worst six miles I will ever run. From now on, pain is a constant companion. The slightest downgrade is a torture to my thighs. My legs get heavier and heavier.

The same effort that made a romp of a seven-minute mile outside of Hopkinton barely gets me through a ten-minute mile on Commonwealth Avenue. I experiment with strides and body positions to see if there are any muscles still willing to respond.

By now I can see the Pru Tower, and then come the unkindest miles of all. Miles where I must will every step toward a goal that never seems any nearer. I spend a mile in agony and bring that tower not one inch nearer. Minutes pass, and the Pru and with it the finish and the relief from pain and my chance to get into a hot tub seem just a mirage.

But somehow I reach Beacon Street and I know I have made it. Like a horse who smells the barn, I am suddenly refreshed.

The last mile brings with it a joy, an elevation of the spirit, that makes everything that went before worthwhile.

And worth doing again next year. One mile at a time.

Like most distance runners, I am still a child. And never more so than when I run. I take that play more seriously than anything else I do. And in that play I retire into the fantasyland of my imagination any time I please.

Like most children, I think I control my life. Believe myself to be independent. I am certain I have been placed on this earth to enjoy myself. Like most children, I live in the best of all possible worlds, a world made for running and racing, where nothing but good can happen. And, like most children, I am oblivious to all of the work done by other people to make it that way.

This is more than faith. Faith is the Breton peasant praying for rain and then taking an umbrella with him when he leaves the house. Faith is a nun friend of my grandmother's who periodically herded thirty to forty orphans onto a train at Poughkeepsie and set out for Coney Island without a penny in her purse. "God will provide," was her motto. That's faith.

Faith is an act of the will made by an adult. The child acts before will and reason and dogma. He simply knows. And the child in me knows that I am in a game that will always have a happy ending. That I can enjoy the anxiety leading up to the race, and the tremendous challenge in the running, and the sweetness or bitterness of the ending, knowing that, whatever happens, I am already a hero, a winner. Knowing that in the end, whatever the crisis, there would always be someone to take care of me.

I hadn't realized this (although it may well have been evident to my family and friends) until the 1976 Boston Marathon. The official temperature on Patriots' Day was ninety-two degrees, a level listed as dangerous for livestock and death-dealing to runners. Any thinking adult would have sat this one out. But there I was with 1,800 others dressing at the Hopkinton High School gym.

Then, walking to the starting line, I passed a gasoline station with a thermometer on the wall. It read 116 degrees. I passed by undeterred.

At the starting line there were hoses to fill our cups, to douse our heads and caps and the shirts we wore. The family of man was already operating. The people were already taking care of their children.

And that was the way it was. The whole thing was absurd. The race should have been postponed or set for later in the day. There was no way for a runner to go those twenty-six sunbaked miles to Boston relying on official help. Yet I set out knowing I would get whatever help I needed. Knowing I would survive.

For one thing, Boston Marathon crowds are special. I recall my first Boston and how astounded I was that people called me George all along the way. They stood in groups with one person picking the names out of the *Globe* so that when I got to them there would be cries of "You can do it, George," or "George, you're looking strong," or, in the late stages, "Keep it up, George, there's only three miles to go."

What that can do to a childlike runner previously known only to his own family is unbelievable. I felt capable of anything, even completing the Boston Marathon.

This year the crowd outdid itself. Within two miles we were running in the rain. It was ninety-two degrees and a cloudless sky, and we were running in a rain provided by hose after hose after hose. There was water everywhere. Mile upon mile of people and children offering water to drink and pour on me. Swarms of young boys giving out Gatorade, with the same enthusiasm they had shown an hour before supplying the leaders. Others with buckets of ice. Some with the traditional orange slices, many of the children just holding out their hands to be touched by the heroes passing by.

From Ashland on, there was nothing but applause and cheers. Then came the reception from the girls at Wellesley, and farther on the children in the Newtown Hills outdoing each other to get us ice and water. And there I saw this solemn four-year-old, just standing with a tiny cup, hoping someone would stop. I did and drank the two ounces and told her, "You're my honey." Boston is like that, a voice, a face, a child that you remember forever.

I was in Boston now and should have been home free. I wasn't. I was running a poor marathon, and when you run a poor marathon you not only hurt, you hurt longer. I had been out on the roads longer than any time in my fourteen years of running. But through all the pain and not knowing whether I would finish, the dragging out those last terrible miles, I always felt safe. I knew I was surrounded by friends and family and those who would take care of me no matter what happened.

And knowing, too, that if I stopped they would say, "You gave it your best, George." Knowing that whatever I did, I would not disappoint them. There would always be a meal and a soft bed and a good day of running tomorrow.

Only the child still lives in a world where such days are possible.

The year my daughter entered college in Boston, she came to see me in the marathon. She was, she told me later, the only calm and rational person among those thousands that jammed Prudential Center.

They cheered and yelled and applauded every finisher. They cheered the young, cheered the old, cheered those from Harvard, cheered those from California. And they cheered even more wildly when someone they knew came into sight. Through it all, she stood as quiet and as staid and withdrawn as an Episcopalian at a revival meeting.

Then I arrived. I made my turn into that long wide plaza, which at that moment was completely empty except for me and the cheering group. The finish line was still an eighth of a mile away, but it didn't matter. The race was over. The crowd's cheers told me that. I had made it. And this was my victory lap. Almost an hour behind the winner, having nailed down 312th place, I was suddenly renewed and refreshed. I was running my home run home, and every stride I took revealed my joy.

Then I saw a figure break out of the crowd into the white expanse that lay between me and the officials at the finish. It wasn't until another fifty yards that I recognized who this yelling, waving, cheering person was. My daughter.

The finish of any marathon can be that kind of emotional experience. Somewhere along the way the runner has been challenged. He has met pain fairly and overcome it. He has had a real deliverance. And at the end of that ordeal, both runner and spectator are aware that something very special has happened.

Sometimes this awareness is expressed in ways that neither runner nor spectator will ever forget. For me that occurred in Boston. For a friend of mine the setting was the Scottish Games at Grandfather Mountain. The marathon there is one of the most difficult in this country. Its 26.2 miles through mountainous country test a runner as almost no other race does.

My friend survived that test and ultimately conquered the course. And when he came to the last climb where the finish was supposed to be, he heard the sound of bagpipes. Now, as everyone knows, the skirling of bagpipes stirs passions and emotions inaccessible in other ways. So my friend, already overcome by reaching the end of this ordeal, was in tears when he breasted the hill.

And now he saw he was on a great plain encircled by the camps of the various Scottish clans. And each sent up a great shout as he passed them.

What place he took, he sometimes forgets. But he will never forget when time stood still on that plain atop Grandfather Mountain and all around him were happy cheering people and the sound of bagpipes.

All this has, of course, nothing to do with winning and losing. Winning and losing is what you do in team games. The runner is not in a game; he is in a contest. And that is a word whose Latin root means to witness or testify. The other runners are wit-

nesses to what he is doing. And therefore, anything else than all
he can give is not enough. When you race, you are under oath.
When you race, you are testifying as to who you are.

The distance runner understands this. He is the mildest of
men. Quiet and even-tempered and rarely given to argument. He
avoids confrontation and seeks his own private world, but in a
marathon he becomes a tiger. He will go to the end of his physiology to find who he is and what he can do. Put himself deeper
and deeper into a cauldron of pain. What is necessary becomes
possible, however absurd the effort may be.

But such interrogations, if they are to mean anything, should
be infrequent. If the marathon is to measure a man, it should
synchronize with the cycles of his growth. Maturity is an uneven, discouraging process. Becoming who you are is not done
on schedule. There are years when nothing seems to happen.

But one must still say that marathons can make memories like
no other event in your life. And that could be an argument for
running one every month. When rocking-chair time comes,
you'll be all set.

Somewhere east of Wellesley, past the church tower at the
halfway point, the Boston Marathon ceases to be a race and
becomes an experience. Forgotten now is the camaraderie of the
gym; the banter at the starting line; the ease of the 7:30 pace
through Framingham and Natick. All that was preparation for
the encounter the runner will have with himself and his world as
he heads for the Newtown Hills.

Those hills and the miles beyond will challenge everything he
holds dear, his value system, his life style. They will ask nothing
less than his view of the universe.

Yet he moves toward this meeting unhurried, relaxed, in complete tune with his body rhythms. He is rediscovering that precious reward of countless hours of training—those moments
when he and the running are one. He becomes the running as
the golfer becomes the swing. To reach this mystical place, time

must be ignored. He must act as Zorba said he always did: "As though I were immortal."

Past Wellesley, then, the runner moves toward the action he is performing, gradually becoming more and more the action until he is the running. And then he reaches even further into these mysterious areas. Like the swimmer who becomes one with his world of water and sky, the runner finds a total relationship with earth and air and wind and rain.

These events are difficult to describe. "Truth and fact," wrote William James, "well up in our lives in ways that exceed verbal formulation."

And almost always this truth occurs in action. When the philosopher Herrigel went to study Zen, he was told to learn archery and use that as the way to wisdom. We learn through our muscles. We learn through the perfecting of our bodies, and stretching them to the utmost. "There are thresholds which thought alone can never permit us to cross," wrote Gabriel Marcel. "An experience is needed."

The Boston is just such an experience. The runner passing Boston College and seeing the last six miles flat before him has reached an understanding he could not gain through his brain alone.

The runner who started in Hopkinton competitive and independent now nears the finish with a sense of dependence and community that is almost overwhelming.

One runner spoke of this feeling between the runners and the spectators as a family. "I know now," he wrote in a letter to the *Boston Globe*, "that the Boston is more than a race, and more than a club. It is a family and I'm proud to be part of it."

The runner is coming to know, or will know if he runs enough Bostons, that it is more than a family. He knows, or will know, that the universe is the smallest divisible unit. And he will know that Assisi is right, that Christian ethic is livable. It has failed because we have regarded our neighbor as Other. As separate. But no one is separate going down Commonwealth Avenue.

The runner has gone beyond the golfer and his swing, beyond the swimmer and his world. The runner has joined common humanity, the seas of anonymity moving toward Pru Center. He has reached the consciousness the Buddhists call Metta, the absolute identification with another suffering human being. He sees a weary, tiring runner and addresses him, if only mentally, "Oh, myself."

Fantasy? Perhaps. Sentimental nonsense? Maybe. But before you write it off completely, read Joyce Carol Oates's wonderfully optimistic essay "New Heaven and Earth."

"Instead of hiding our most amazing, mysterious and inexplicable experiences," she writes, "we must learn to articulate and share them."

Even more to the point is her suggestion that we are coming to a transformation of America. "Our minds," she writes (echoing the early Church Fathers' "The multitude of the faithful have only one heart and one soul"), "belong to a collective mind and the old boundary of the skin is no boundary at all but a membrane connecting the inner and outer experiences of our existence."

The runner relaxing in a shower at Pru Center senses he has united these two existences (his own and the world's). He has a new and radically altered relationship with other people, the earth, the universe.

That's the sort of thing that can happen almost any Patriots' Day somewhere east of Wellesley on the way to Boston.

They gave me the business at Mort's Corner the next morning. "Why don't you write about the human-interest stories in the Boston Marathon," someone asked, "instead of a column that no one will understand, including yourself?"

It was a good question, but it held its own answer. Because there are two Boston Marathons. One is the outer event. The Boston of the sports writers. The World Series of distance runners, attracting athletes and characters from all over the world.

The Patriots' Day event filled with funny and odd and touching happenings all the way from Hopkinton to Boston.

The other Boston is an inner event. It concerns itself with what these thousands of runners are looking for. The search, whether they know it or not, for one's "true gravity." And that is already, as they say at Mort's, something no one understands, including myself.

The first I had learned of "true gravity" was in a remarkable book I had read before leaving for Boston, *Golf in the Kingdom,* by Michael Murphy. Shivas Irons, the golf professional who takes Murphy on this extraordinary golf round, is a disciple of Pythagoras and says we must know the world from the inside; that we can come to know the deeper structure of the universe only through our own body and senses and living experience.

With a shillelagh and some primitive golf balls Irons teaches Murphy to find his "inner body." To forget his images of disaster, the hook, the ever present rough, the familiar curses and excuses. So that, in Murphy's words, he "played the remaining holes in this state of grace," and, as he put it, "those final holes played me."

Somewhere past Wellesley, the halfway point, I suddenly found that Murphy had written something that had an equal application to running and especially to marathons.

This marathon had begun no different from other Bostons. As usual, the weather was bad. The bright Hopkinton sun told of midday heat farther on. The course would run long and slow today. Nine Bostons had made me a realist. And a realist in a hot Boston will wear light clothes, and a handkerchief to shield his scalp from the sun. He will drink everything handed to him and pour what's left on his head. He will run well within himself for seventeen miles, take the hills as best he can and let it all hang out in Boston.

That's the way it went. I started near the leaders (one year I stayed at the back and it took me over a minute to get to the starting line after the gun went off). And at least eight hundred passed me in the first ten miles. My pace, however, was just right for me and I had survived an anxious moment in Natick at the first Gatorade station, which was empty when I got there. For a hundred yards the street was filled with discarded-Gatorade cartons. I noticed an upright one and picked it up. It had some Gatorade left. So, stopping here and there and now and then, I left Natick almost fully revived.

By Wellesley I knew it was going to be a good one. Not in time, perhaps. The three-hour marathon would have to wait another year. But it would be good for this heat.

And then it happened. After nine agonizing Bostons, nine Patriots' Days of worrying about pace and time and even finishing, I finally found, if only for a few miles, what running was all about.

Now, people will tell you why they run. And the reasons will change from day to day, because it is like peeling an onion. They get down to deeper and deeper reasons but always failing to reach the essence of the running experience.

But now, heading out of Wellesley toward Lower Newton Falls and the beer drinkers at Mary's Bar, I suddenly found what must be the essence of running. I was thinking then of Murphy's golf game. I would, I said to myself, just concentrate on finding the perfect running form. I would find the pace at which I could run forever. Then let my inner body take over.

I ran then oblivious of the other runners. Only half hearing a nine-year-old philosopher sitting on the curb who shouted, "Smile and it won't hurt as much." Still looking, of course, for every orange slice, every cup of water. Still touching the children's outstretched hands. But in a world of my own where my running became me. I have on occasions in practice been lost in thought, oblivious of my surroundings but oblivious, too, of the running, so that I could not recall how I got to where I was. But this was entirely different. I was entirely occupied with this magic thing I was doing. I was one with what I was doing.

Past Boston College and through Brookline I went, full of run-

ning. The course, as Murphy had said, was now running me.
Three blocks to go and the crowds were building up to the ten
thousand waiting at the Pru Center. Two blocks to go and there
were my daughter and her college classmates giving me a reception even Ted Williams would have acknowledged.

It was too much. The day. The run. And now this. Suddenly I
had the handkerchief off my head and I was twirling it in the air.
I ran laughing past those girls toward the finish line, still twirling
the handkerchief like Zorba the Greek telling those wonderful
affectionate Bostonians that in some way I had found what running and the Boston Marathon were all about.

Mort, I'll have the coffee black and no chatter.

16. Meditating

In this ease of movement, this harmony, this
rhythmic breathing of life into life, I am able to
let my mind wander. I absent myself from road
and wind and the warm sun. I am free to
meditate, to measure the importance of things.

"SINCE PAIN AND BOREDOM are the chief enemies of human happiness," wrote Schopenhauer, "Nature has provided a protection against both. We can ward off pain by cheerfulness; and boredom by intelligence."

Unfortunately most of us are equipped to handle one but not the other. The cheerful people are those who need people. They need people to love or be friends with or to help or master or rule. For them life without other people would be pure boredom, the ultimate torture. Solitary confinement, the supreme punishment. A monk's cell, a slice of hell. They look on loneliness as a disease and find "unoccupied leisure," Schopenhauer said, "altogether unendurable."

Others, like myself, see things the opposite way. We are rarely if ever bored but feel pain at ranges imperceptible to most people. I feel pain as a dog hears sound. I am an early-warning system for discomfort, a mass of nerve endings, a being dominated by my nervous system. And this intolerance is not only to physical pain but to psychic pain as well. The real pain in everyday life.

On the other hand, I like being alone. I enjoy my own company. I am satisfied running the roads far from any other human being. For me loneliness is the desirable state. Solitary confinement, a touch of heaven. I am never bored. People and the pain they cause are what I cannot stand. The pain of relationships made and broken. The pain of leaving. The pain of being left.

I am built to be alone. I am an intellectual, which I suppose is what Schopenhauer meant when he wrote "intelligence." But being an intellectual has really nothing to do with intelligence, it simply describes the way I think. My mind works through association rather than logic or reason. When I run those miles over the roads there is all the while a stream of consciousness, a torrent of ideas, coursing through my brain. One idea after another goes hurtling past like so much white water. Giving me here and there a new insight, a new intuition, a new understanding. Each in turn soon replaced by yet another thought, still another idea.

At those times I can believe Erich Segal's story of wanting to dash up to a house and ask for a pen and paper to write a thought down. For he knew as surely as I that the thought, however clear, would soon be forgotten. And since there is no logical progression, no amount of reasoning would bring it back.

By that rushing stream I come alive. The world's thinkers have known this and blessed this solitary state. The yardstick of a human being, said Kierkegaard, is his ability to bear being alone. You can find similar passages in Emerson, Nietszche, Schopenhauer and many others. But for myself it is sufficient to justify myself, not to put anyone else down. Either everyone is normal or no one is. The people who need people, and the people who don't need people. Where I do well, some do badly, but the opposite is also true.

The intellectual does badly as a lover and almost as poorly as a friend. It is the payment I must make for a life free of boredom. The price I must meet for my precious stream of consciousness, my river of ideas, and the growth that goes with it.

Love, you see, dams this torrent, obstructs this flow. Love is, among other things, abnormal attention. It is attention to one person, one idea, and I cannot have that. "What happens to a person in love," said Ortega, "is to isolate on one object and remain on it alone, fixed and paralyzed like a rooster before a hypnotic white line." It was therefore, to that Spanish intellectual, "an inferior state of mind and a form of transitory imbecility."

Nor am I better with friendship. For one thing, anyone who would accept me is suspect. Of any friend I feel like Santayana when told that William James had a high regard for him. "If he knew me better," he said, "he would like me less." With me it works both ways. As soon as I reach friends' limits I am gone. As soon as they no longer contribute to my growth I must leave.

Emerson was on to this. "A man's growth," he said, "is seen in the successive choirs of his friends." Jung made much the same observation. He was saddened, he said, by the friends he had to abandon, but there was nothing else to be done. When they no longer were in his orbit they had to be left behind. "As soon as I had seen through them," he said, "the magic was gone." An odd way to live, you might say. And truly it is. Never boring, to be sure, but frequently depressing and filled with pain and an aching emptiness. And there are times when that rush of white water bubbling through my brain doesn't seem worth the people it costs me.

Perhaps Jung felt the same. "I need people to a higher degree than others," he said, "and at the same time much less."

Let me take that idea and run on it.

You come, too.

The distance runner, I have said, does badly as a lover and almost as poorly as a friend. It is the price I must pay for my stream of consciousness, my river of ideas. It is my payment for the growth that goes on in my brain, for the knowledge I have yet to attain. I cannot attend to anything that would obstruct that flow or keep me from those goals.

On the road I become a philosopher and follow the philosophers' tradition. I affirm my own existence and no one else's. I am occupied with my own inner life. I am constructing a system which will justify my own way of being in the world. And discovering, as Emerson said, that there are thoughts in my brain which have no other watchman or lover or defender than me.

So I have no time or attention or energy to throw away on anything else, be it person or cause or country. I have no time for love; nor do I have time for hate. Hate, you see, takes the same attention and time as love, and even more energy. When you hate, energy flows out of you toward the hated person, the hated cause, the hated country. Nothing burns one up faster than hate and anger and revenge. There is no quicker way to be drained of emotion and energy.

And hate no less than love stops my stream of consciousness. It prevents my exploration of myself, my passage through my inner world. It takes time of which I have so little, and none to waste. There is no deadline more insistent than the riddle of life.

So hate is something I do as little as possible and never with relish. I will not be forced into that state. Cross me and I will put you out of my mind. Injure me and I will drop you out of consciousness. Vex me and you will no longer exist. Insult me and I will not respond.

You might see this failure to react as making me a pacifist. To an extent you might be right. I am ready to flee at the slightest indication of violence. Under no circumstances will I fight, and I seldom argue. Like Galileo I say to myself, "It is so nevertheless, whether I say it or not."

But I am no pacifist. Pacifism is just another cause. Another object that requires attention and time and investment of myself. What I am is neutral. I reserve the right never to take sides. I continue to deny, to doubt, to analyze, to suspend judgment. In me you see the epitome of the neutral, the outsider, the uninvolved. I am not interested in either sin or the sinner, unless it is my sin and I am the sinner.

When I run I am a neutral. My road is a neutral zone. It is an area no one violates. A territory everyone respects. No one bothers me. No one asks me for an opinion, or a contribution. No one wants me to sign a petition or stand up and be counted. No one asks for love, or deserves hate.

During fifteen years and thousands of hours on the road I cannot recall being angry for any length of time. Or indeed spending any of those miles thinking of revenge or experiencing envy or jealousy, or whatever might alienate me from other humans. On the other hand, neither can I remember many times I have thought of other people except for their ideas.

My involvement, like it or not, is all with myself.

I devote all my care and endurance and intensity to my own thoughts and imagination and self-analysis. My temptation is delight in thought itself, in the intricate dance of my mind. The pleasure in the process that might stop me from reaching the End. My danger is not that I will fail my fellows (I have already done that); or in making the world work (which doesn't interest me.) My danger is that I will fail to reach my limits and find God.

But here my body helps. Running is an awareness and a perfection that I find unrivaled. Nothing else, mental or physical or spiritual, do I do as well. And it is that feeling of being totally whole and satisfied in my body that keeps me dissatisfied with what I think. I cannot accept less from my mind than the perfection that I experience in my body.

And since that perfection is not to be gained this side of the divide, I keep running and seeking the truth which lies beyond love and hate. And I accept the paradox philosophers know only too well: My unity will be found in division from my lovers and friends.

The first half hour of my run is for my body. The last half hour, for my soul. In the beginning the road is a miracle of solitude and escape. In the end it is a miracle of discovery and joy.

Throughout, it brings an understanding of what Blake meant when he said, "Energy is eternal delight."

I always start in optimism. For one hour I feel capable of being a hermit, an anchorite. On the road I can seek my own desert, my own mountain, my own little cell. I am alone and away from the world, in an area, a pace and a silence that allow me to be myself. More than an hour might be too much. Few of us, and certainly not I, have the self-discipline and control to fill the hermit's day—with prayer and reading and meditation.

But for that hour I am a solitary. And I begin with that same discipline and control, now needed for the strong, steady pace against the headwind and the hills along the river road. In that first half hour I become my body. My body is me and I am my body. And I know that only in its fullness will I be all that I will be. I delight in my energy, my strength, my power as I pass by the freshly greening fields. In a world coming alive with the energy in spring, I feel myself come alive, come back from being split and splintered, and becoming whole. I am a total and perfect runner.

And in this perfection, this ease of movement, this harmony, this rhythmic breathing of life into life, I am able to let my mind wander. I absent myself from road and wind and the warm sun. I am free to meditate, to measure the importance of things. I am purified by the effort that has gone before, drained of pride, filled with childlike grace and innocence; the energy of my body becomes an energy of the mind. An energy that becomes delight, however, only to the degree I understand what Bernanos warned about: the impotency of power, the ignorance of learning, the idiocy of machination, the frivolity of being serious.

But those are the insights of a free mind. Thomas Merton, another solitary, understood that. The beginning of freedom, he wrote, is not liberation from the body but liberation from the mind. We are not entangled in our own body, we are entangled in our mind.

I am now turned from home. I am going downwind and in

those miles I become unentangled. I move out of thickets that have constrained me. Out of underbrush that has reduced me to futile plans and more futile action.

I move beyond ambition and envy, beyond pleasure and diversion. In those miles downwind, I have a new vision of myself and the universe. The running is easy, automatic, yet full of power, strength, precision. A tremendous energy pours through my body. I am whole and holy. And the universe is whole and holy and full of meaning. In the passion of this running, truth is being carried, as the poet says, alive into my heart.

So in those final miles meditation becomes contemplation. What has been a measuring of things becomes an awareness of the sacred. The road now becomes sacred ground, the temple the word contains. There are cars and traffic, noise and exhaust, but I am past sight and sound, past this disturbance. I know or, better, I experience the whole of what Blake said.

Man has no body distinct from the soul. Energy is the only life and is from the body; and reason is the outward circumference of energy. And energy is indeed eternal delight.

So as my run ends I am back in my body. The energy I felt at the beginning of the run gradually filling my mind and soul, gradually creating a unity, a wholeness, a peak feeling of being one with myself and the universe. What they call "in zen," satori. And if at that moment I still don't know the answers to the last dramatic questions of my existence and yours and the existence of the universe, at the very least I know now these answers do exist.

And tomorrow I will be out on the roads seeking them once more.

Today I took Truth and ran with it on the ocean road. I do that every day. For one hour, it is yesterday, today and tomorrow. At eight minutes a mile, I am, I was, I will be. On the ocean road, I experience what I cannot know. Because for me and you and the common man, revealed Truth must be experienced. Only the giants can come to know through reason what Moses brought down from Sinai. The rest of us must learn with our bodies.

So we begin in fear, which is the beginning of wisdom, and seek understanding. And our bodies, our senses, teach us that law is how a thing works. That the Ten Commandments describe how the universe works. And we discover that the closer we become to just being, the closer we come to understanding "I am who I am."

This is probably not true about everyone, but the runner would agree. He possesses himself in solitude and silence and suffering. He is gradually stripped of desires and attachment to things. As I run, I get closer and closer to requiring nothing more than life supports, air and water and the use of the planet. I surrender to something greater than my will. My design? His will?

Such moments do not come easily or for the asking. Running is a serious thing and must be taken seriously. I will not find truth in something I use to avoid it. I will not find it, either, in something I do as a means and not an end. To use running to become fit or lose weight or calm my nerves would lead not to truth but to heresy.

So I take that hour and run as if my life depended on it. I run into being and becoming and having been. Into feeling and seeing and hearing. Into all those senses by which I know the world that God made, and me in it. Into understanding why a Being whose reason to exist is "to be" should have made me to His image.

Am I operating at too low a level this too physical body? I can only answer that is the way I know. And whatever happens, revealed Truth must be experienced Truth. If not through intelligence or some special ability to alter consciousness, then through hard work and effort, however mediocre. Through desire and determination and qualities accessible to every man.

The body does all this. The body which is the stumbling block to the philosophers. The body they have separated and discarded. That body brings the messages.

It lets us see that the New Testament, which changed the law to love and made the Word flesh, is a hymn to the body. The blind see, the lame walk, the deaf hear, the dumb speak. People are hungry and thirsty and indulge in sex. There is color and sound and wind and water. There are tempests and droughts. And a climax of pain and suffering and torture and death.

This is something the runner in me understands. I start with the guilt and doubt and despair that possess most of us. But I am soon exploring the limits of my body, of my sensory powers. I run in complete touch with myself. I can tell you the wind speed, the temperature, the humidity and whether I'm on a grade and how steep it is. I take the universe around me and wrap myself in it and become one with it, moving at a pace which makes me part of it.

And then I add the sound of wind and the changing pitch of my footstrikes as I go from surface to surface. And I take in the sight of light and shadows and the road itself, the road that Bernanos called a miracle of solitude and escape. "The man who has not seen the road in the early light of morning, cool and living between two rows of trees," he wrote, "does not know the meaning of hope." But then Bernanos was one who believed that man must possess himself in solitude and silence before he is of any use to society.

The runner need not break four minutes in the mile or four hours in the marathon. It is only necessary that he runs and runs and sometimes suffers. Then one day he will wake up and discover that somewhere along the way he has begun to see order and law and love and Truth that makes men free.

It could happen to you or me on the ocean road.

"Do you believe in personal immortality?" a Unitarian friend asked me at lunch the other day. Not an everyday subject, but if you have Unitarian friends (being nonjudgmental, they are the best kind) you become accustomed to such questions. Even at lunch. Unitarians, it appears, are ready to discuss the Eternal Verities any time, day or night. In fact, my friend assures me, they would rather go to a discussion about heaven than to the actual place.

This time I was ready for the hard question. Just the previous day personal immortality had changed for me from a childhood belief and an undergraduate theory to actual fact. It had become a reality. On my afternoon run I had suddenly overreached the confines of time and space. I had become the perfect runner moving easily and surely and effortlessly toward infinity. My ten years of almost daily running had brought me to an area of consciousness, a level of being, that I never knew existed.

For the runner, running has always been a form of contemplation and meditation; an activity with the saving grace, as Santayana said, of football, of purging, rinsing and exhausting the inner man; a time when the movements of his body in concert with his mind and heart gave him an appreciation of what was good and true and beautiful. But it is now evident it can do even more.

Running that day became for me, as I'm sure it has for others, a mystical experience. A proof of the existence of God. Something happened and then, in the words of a recent letter writer to *Harper's,* "One simply knows, and believes, and can never forget."

There is no way of documenting this. Such states are difficult to describe and impossible to analyze. Conversely, there is no use denying them. "Mystics," wrote William James, "have been there and know." The mystic, James declared, is invulnerable.

He is also, for the most part, unchallenged. Although we may not have been there ourselves, we suspect what he says is true. We simply do not know how to make it true for ourselves.

That way now seems open. Where once it was so that not more than a thimbleful of meditation was going on in America, we are now becoming a nation of meditators. And in our new-found leisure we are discovering the salvation and liberation that exist in play. For it is sport that is finally giving the common man a true picture of himself. Freeing him from authority and allowing him to find and fulfill his own design. For the runners this meant the realization that solitude is the staff of life and not a mark of failure. That, for him at least, community is a myth. He became able to pursue his asocial ways. To change his life to accommodate to his inner reality.

(When a psychiatrist-marathoner friend asked me recently, "What was it like before we started running?" I could not remember. If there had been a life before running, it was imperfect and unfulfilled.)

Play is truly the answer. "There are many routes," wrote poet Jonathan Price, "in fact, any way the serious world calls play." So it is running for those who are runners. Other forms for other people.

What route you take depends on yourself. I cannot bring visions of immortality to a nonrunner by dragging him along on my afternoon runs. What you do must absorb you utterly and intensely; and to do that it must be your game, your sport, your play. "How we play," writes George Leonard, "signifies nothing less than our way of being in the world."

For the dancer, the dance brings this feeling for life, this intimation of immortality. ("When a jump works," says Jacques d'Amboise, "it feels like forever. I'm riding on top of time.") Others get the same sort of experience from skiing, surfing, karate, golf, football or what have you.

How long it will take is another story. One must go through discipline to get to freedom. Be assured it does not occur to beginners. Only when how you do a thing surpasses the thing you are doing can you break through the barriers to these levels of consciousness, your own inner depths.

But then when they ask you the real question that is bothering everyone in this age, "Is this all there is?" you can answer, "You've got to be kidding."

17. Growing

I am in that first Paradise, the Paradise given.
The danger is that I will be content to stay
there. That I will never reach for the Paradise
that must be won or lost.

RUNNING IS a dangerous game. At one pole the danger is contentment. Running becomes so addictive physically, so habit-forming psychologically, that it takes willpower for me not to run. And it has a solitude so satisfying that I sometimes wonder if the hermit isn't the supreme hedonist.

So there is this absolute contentment. This willingness to absent myself from everything else. To see little else as worth the effort. When I run I take the risk of that contentment. Of becoming what Updike described as the contented man, "an animal with clothes on."

Running can do that. When I run I am completely content. I cease growing. I live just for those moments on the road. After all, what else do I do as well? Where else do I feel as invulnerable? How else can I know such peace?

So I know this contentment all too well. The road becomes my place to hide. There I withdraw from the world. I retreat into a universe bounded by my line of sight, the sound of my footsteps, the feelings of heat and cold, of sun and rain and wind. I narrow the cosmos to this hour, this road, this running. Naught else occupies me. I am content.

This is one pole. If I am not Updike's animal, I am a child in running gear. I am in that first Paradise, the Paradise given. The danger is that I will be content to stay there. That I will never reach for the Paradise that must be won or lost. The danger is that I will never move on, never grow up.

But that movement, that growing up, is even more dangerous, perhaps the most dangerous thing a human being can do. And that is precisely what happens when running becomes a meditation. When I become a thinker and leave the freedom of childhood; and, in my hour on the road, begin the lifelong journey whose goal is self-knowledge.

When a person thinks, he inevitably separates himself from prevailing opinion. And, by hidden and secret ways, will eventually end, according to Ortega, in some secluded spot filled with unaccustomed thoughts. Thinking will put his stable universe in peril. He will be alone with no one else to help him.

I know this to be true. When I run and meditate, I forsake the shelter I had in the pure simplicity of running. I abandon the certainties built into my everyday life. I leave in my wake my ancestors, my traditions, my church, my society, my family, my friends, everyone and everything I hold important to me. I jettison everything I have not made authentic by my own experience. Everything, as Thoreau said, I have not learned by direct intercourse and sympathy. I put all this at stake in that seemingly playful carefree hour on the river road.

It is a gamble I must take. No one can substitute for me in deciding for myself, in deciding on my life. No one can think for me. Nor needs to. Of the common man, Emerson said: "What Plato has thought, he may think; what the saint has felt, he may feel; what has befallen any man, he may understand."

This is my ball game to win or lose. And what I must deal with is not luck or chance, but choice. It is choice that is omnipresent in life, not chance. What I can see and feel and almost taste is choice. Choosing my self, my values, my universe. Choosing my own drama, my own life, my own heroism. Seeking through imagination and reason and intuition that unique something that I, and no other, am here to do.

No one ever said it was easy or safe. We have no contract with life. But neither are we here simply to avoid pain and enjoy pleasure. At some time or other, I must leave my childlike existence. However reluctantly, I must chance it and risk the contentment; knowing that to be reborn I must first be ejected from Paradise.

And knowing also that I may never come back. That I may wander forever in search of a self I will never find. Yet never being able to return to the easy theologies, the painless salvations I left behind.

I want no other choice. In this game, the only sure way to lose is to sit it out.

I am a lonely figure when I run the roads. People wonder how far I have come, how far I have to go. They see me alone and friendless on a journey that has no visible beginning or end. I appear isolated and vulnerable, a homeless creature. It is all they can do to keep from stopping the car and asking if they can take me wherever I'm going.

I know this because I feel it myself. When I see a runner, I have much the same thoughts. No matter how often I run the roads myself, I am struck by how solitary my fellow runner appears. The sight of a runner at dusk or in inclement weather makes me glad to be safe and warm in my car and headed for home. And at those times, I wonder how I can go out there myself, how I can leave comfort and warmth and that feeling of intimacy and belonging to do this distracted thing.

But when finally I am there, I realize it is not comfort and warmth I am leaving, not intimacy and belonging I am giving up, but the loneliness that pursues me this day and every day. I know that the real loneliness, the real isolation, the real vulnerability, begins long before I put on my running shoes.

The real loneliness begins with my failures as son, husband, father, physician, lover, friend. The real loneliness begins when those other gods have failed, the loved ones, the career, the triumphs, the victories, the good life.

The heartbreaking loneliness begins when I realize that no one can think for me; no one can live for me; no one can die for me. I can count on no one for help.

The true loneliness, then, is me seeing that nothing I do is true. Me and this inner emptiness, me and the abyss, me and the false me I am with other people, me being what I do, what I accomplish, the clever things I say. Me and that living of a lie, a long, lonely lifetime lie.

When I'm about overwhelmed by all this, I take this loneliness out on the roads, there to find my true self, to hear my own message, to decide for myself on my life. But most of all, to know certainty, to know that there is an answer even though I may never find it.

All this is not new. Hell may be other people, but the final enemy is within. "Will I always torment like this?" wrote Gide. "I worry from morning to night. I worry about not knowing who I will be: I do not even know who I want to be."

And then hear R. D. Laing, the psychiatrist: "Whoever I am is not to be confused with the names people give me or what they call me. I am not my name. I am a territory. What they say about me is a map of me. Where O! Where is my territory?"

When you see me, that lonely figure out on the road, I am looking for my territory, my self, the person I must be. There I am no longer the observer watching myself think and talk and react. I am not the person others see and meet and even love. There I am whole; I am finally who I am.

And there I encounter myself. That encounter is a deep place totally isolated which cannot be understood or touched by others, a place that cannot be described as much as experienced, a state that philosophers could define as solitude. It is no longer me and the abyss; it is me and my God.

But of course this is only the outline, the game plan. In actuality, it is not that easy. Like all pilgrimages, this one is filled with stops and starts, with peaks and valleys, with pains and pleasures. There are periods of depression and elation, times when I overflow with joy at this conjunction of action and contemplation. Other times when I am so tired I must stop and walk. But in that hour I know certainty. I know there is an answer to my odd union of animal and angel, my mysterious mixture of body and consciousness, my perplexing amalgam of material and spirit. And if for now that answer is only for the moment and only for me in my lowest common denominator, me the runner, it is still enough.

By abandoning myself to this, as Emerson said, by unlocking my human doors, I am caught up in the life of the universe. Then, finally, loneliness is dispelled. I know I am holy, made for the greater glory of my Creator, born to do His work.

Which for this day and this hour is running, a lonely figure on a lonely road.

When I became a runner, it seemed a small step to go from a sound body to a sound mind. Altogether natural that muscular strength be converted into virtue. That the ability to handle pain and fatigue would allow me to come to grips with guilt and anxiety. It seemed inevitable that the well-working body would become the well-working of the mind and the heart. And somehow necessary that the maximal steady physiological state should have its quickly attained psychological counterpart. Physical fitness, I thought, would give me back not only my body but my soul as well.

It never happened. As I became sound of wind and limb, as I neared my physical perfection, I became more and more aware of my mental imperfections. I was not normal, healthy and happy. I was, on the contrary, confused, angry, ambivalent, blaming others, denying responsibility. As my pulse slowed and my heart became more efficient, I knew my character to be a lie and my life style a shield from my own reality.

As my endurance increased and my performance improved, my day-to-day living became an ordeal of guilt and anxiety. Instead of life becoming routine and automatic and secure, I found myself unable to cope and adjust, and know now I never will. The normal life, I discovered, is for others, not me.

Meanwhile, my body went blithely on its way. I still run close to five minutes for the mile. At other distances, I am usually within a minute a mile of the winners. I sleep well and can eat anything this side of a bathtub stopper. My bowels are regular and I rarely have a headache or a muscle pain. My energy level is high enough to do anything I like to do for as long as I like to do it. My body is at the top of its powers. It is tuned to an exquisite clarity and has a wide range of perception.

But all this does nothing for my mental health. In fact, it probably helps destroy it. Mental health disappears when we see ourselves as we are. And my level of fitness has made me see myself as I am, warts and all. The intensity of my physical life tells me all the old sayings are true.

Sin *is* the failure to reach your potential. The answer to life *is* more life. You must seek the limits of the possible and then go beyond. Guilt *is* the unlived life. When I became fit and lean and uncompromising in my running, I saw myself as I really was without disguise or defense. I could no longer accept the person I had pretended to be. And I was unprepared to deal with the person I really was.

All of which means there are interesting years ahead.

There is at least one thing to be said for being a neurotic and living with guilt and anxiety: it is never boring. It may, in fact, be exasperating, especially for those around me who had to put up with my irrational discontent. The search for self-esteem, for the heroic action, by anyone as disorganized and transfixed by choice as I am, can occasionally push friends and family to verbal abuse. But there is no epithet I haven't already used on myself.

Still I know, and they should, that I will eventually find in real life the unity I feel during my hour's run on the roads. There I am in the palm of God's hand, running with my angel. And at those times I know what Yeats meant when he wrote: ". . . my body of a sudden blazed/And twenty minutes more or less/It seemed, so great my happiness/That I was blessed, and could bless . . ."

And then in the race I go through the penance of a three-mile run, accepting the painful grip of lactic acid and knowing what going without oxygen does. And at the end is the absolution, free from fear, free from anxiety. The marathon is much the same. A purgatory of mile on mile and then at the finish the peace beyond understanding. A time when even death becomes acceptable.

Those hours, those races, sustain me. The rest of the day, I am caught in my own inadequacy. So it seems that being sound of body does not automatically make you sound of mind. It may even delay the process. But in the end, it is vital to the synthesis of body and mind and spirit that makes the whole person.

Until then, I am like Nijinsky. I am kept alive by movement. When I am immobile, I risk all that I am. Even my sanity.

My friend Tom Osler, who is a fifty-miler and teaches math at a state college, says that depressions are a part of life. The runner, he says, must expect them; even welcome them. They are just as normal, just as inevitable and just as necessary as the happy times.

And now in the depths of my semiannual, or is it quarterly, depression, I am inclined to agree. Periodically, no matter how I try to avoid it, I run myself into this growing inner discontent. Every six months or so, I develop this feeling that every task is too difficult to do and not worth the effort anyway.

My running suffers most. In fact, it is the first indication that things are amiss. I no longer look forward to my daily run. And should I ignore this lack of zest and run anyway, I tire easily and don't enjoy it. But the running and this loss of enjoyment are only part of it. My emotions, my moods, my concentration, my attention span, my attitude toward myself and others are all affected. Instead of battling anoxia and lactic acid and muscles depleted of sugar, I am in hand-to-hand combat with dejection and dependency, with rejection and self-pity, with guilt and loneliness. I am truly in the dark night of the soul.

In the real night, I awaken repeatedly for no apparent reason. And in the morning I am not refreshed or ready for the new day. I would like to pull the covers over my head and wait for this terrible state to pass over.

Is all this something inevitable, as Osler states? Or is it simply because I have run myself into some temporary physical state? And could I not, with a little prudence, avoid all these unnecessary sufferings?

I think not. Such periods are inescapable. Ecclesiastes was right. There is a time for everything. A time for running. A time not to run. Human nature frowns on prudence. It demands that we maximize ourselves. That whatever we do, we do it with all our might. And, predictably, this means periodic exhaustion, periodic failure, periodic depression and, as happily, periodic reevaluation.

I am now in those days of Ecclesiastes. "The fine hammered steel of woe," Melville called this book. I believe it. Now words cannot describe the weariness of things, and days give me no pleasure. And now it does seem as it did to him that "all effort and achievement come from man's envy of man."

The peculiarity, as Ecclesiastes noted, is that these depressions occur not when things are going badly, but when they are going well. Not in times of failure, but in times of triumph. These depressions are not preceded by tragedy, but by celebration. Not by the worst race I have run, but by the best.

Less than two weeks ago, I ran a taxing and courageous and outlandishly fast ten-miler in Central Park. I ran to my limits, met the challenges of several runners who might normally have beaten me; and then ran the last five miles faster than the first, never giving an inch to those trying to catch me. It was an hour and four minutes and fifteen seconds of being as good a runner as I could be.

Later, as I sprawled on a chair in the parish hall of the Church of the Heavenly Rest, watching my fellow runners fill up on coffee and doughnuts, I felt warm and tired and satisfied. I turned to a friend next to me and said, "George, right now I could pull the sword out of the stone."

Today, if I said that, it would be presumptuous. I have lost what Yeats called "radical innocence." But I know there is and there always will be a time of running. A time when running is enough. When it is enough to race the same races, run the same roads. Enough to live out the cycle upon cycle of the running year. And thereby to fulfill myself in the many ways I do when running is the focal point of my life.

But there is also a time of not running. Time to see that the good can be the enemy of the best. That it is not merely the trivial that clutters up my life, but the important as well. I have, as Anne Lindbergh wrote, a surfeit of treasures. And it is time for me to answer the question of Ecclesiastes, "What is best for men to do during their few days of life under the sun?"

If it were not for the depression, I would have thought that unanswerable question answered. But now I know that running is not enough. The answer "Sheehan's my name, running's my game" is not enough. There are more ways to understand life, it now appears, than running.

Or business or politics or the arts or the sciences, for that matter. I am reminded that Bernard De Voto once said to Robert Frost, "You're a good poet, Robert, but you're a bad man."

Perhaps he was and perhaps he wasn't. To me, it seems that could be almost anyone's epitaph, including my own. And my periodic depressions make me realize that life may well be a game, but God judges the player, not the performance.

Not the race, but the runner.

The enemy, as always, is within.

It is Christmas morning. The day the Word was made Flesh. The birthday of the Incarnation. The day of Joy to the World, peace on earth, goodwill toward men. And I am running my river road, celebrating my flesh, rejoicing in my nativity, experiencing my incarnation. I am finding my peace in the rhythm of my thighs and lungs and pulse. Discovering my joy bounding over hills of virgin snow.

Elsewhere, people of goodwill are exchanging gifts, going to worship, preparing feasts. The day wears a halo of compassion and love. This is the day of the family of man. A day no one should be alone. A day that reveals your view of yourself and your universe and your fellow man.

I am alone and happy with myself and my view of the universe. I occupy my body with delight. And the universe is not only the message, it is my medium. My body is made to accept the message, to create in the medium. I am slim with good legs and a small trunk, a social introvert but a biological extrovert. I resemble Martha Graham's description of the new dancers.

"They are built," she said, "more for air, swiftness, than for argument." And through the dance they discover themselves.

I am discovering myself on this run. Beginning again at the beginning. Beginning with my body; the body that Coventry Patmore called "creation's and Creator's crowning good . . . So rich with wealth conceal'd that Heaven and Hell fight chiefly for this field."

I begin to sing myself and hope, like Whitman, not to cease till death. And hoping always to find what others have and I have not, a faith in love.

Love requires muscles I have never used. It is not easy to make feeling somehow transcend itself to emotion and then further to tenderness and sometimes love.

It is even more difficult if you lack the buoyant enthusiasm so common in most people or the courage obviously resident in others. My dominant quality is neither enthusiasm nor courage; it is the power of relinquishment, of withdrawal, of doing with less. I avoid risk, and making myself vulnerable. I am unwilling to stake anything on anyone else. I live in a fantasy world shut off from other people.

Yet where I am now is no fantasy. It is beautiful and real and a delight. The snow crunches underfoot. The pure light of the sun flashes off the white surface, the sky is high and blue. The air is dry and clean in my lungs. My senses are filled with these realities, with the sound of my breathing, the soft noise of my passage. I am living time and I am living space. The time and space Blake described, when a pulsation of an artery is equal to six thousand years and where a space no bigger than a globule of a man's blood opens into eternity.

But it is a time and a space into which I will admit no other. I am still alone, not daring to let my solitude join another solitude. Still not having the patience, the forgiveness and the acceptance that living with and loving other people demands.

So, for this distance runner at least, the holidays are too much. When socialization and celebration are at their height, I am most miserable. When, in addition, gifts and in them the secret knowledge of the Other are exchanged, it becomes too much. I am inclined to rise in defense of Scrooge. Leave us alone in our misery. Let us work out our own salvation.

This Christmas morning, I run far from family and friends, hoping to see my path to what they already have. All the while knowing a freedom I would exchange only for the whole truth. Feeling a delight that I would risk only if there was a promise of eternity. Living with a peace that perhaps no one else can share.

Like other solitary men who concentrate on thought and imagination and self-analysis, I am afraid to invest myself in anything less than perfection either in an idea or in a person. Like them, I have a great need for affection, but cannot give it. I am fearful of not being loved, but even more frightened of having to love.

When I think on that, the running is not enough. I am alone and lonely running the river road.

I am in debt to anyone who can make me cry. To anyone who makes me know joy. I owe for those moments when I see the world beyond this world. And know that I am not a biological animal or a social animal, but a theological animal. That the answer to my existence must somehow contain God.

I met such a person last week. Miss Emily Dickinson. Or rather Miss Julie Harris as Miss Emily Dickinson. And for an hour and a half was in her company. A short way into those ninety minutes, I had given up any pretext of composure. I had stopped holding back the tears. I sat with handkerchief in hand, keeping Miss Harris and her Emily from becoming a blur on my TV tube.

"I know it is poetry," Emily had said, "if I feel physically as if the top of my head were taken off." My ways may be different, but they are just as physical, just as uncontrollable. When I am in the presence of poetry and genius and the real world we came from, I know it. When I see clearly life is not a biological game or a social game or a political game, but a theological game, I know it, too. And know it with every blood vessel and nerve ending and muscle fiber in my body.

Emily played that theological game. Reduced the world to herself, her family, nature and God. The longest trip she took all day was from her bedroom door to the head of the stairs. Others have also taken that narrow focus. Rodin, for instance. He once told Rilke that he had read *The Imitation of Christ* and that in the third chapter wherever the text had the word "God" he had substituted "sculpture." It read just as well, he said.

So Emily took poetry and played her game with God. Emerson put it this way: "Take what you want, God said, and pay for it." But better would be to take what you want and play for it. The stakes? Your soul, yourself, your life. "I'll tell you what I paid," she wrote. "Precisely an existence."

And in the end she won, of course. She won the game with the "burglar, banker, father." She accepted Him and apologized with tongue in cheek "for Thine own Duplicity." She challenged, complained. Yet she knew that in heaven there would be a new equation. Somehow it would all be even.

But her answer here was to become as good at her game as God was. To approach His perfection by perfecting her imperfections. She knew all along that God is Himself a poet.

The runner knows God is a runner. "Some keep the Sabbath going to Church," Emily wrote. "I keep it staying at home." I keep it in company with some hundreds of others, running races in Central Park.

We congregate at the Ninety-first Street entrance, just north of the Guggenheim and across the street from the Church of the Heavenly Rest, our postrace meeting place. And we stand around like so many souls waiting in an antechamber while somewhere else the process of birth is about to happen.

The gun goes off. I have prepared for this race, known the ordeal to come. But it is always worse than I had imagined. Only a mile or so out and I wonder why I ever started.

I have sacrificed, denied appetites, fought desires, avoided pleasures for this? I am not only in pain, but I know it will last until the race ends. And, despite the effort, being passed and passed, continually losing ground. Can this possibly be the thing I do the best?

And then, a mile or so farther, a worse temptation. To quit. No one will know. Quitting does not mean stopping. It means giving just a little less than my limit. Slowing the pace to where I can breathe without pain and where the legs (is it possible?) feel comfortable.

And then it is over. The last stretch is survival, a counting of each step, head down, not daring to see how far it is to the finish line. But when I finish, I know what it is to race 6.2 miles in thirty-seven minutes and eleven seconds. What it is to go to the absolute limit. What this biological social theological animal can do.

I have made my move. I await His. I am with the others in the Heavenly Rest. Purified. At peace. The appetites no longer appetites. The desires no longer desires. Tea is enough. And the Other becomes someone to touch and embrace and congratulate. The body becomes a person, my neighbor.

A very small life, you might say. So was Emily's. Yet so full I can but envy her. Others, of course, see it so empty they can feel only pity. She saw no moor. Saw no sea. Saw few people. The few she loved died. But all the while, she played her game with God. Put out the pieces every day and took her position. Made her move and waited for His.

And for me on the way home, the Turnpike clouded with my tears, Amherst, Massachusetts, a century ago seems but minutes away.

I have raced and I will be back next week. This week coming, I will be a sinner. I will know food. Give in to the body. Ignore beauty. Forget truth. This week, God will be burglar, banker, father.

But come Sunday, He will be my friend and lover, and runner. And I will beat Him at my game. And I'll know it if I do. Because I will end in tears. I will know joy. And I will feel as if the top of my head were taken off.

18. Seeing

*And in those moments there is a light and joy
and understanding. For a time, however brief,
there is no confusion. I seem to see the way
things really are. I am in the Kingdom.*

WE WERE NOT created to be spectators. Not made to be onlookers. Not born to be bystanders. You and I cannot view life as a theatergoer would, pleased or displeased by what unfolds. You, as well as I, are producer, playwright, actor, making, creating and living the drama on stage. Life must be lived. Acted out. The play we are in is our own.

There are reasons, of course, to observe others. To learn how something is done. And to see the human body or soul or intellect in its perfection. We watch others so that their skill becomes our skill, their wisdom becomes our wisdom, their faith becomes our faith. But eventually we must go it alone. Find our own skill, our own wisdom, our own faith. Otherwise we will die without having learned who we are or what we can accomplish. And we will die without having an inkling of the meaning of it all.

I look for those answers on the roads. I take my tools of sight, hearing, touch, smell, taste and intellect and run with them. And I leave behind whatever I own, forgetting whatever I thought valuable, whatever I held dear. Naked, or almost, I come upon a new world. There on a country road, moving at eight miles an hour, I discover the total universe, the natural and the supernatural that wise men speculate about. It is a life, a world, a universe that begins on the other side of sweat and exhaustion.

I am purified by that sweat. I am baptized in my own water. I move again through a new Eden. I am fallen man restored, not yet knowing he will fall again. For now, at least, I am a child at play, at home in a home made for me. I am saturated with the goodness of the world, filled with the sight and the sound and the smell and the feel of the land through which I run. I sing with the poet Hopkins, "What I do is me; for this I came."

But then comes the Hill, and I know I am made for more. And by becoming more, I am challenged to choose suffering, to endure pain, to bear hardship. And in that becoming, I must live the mysteries of Sin and Free Will and Grace. All this I feel as I leave the beautiful endless time of running on the flat to risk everything on the ascent of the Hill.

At first the gentle swell carries me. At that level, nature is a help. The same nature which Bucky Fuller says is so prepared for us that whenever we need anything we find it has been stockpiled from the beginning of time.

But gradually the Hill demands more and more. I have reached the end of my physiology. The end of what is possible. And now it is beyond what I can stand. The temptation is to say, "Enough." This much is enough. But I will not give in.

I am fighting God. Fighting the limitations He gave me. Fighting the pain. Fighting the unfairness. Fighting all the evil in me and the world. And I will not give in. I will conquer this hill, and I will conquer it alone.

Of that moment, Kazantzakis tells a story: When God was asked when he would forgive Lucifer, He replied, "When he forgives Me." Kazantzakis in *Report to Greco* made his own Ascent, leaving, as he said, "a red track made by drops of my blood." And finding in the crucifixion the strength to persevere.

I cannot live the life of this genius. My Hill is but a mound to his mountain, my pain a shadow of his torment, but the human mystery is still there.

And still striving for that impossible summit. I forgive God. I accept the pain. I pass the crest. And for the briefest of eternities, I am God's child, brother to Christ, filled with the Holy Ghost.

The world belongs to those who laugh and cry. Laughter is the beginning of wisdom, the first evidence of the divine sense of humor. Those who know laughter have learned the secret of living. Have discovered that life is a wonderful game.

Crying starts when we see things as they really are. When we realize with William Blake that everything that lives is holy. When everything is seen to be infinite and we are part of the infinity. Tears come when we are filled with the joy of that vision. When we finally and irrevocably say yes to life. When we reach past reason and logic and know that the test of what we do and how we do it is delight.

For most of us these feelings are long in coming. We fail to touch or hear or see the real world. "Anything can make us look," writes Archibald MacLeish; "only art makes us see." Art and other things, but more of that later. We do not see because we are occupied with the doing and the getting and the spending. With Blake's unholy things, the lethargies, the cruelties. We fail to love. We lack passion. We feel no urgency. We have no intensity. We possess no enthusiasm.

This is as evident from our faces as our souls and intellects. George Burch, the cardiologist, once remarked that watching the expressions of the people on the street made him pessimistic about the medical profession being able to help them in any way.

Yet each of us, if Blake is right, has the faculty of seeing things as they really are. The visionary faculty is a natural gift. But this perception must be cleansed, otherwise we remain in the world of reason and mortality. This cleansing, it seems to me, must start with a cleansing discipline, a purifying effort. And for me, that means running, distance running.

Running keeps me at a physical peak and sharpens my senses. It makes me touch and see and hear as if for the first time. Through it, I get past the first barrier to true emotions, the lack of integration with the body. Into it I escape from the pettiness and triviality of everyday life. And, once inside, stop the daily pendulum perpetually oscillating between distraction and boredom.

But most of all, running gives me that margin Colin Wilson spoke of in *The Outsider*. There is a margin, he wrote, that can be stimulated only by pain and inconvenience, but which is indifferent to pleasure. It is only after that pain and inconvenience, after that challenge, that occurs the momentary and passing clarity in which things are seen as they eternally are.

Of all this, Blake is the great reporter. When asked if he saw the sun as a great red disk, he said: "Oh, no, no. I see an innumerable company of the heavenly host crying: "Holy, holy, holy, holy is the Lord God Almighty." No wonder his wife, when asked about him, said she never had much time to talk to him. "Mr. Blake," she said, "is almost always in Paradise."

For me such moments come more easily now. Goodness and truth and beauty suddenly possess me. I am surprised by joy, filled with delight, and there is nothing to do but exult in tears. And I think of Housman, who said he was careful not to think of a poem while shaving, lest he cut himself. And I must be careful while in company not to think on my dear dead friends who wrote so truly and so beautifully of what moved them to tears, lest I be thought senile and childish sitting there weeping.

On my runs, I am not so constrained. They have become shameless hours with tears streaming down my cheeks. I am now one with Nietzsche, who wrote of being unable to leave his room for the "ridiculous reason" that his eyes were swollen. "I have wept so much on my walk the day before," he wrote, "not sentimental tears, but tears of joy. I sang and cried out foolish things. I was full of a new vision."

Such tears cannot be manufactured, neither in myself nor in

those who wrote for me or for you reading this piece. "If you would have me weep," wrote Horace, "first you must grieve yourself." Only someone who has wept in joy and truth and beauty, who has had the vision, can make us weep also. Only those who have gone through the cleansing and purification in a long apprenticeship of discipline and effort can speak to our innermost hearts.

The total process is perhaps best described by poet John Hall Wheelock. "The long lonely effort and the self-discipline," he wrote, "are the poet's prayer that he may be the instrument of that voice [the voice of the race or the unconscious in all of us]. And thereby to speak words and wisdom beyond his own scope and clairvoyance."

The world belongs to those who make this effort. Those who laugh and cry, who sleep with the angels and, like Blake, are almost always in Paradise.

"Time and freedom," wrote Nikolai Berdyaev, "are the fundamental and most painful of metaphysical problems." But he reserved his most disturbing observations for the problem of time. "It is the child of sin," he states, "of sinful slavery, of sinful anxiety." And, in his way, he agrees with the words of Buddha: "As long as you are in time there's suffering."

But suffering we can take. It is the swing from boredom to anxiety, from depression to worry, that exhausts and defeats us. The sure knowledge that we can be much more than we are frustrates us.

But how does one get out of time? How does one escape from this slavery, this anxiety? How does one find his creativity? If the experts don't know, what are we common folk to do?

Well, I don't know about you, but when I have a problem, I run with it. And so on this clear October day I am heading north toward the Hook on the ocean road. Ready to live the questions. Trying to find answers. Searching for a new response to the human condition. For insights I am sure will not come through my senses or rational mind.

But at first the day floods my senses. The sky is as high as heaven. The bay and the ocean on either side are a deep blue to the horizon. I am framed in the bright whites and the clean colors that sea and sun and sand possess in the fall. There is a breeze at my back and the sun is warm between my shoulder blades. I am already bathed in pleasant sweat.

But now I begin to get beyond this sight and sound, of observing the road ahead and the water to the side. The running alone occupies me. Fills my awareness. I am a steady flow. I am pure involvement. Total concentration. I am comfortable, calm, relaxed, full of running. I could run like this forever.

And during all this I narrow my consciousness to the immediate moment. I am moving from time measured to where time stands still. I am giving up past and future for this now. I am leaving the linear time where my footsteps are a metronome, my pulse and respirations are in harmony, and every eight minutes I move my body one mile.

And for a while I alternate. Briefly, I return to sweat and movement and sun warm between my shoulder blades, the sight of sea and sky. Then once again I am in the now, the eternal present where literally nothing happens. I am suspended, content with the nothing. And the peace that comes with it.

And that perhaps is the essence of the running experience for me, and any number of different experiences for other people. The lack of anxiety, the complete acceptance, the letting go and the faith that all will be well. In running, I feel free. I have no other goal, no other reward. The running is its own reason for being.

And I run with no threat of failure. In fact, with no threat of success. There can be no consequences to make me worry or doubt. I am secure whatever happens. And in that security I reach a wholeness that I find nowhere else.

I have moved that little more out of the nothing into the now, the present moment that Aldous Huxley said was the only aperture through which the soul can pass out of time into eternity. That may or may not be. I do think there is aperture and when I run I move through it into fields of words and thoughts, of ideas and concepts I was never conscious of before. And I plunder the past of my race in this place which is outside of time.

And when I once again feel sweat and movement, once more see water and sky, I am a quarter of a mile farther on. My body is always on time and it stays on course. But somewhere on the way to the Hook, I have escaped guilt for the past and boredom in the present and anxiety for the future.

I have, as the poet Blake sang, held infinity in the palm of my hand and eternity in an hour.

For most of us, the meaning of life will remain obscure this side of the resurrection. Until then, what we do know or believe must be conceived in contemplation and born in action. It must be given substance by our bodies. Fleshed out by our flesh.

It has to be a total intellectual and spiritual and physical reaction to the human predicament. Which is no less, as Ortega said, than the perpetual surprise of existing without any previous consent on our part, castaways on an unpremeditated globe.

These reactions are sometimes thrust upon us. When we are in danger, for instance. When we are, as the Spanish saying goes, "between the sword and the wall." G. K. Chesterton reported on such an experience in a runaway hansom cab. "I had, so to speak," he wrote, "five religions in as many seconds." He went, he said, from pure pagan fear to what he hoped was Christianity.

But all such revelations need not begin in fear. Need not be set in action by the thought you have only a minute or hour or day or six months to live. They may, as I have discovered, occur in the course of an afternoon's run.

Before I run, I am a Cartesian. The body is simply a machine. I must take it for a run and tune it up. I must improve my body so that I can fulfill my real purpose, which is to think. It isn't until I get on the roads that I know again, as I have known for fifteen years, that I am my body and I am my soul, and I exist as a totality.

At first, however, I am all body. Where finally I hope to become aware of the surrounding universe and the self and finally my place in the scheme of things, I am now completely occupied with my body.

Finding rhythm and speed. Making adjustments for wind and hills, for heat and humidity. Attending to the sensations from feet and joints and muscles. I am a thinking animal using my brain instead of my mind.

Then, quite mysteriously, I am in the second wind. Like a jet suddenly settling into cruising speed after the surging of the takeoff, my running becomes easy, automatic. It has become play. And I have moved from being animal to being a pleasure-seeking adult. A castaway enjoying what he can.

But that euphoria, that glow, passes. The running asks for effort. It is no longer easy. The next quarter hour will demand more and more. I will be tempted to turn and head back to town. Being human, it seems, is more than enjoyment, more than pleasure. Life is also pain. And because of that, it is perplexity, essential and continual perplexity.

Some of that perplexity clears when I reach the third wind. The second wind is physiological and has to do with the heart and blood vessels and core temperature. The third wind, which comes after half an hour, is psychological, and has to do with the mind and the spirit, with joy and peace, with faith and hope, with unity and certainty.

Sometimes, this state, this awareness, comes at the best part of my run. I am at the crest of my hill, looking down on my river and seeing in the distance my town, where people are right now working and sustaining life, theirs and mine.

And now that hill becomes every hill, the river every river, the town every town, and the people all humanity. And in those moments there is a light and joy and understanding. For a time, however brief, there is no confusion. I seem to see the way things really are. I am in the Kingdom.

Just once, I have gone beyond this. My running became my offering. A dozen years of training and discipline, hours upon hours of perfecting the art and purifying the artist, came to this: I was a child before his Father, offering what I did best. Asking that my Father be pleased. That I be accepted. And I found myself, this little child, with tears streaming down my face, running the river road back to town.

A happy few have known it all. Have known that acceptance. Hear the words of Aquinas, who said all his work was straw. And the words of Pascal: "From about half past ten in the evening to about half an hour after midnight. Fire. God of Abraham. God of Isaac. God of Jacob. Not the God of philosophers and scholars. Absolute certainty; beyond reason. Joy. Peace."

We begin in the body and end in the Vision.

The flight home was depressing. The weekend in Crowley, Louisiana, had been a peak experience. Had been, in fact, a climax of my life as a runner and as a writer, and perhaps as a person. I had worn the number "1" in the National AAU Championship Marathon and finished in the top third of the field.

Before the race, runner after runner had come and shook my hand, saying, "Dr. Shee-han, I loved your book and just want you to know it." One said he had given eighteen copies as Christmas presents. All weekend, they sought me out to tell me how much I helped them.

Later, at the awards dinner, I was given a plaque. I was, the inscription said, the outstanding distance runner of the year. A similar plaque the previous year had said the same thing about Frank Shorter. I was being classed with the immortals. And then, as a final gesture of esteem, I was permitted to talk.

The talk was more than a talk. It was a love affair. I spoke to each face in turn. And saw in each a reflection of my feeling for them. I told them of the beauties of our bodies, and how we needed play. I told them we were all to be heroes in some way and if we were heroic enough we would see God.

And when I finished, I was in tears and so were they. And

then we all stood and applauded who we were and what we had done and the feeling that was in that great room.

And now I was flying away from all that. Flying toward what? Where was I to go from here? What was there to reach for that would surpass where I had been? Where would I get the size and strength and presence to be more than I was that day?

Life, I saw again, was a problem that will never be solved. At no time is this more evident than when we are close to the solution. No time more evident than when we succeed. When we have come far, but not far enough.

The wise men have spoken of this. For every hundred men who can handle adversity, they concluded, there is but one who can handle success. Flying home, I knew I was not that one. My elation had disappeared. I was fearful of the future. I had exhausted my potential and could see nothing ahead but repeating what I had already done. Doing the few things I did well over and over again for the rest of my life.

The man next to me was a runner who had completed his first marathon. "What do I do now?" he asked, echoing the thought in my mind. His answer would be my answer.

What do I do now? More of the same, only better. Run another and learn that much more about myself and the world and Who made me. Run another and another. Bathe myself in pain and fatigue. Reach for energies I have yet to use. Run another and another and another. Make my truth out of that experience, out of what happens.

What do I do now? No matter what I have done, there is still more to do. No matter how well it has been done, it can still be done better. No matter how fast the race, it can still be run faster. Everything I do must be aimed at that, aimed at being a masterpiece. The things I write, the races I run, each day I live. There can be no other way.

I thought then of the ancient Egyptians who believed there was a judgment after death and the initial step was to weigh the heart. It seems so true. The heart is the measure of our energy, our courage, our intuition, our love. It is the measure of our days, of what we have done, of who we are.

Was I ready, then, to have my heart weighed? Was this as far as I would go? Was I ready to rest, to obey the commandments and await my reward?

The plane was bringing me back to earth. Without thinking, I took my pulse. A slow, steady forty-eight, and only a day after a marathon. And I knew then, as every runner knows, my heart is capable of anything. All it asks is the time to do it.

When I have run my best marathon and written my best piece and done my best deed of love for myself and my neighbor, I know the cry will still come from my heart: "There is more, there is more. I Who have made you know." What else is a heart for, then, but to be uneasy, to ask for what seems impossible, and never be satisfied? So my heart will be restless until it finds its final rest.

Then they can weigh it.